ISAIAH: THE KINGDOM PREVIEWED

Heart and Mind Series

Tony Portell

Helping Others Heal

Isaiah: The Kingdom Previewed

Heart and Mind Series

Published by Helping Others Heal

Indianapolis, Indiana

Copyright © 2025 by Tony Portell

Helpingothersheal.org

ISBN: 979-8-9897593-8-5

This title is available in ebook and paperback formats.

All scripture quotations unless otherwise indicated, are taken from the Holy Bible New Living Translation NLT copyright 1996, 2004. Scriptures marked TPT are from The Passion Translation.

For inquiries about the book, media or speaking request, contact Tony@HelpingOthersHeal.org

All rights reserved.

No part of this publication may be reproduced, distributed, or transmitted in any form or by any means, including photocopying, recording, or other electronic or mechanical methods, or by any information storage and retrieval system without the prior written permission of the publisher, except in the case of very brief quotations embodied in critical reviews and certain other noncommercial uses permitted by copyright law.

First Printing December 2025 / Printed in the United States of America

Maps "Copyright Ralph F. Wilson . All rights reserved. Used by permission."

CONTENTS

Background of Isaiah's Writing	1
Heart and Mind Series	3
How to Get the most out of this book	5
Day 1 Isaiah 1:1-2	6
Day 2 Isaiah 1:3-6	8
Day 3 Isaiah 1:7-10	9
Day 4 Isaiah 1:10-15	11
Day 5 Isaiah 1:16-17	13
Day 6 Isaiah 1:18-20	15
Day 7 Isaiah 1:21-31	17
Day 8 Isaiah 2:1-4	19
Day 9 Isaiah 2:5-17	21

Day 10 Isaiah 2:18-22	23
Day 11 Isaiah 3:1-9	25
Day 12 Isaiah 3:10-26	27
Day 13 Isaiah 4:1-6	29
Day 14 Isaiah 5:1-7	30
Day 15 Isaiah 5:8-30	31
Day 16 Isaiah 6:1-8	33
Day 17 Isaiah 6:9-13	35
Day 18 Isaiah 7:1-6	36
Day 19 Isaiah 7:7-9	38
Day 20 Isaiah 7:10-16	40
Day 21 Isaiah 7:17-25	42
Day 22 Isaiah 8:1-10	44
Day 23 Isaiah 8:11-17	46
Day 24 Isaiah 8:18-22	47

Day 25 Isaiah 9:1-7	49
Day 26 Isaiah 9:8-21	51
Day 27 Isaiah 10:1-4	54
Day 28 Isaiah 10:5-11	56
Day 29 Isaiah 10:12-19	58
Day 30 Isaiah 10:20-27	60
Day 31 Isaiah 10:28-34	62
Day 32: Isaiah 11:1-5	64
Day 33 Isaiah 11:6-9	66
Day 34 Isaiah 11:10-16	67
Day 35 Isaiah 12:2-3	69
Day 36 Isaiah 12:4-6	71
Day 37 Isaiah 13:1-12	72
Day 38 Isaiah 13:13-22	74
Day 39 Isaiah 14:1-11	76

Day 40 Isaiah 14:12-23	78
Day 41 Isaiah 15:1-9	80
Day 42 Isaiah 16:1-13	82
Day 43 Isaiah 17:1-6	85
Day 44 Isaiah 17:7-14	87
Day 45 Isaiah 18:1-7	90
Day 46 Isaiah 19:1-10	92
Day 47 Isaiah 20:1-6	95
Day 48 Isaiah 21:1-10	97
Day 49 Isaiah 21:11-17	99
Day 50 Isaiah 22:1-14	101
Day 51 Isaiah 22:15-25	104
Day 52 Isaiah 23:1-17	106
Day 53 Isaiah 24:1-13	109
Day 54 Isaiah 24:14-23	112

Day 55 Isaiah 25:1-12	115
Day 56 Isaiah 26:1-21	118
Day 57 Isaiah 27:1-6	122
Day 58 Isaiah 27:7-13	124
Day 59 Isaiah 28:1-19	126
Day 60 Isaiah 28:20-26	130
Day 61 Isaiah 28:27-29	132
Day 62 Isaiah 29:1-14	134
Day 63 Isaiah 29:15-24	137
Day 64 Isaiah 30:1-5	140
Day 65 Isaiah 30:8-11	142
Day 66 Isaiah 30:12-17	144
Day 67 Isaiah 30:18-22	146
Day 68 Isaiah 30:23-33	148
Day 69 Isaiah 31:1-5	150

Day 70 Isaiah 31:6-9	152
Day 71 Isaiah 32:1-2	154
Day 72 Isaiah 32:3-20	156
Day 73 Isaiah 33:1-6	159
Day 74 Isaiah 33:7-16	161
Day 75 Isaiah 33:17-24	164
Day 76 Isaiah 34:1-17	167
Day 77 Isaiah 35:1-4	171
Day 78 Isaiah 35:5-10	173
Day 79 Isaiah 36:1-22	176
Day 80 Isaiah 37:1-29	180
Day 81 Isaiah 37:30-38	184
Day 82 Isaiah 38:1-6	187
Day 83 Isaiah 38:7-22	189
Day 84 Isaiah 39:1-8	191

Day 85 Isaiah 40:1-5	193
Day 86 Isaiah 40:6-11	195
Day 87 Isaiah 40:12-25	198
Day 88 Isaiah 41:1-7	203
Day 89 Isaiah 41:8-14	206
Day 90 Isaiah 41:15-29	209
Day 91 Isaiah 42:1-6	213
Day 92 Isaiah 42:7-12	215
Day 93 Isaiah 42:13-20	218
Day 94 Isaiah 42:21-25	221
Day 95 Isaiah 43:1-7	224
Day 96 Isaiah 43:8-13	228
Day 97 Isaiah 43:14-28	232
Day 98 Isaiah 44:1-7	237
Day 99 Isaiah 44:8-20	240

Day 100 Isaiah 44:21-28	245
Day 101 Isaiah 45:1-3	249
Day 102 Isaiah 45:4-11	251
Day 103 Isaiah 45:12-15	254
Day 104 Isaiah 45:16-21	257
Day 105 Isaiah 45:22-25	260
Day 106 Isaiah 46:1-4	262
Day 107 Isaiah 46:5-9	264
Day 108 Isaiah 46:10-13	267
Day 109 Isaiah 47:1-10	269
Day 110 Isaiah 47:11-15	273
Day 111 Isaiah 48:1-6	276
Day 112 Isaiah 48:7-15	279
Day 113 Isaiah 48:16-22	282
Day 114 Isaiah 49:1-4	286

Day 115 Isaiah 49:5-9	289
Day 116 Isaiah 49:10-14	292
Day 117 Isaiah 49:15-18	295
Day 118 Isaiah 49:19-26	297
Day 119 Isaiah 49:19-26	301
Day 120 Isaiah 50:1-7	305
Day 121 Isaiah 50:8-11	309
Day 122 Isaiah 51:1-3	312
Day 123 Isaiah 51:4-7	314
Day 124 Isaiah 51:8-12	317
Day 125 Isaiah 51:13-18	320
Day 126 Isaiah 51:19-23	323
Day 127 Isaiah 52:1-6	325
Day 128 Isaiah 52:7-10	328
Day 129 Isaiah 52:11-15	330

Day 130 Isaiah 53:1-5	333
Day 131 Isaiah 53:6-9	336
Day 132 Isaiah 53:10-12	339
Day 133 Isaiah 54:1-5	342
Day 134 Isaiah 54:6-10	345
Day 135 Isaiah 54:11-17	348
Day 136 Isaiah 56:1-5	351
Day 137 Isaiah 56:6-12	354
Day 138 Isaiah 57:1-5	358
Day 139 Isaiah 57:6-10	361
Day 140 Isaiah 57:11-15	363
Day 141 Isaiah 57:16-21	366
Day 142 Isaiah 58:1-5	369
Day 143 Isaiah 58:6-10	371
Day 144 Isaiah 58:11-14	374

Day 145 Isaiah 59:1-5	377
Day 146 Isaiah 59:6-12	379
Day 147 Isaiah 59:13-17	382
Day 148 Isaiah 59:18-21	385
Day 149 Isaiah 60:1-4	388
Day 150 Isaiah 60:5-9	391
Day 151 Isaiah 60:10-14	394
Day 152 Isaiah 60:15-18	397
Day 153 Isaiah 60:19-22	400
Day 154 Isaiah 61:1-3	402
Day 155 Isaiah 61:4-7	405
Day 156 Isaiah 61:8-11	408
Day 157 Isaiah 62:1-5	411
Day 158 Isaiah 62:6-9	414
Day 159 Isaiah 62:10-12	417

Day 160 Isaiah 63:1-6	419
Day 161 Isaiah 63:7-10	422
Day 162 Isaiah 63:11-16	425
Day 163 Isaiah 63:17-19	429
Day 164 Isaiah 64:1-5	431
Day 165 Isaiah 64:6-7	434
Day 166 Isaiah 64:8-12	436
Day 167 Isaiah 55:1-5	438
Day 168 Isaiah 55:6-10	441
Day 169 Isaiah 55:11-14	443
Day 170 Isaiah 65:15-18	446
Day 171 Isaiah 65:19-20	448
Day 172 Isaiah 65:21-25	450
Day 173 Isaiah 66:1-4	453
Day 174 Isaiah 66:5-9	457

Day 175 Isaiah 66:10-13	461
Day 176 Isaiah 66:14-17	463
Day 177 Isaiah 66:18-21	465
Day 178 Isaiah 66:22-24	466
Glossary of Key Words	469
The Isaiah Pauline Connection	473
More Mind and Heart Series Works Helping Others Heal	475
About the Author Tony Portell	477
Books by Tony Portell	479
A Final Favor…	481

BACKGROUND OF ISAIAH'S WRITING

The Book of Isaiah is far more than an ancient historical document; it is a sweeping prophetic vision filled with messages of judgment, profound hope, and the amazing prophetic anticipation of Jesus' coming. Written by the prophet Isaiah, it addresses a nation in crisis, but its themes resonate with a timeless power, offering life-changing insight to those who explore its pages.

To understand Isaiah's message, we must first understand his world. The nation of Israel was in a precarious political state, marked by division and external threats:

• **A Divided Kingdom:** Following a civil war nearly two centuries before Isaiah's time, the once-unified kingdom of Israel had split into two separate nations: **Israel** in the north and **Judah** in the south.

The Assyrian Empire conquered and scattered the people of the northern kingdom of Israel.

• **A Threatened Remnant:** This left Judah, the southern kingdom where Jerusalem was located, as the small, vulnerable remnant of God's people, facing constant threats from surrounding empires.

At the time of Isaiah, Israel had been in the Promised Land for almost 700 years. Remember, God had freed them through miracles through Moses. For their first 400 years in Canaan, judges ruled Israel. Then, for about 120 years, three kings reigned over Israel: Saul, David, and Solomon. In 917 BC, Israel had a civil war and remained divided into two nations, Israel (to the north) and Judah (to the south).

Assyria absorbed most of the scattered people from the northern kingdom of Israel. Judah and Benjamin are all that remain, and they're reduced to the lands just around the city of Jerusalem. The kingdom, once great, shrank to about the size of Indianapolis and a few surrounding counties.

What's left of the Jewish nation is about to be conquered by Assyria, and Isaiah is predicting its demise. He is also warning them of the removal of God's protection because of their rebellion.

Isaiah is a series of prophetic messages about what will happen to the Jewish nation.

Isaiah is also called the fifth gospel because it offers a wonderful promise of hope about future restoration and a King who will reign forever. The book is filled with amazing prophecies that anticipate Jesus' coming.

Isaiah is a message of warning and hope. Warning against rebellion and hope because God is faithful even when we are not.

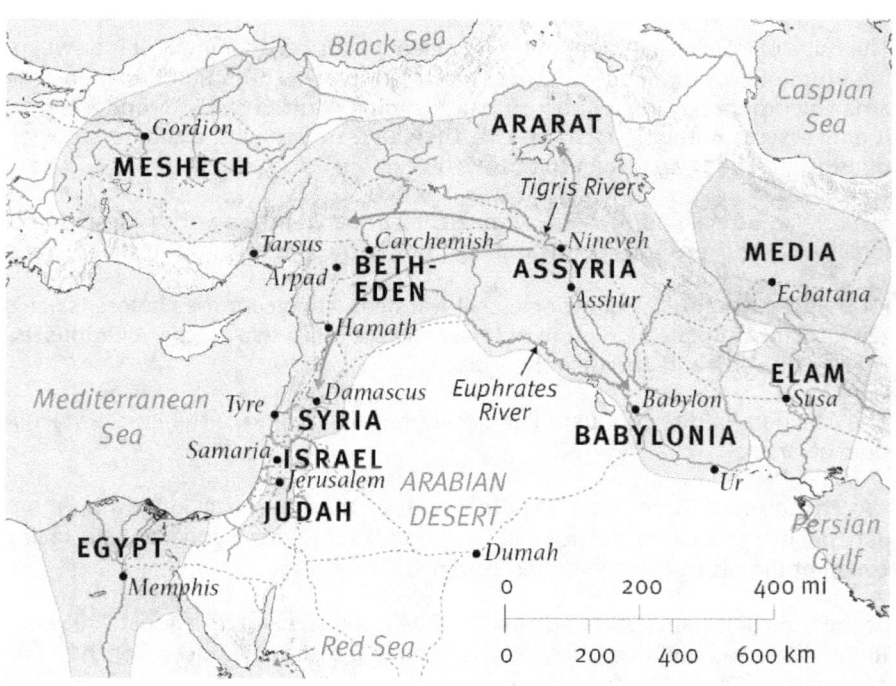

HEART AND MIND SERIES

Discover a journey that bridges knowledge and experience, inviting you to encounter God with both your heart and your mind. This book offers more than information—it's an invitation to transformation. Each day, you'll explore the timeless wisdom of the Bible, enriched with background, context, and practical insights that help you connect with God. Through thoughtful application and guided reflection, you'll learn how scripture can penetrate beyond intellect, reaching into the core of your being to inspire actual change.

The Heart and Mind Series is designed to help you seek God holistically. By weaving together biblical understanding and personal experience, this series encourages you to pursue both revelation and knowledge. With daily portions of scripture, research-backed insights, and suggestions for meaningful connection with God, you'll discover how faith can engage your entire self—leading to encounters that are not just informative, but truly life-changing.

I encourage you to open God's Word with prayer, humbly asking God to reveal Himself. This is critical when seeking to understand and follow God, who wants to connect with us. If we allow it, the Bible's words can penetrate our hearts and reveal our deepest thoughts.

When we have these supernatural encounters with God, they can be life changing. Otherwise, we are just gaining more knowledge and not applying it to our everyday lives. The Apostle Paul reminds us,

> But while knowledge makes us feel important, love strengthens the church. 1 Corinthians 8:1b

We cannot separate our knowledge of God and our experience with God. We need both. We have a heart and mind. Throughout the Bible, the writers emphasized seeking God's Word as much as they emphasized seeking God's presence.

Solomon described wisdom as revelation from God and knowledge as our pursuit to learn about God.

HOW TO
Get the most out of this book

Always begin any time of Bible study by praying and asking the Holy Spirit to enlighten your thoughts and provide revelation into the text and how it applies to your life today. Because these words are God-breathed, they convey within the context a living message personalized to inspire us to draw closer to God at the moment. This is not simply reading history, *"dates and dead guys."*

Remember the words of the writer of Hebrews,

> For the word of God is alive and powerful. It is sharper than the sharpest two-edged sword, cutting between soul and spirit, between joint and marrow. It exposes our innermost thoughts and desires. Hebrews 4:12

The Hebrews writer defines two distinct aspects of our lives: the head and the heart, the spirit and the mind, or as Solomon referred to wisdom and knowledge. He describes how the Word of God helps us separate God's thoughts and our thoughts. The random thoughts we have floating around in our heads and the will of God revealed to our spirits. Neuroscience refers to this as left and right brain. The left hemisphere handles thought, logic, reason, and communication. The right hemisphere handles creativity, imagination, relationships, and emotions. Just as we need both sides of brain to function, we need revelation from God, which comes through prayer (right brain), and study of scripture (left brain). Healthy faith is Spirit and Word.

I pray that God will open your heart and mind to receive life changing insight as you encounter God through these studies.

DAY 1
Isaiah 1:1-2

These are the visions that Isaiah son of Amoz saw concerning Judah and Jerusalem. He saw these visions during the years when Uzziah, Jotham, Ahaz, and Hezekiah were kings of Judah

Listen, O heavens! Pay attention, earth! This is what the LORD says: "The children I raised and cared for have rebelled against me. Isaiah 1:1-2

Isaiah's visions and words from God start with an indictment against His fellow Jews in Judah and Jerusalem.

By way of background, the northern nation of Israel had already been subdued and destroyed by the Assyrians. The ten tribes of the north of the nation of Israel will now and forever be called the Ten Lost Tribes of Israel. Thus began the dispersion—spreading the Jewish people across northern Africa to Europe.

The only true Israelite nation left is a small portion of land around Jerusalem, now referred to as Judah. It is made up of two tribes, Judah and Benjamin. Far from the great nation under David and Solomon, Judah is the lonely remnant of what is left.

God calls them to account for their rebellion. God is letting them know this is the primary cause if they have not connected their pain with their rebellion. The people are beaten down, sick, and overrun by their enemies; their crops are failing, and God sees their offerings as detestable. Jerusalem, the once great city of David and Solomon, is now in ruins.

What causes rebellion in us. It usually forms through childhood trauma. A lack of unconditional love from a parent or primary caregiver. We call this poor attachment. The inability to bond with someone we should trust to care for us makes us insecure And feeling unlovable. These people tend to grow up to be very independent, self-reliant, and insecure. This not only occurs with people but also with God. If we cannot trust people, we typically cannot trust God.

Notice the relational language God uses. He refers to the Israelites as "children I raised and cared for. " This is not a harsh and angry judge ruling from a distance and demanding a pound of flesh to appease Him. This is a parent, heartbroken over the rebellion of His children who are bringing disaster on themselves.

But with our God, there is always grace. Even in the Old Testament, we will see the head of a God of mercy, compassion, and unfailing love throughout the pages. Seed how He offers these rebels hope.

DAY 2
Isaiah 1:3-6

Even an ox knows its owner, and a donkey recognizes its master's care— but Israel doesn't know its master. My people don't recognize my care for them." 4 Oh, what a sinful nation they are— loaded down with a burden of guilt. They are evil people, corrupt children who have rejected the LORD. They have despised the Holy One of Israel and turned their backs on him. 5 Why do you continue to invite punishment? Must you rebel forever? Your head is injured, and your heart is sick. 6 You are battered from head to foot—covered with bruises, welts, and infected wounds—without any soothing ointments or bandages.

Isaiah's writing will feature this primary theme of the Israelites' rebellion against God. We can identify with their lack of trust in God and their turning to idols, including that main idol of self. Everything they are complaining about, they have brought on themselves. They see themselves as righteous and God failing to protect and provide for them. God points out that people don't recognize how He cared for them.

It is easy to think we are better than we are. God says the problem is "our head is injured." In other words, we don't think clearly. We are not seeing our lives through God's eyes. God also tells them, "Your heart is sick". Not only are they not thinking clearly, but they are also not sensing and feeling God when He is wanting to lead them. The problem is that we do not recognize God or what He has done for us. Our lack of attachment or personal connection with God keeps us from trusting Him, especially in a crisis. Part of our journey toward maturity is to renew our minds, as the Apostle Paul instructs us in Romans 12:2, to grasp and fully embrace God's love.

The Father wants to reveal Himself to our heads and hearts. We must humbly listen, wait, and trust Him to speak and lead us.

DAY 3
Isaiah 1:7-10

> Your country lies in ruins, and your towns are burned. Foreigners plunder your fields before your eyes and destroy everything they see. 8 Beautiful Jerusalem stands abandoned like a watchman's shelter in a vineyard, like a lean-to in a cucumber field after the harvest, like a helpless city under siege. 9 If the LORD of Heaven's Armies had not spared a few of us, we would have been wiped out like Sodom, destroyed like Gomorrah.

You sense God's heart is as broken as the people are for their nation, which lies in ruins. They are being overwhelmed and destroyed. If there is anything good or any victories, they are from God. The only reason God protects them goes back to His covenant with Abraham. God promised always to preserve a remnant whereby he could bless the people of Israel and all the world's nations.

Not only did God promise to preserve the Jewish people, but He also looked forward to the promised Redeemer in Jesus.

> Dear brothers and sisters, here's an example from everyday life. Just as no one can set aside or amend an irrevocable agreement, so it is in this case. 16 God gave the promises to Abraham and his child And notice that the Scripture doesn't say "to his children," as if it meant many descendants. Rather, it says "to his child"—and that, of course, means Christ. Galatians 3:15-16

God calls the people "Sodom and Gomorrah." Things are good when God refers to you as the two greatest symbols of rebellion in the Bible. I appreciate that when God confronts us, He doesn't mince words. He knows how destructive sin is in our lives, and His goal is to point it out clearly, not to shame us but for us to see the truth and find freedom in turning to Him.

DAY 4
Isaiah 1:10-15

10 Listen to the LORD, you leaders of "Sodom." 11 Listen to the law of our God, people of "Gomorrah." "What makes you think I want all your sacrifices?" says the LORD. "I am sick of your burnt offerings of rams and the fat of fattened cattle. I get no pleasure from the blood of bulls and lambs and goats. 12 When you come to worship me, who asked you to parade through my courts with all your ceremony? 13 Stop bringing me your meaningless gifts; the incense of your offerings disgusts me! As for your celebrations of the new moon and the Sabbath and your special days for fasting— they are all sinful and false. I want no more of your pious meetings. 14 I hate your new moon celebrations and your annual festivals. They are a burden to me. I cannot stand them! 15 When you lift up your hands in prayer, I will not look. Though you offer many prayers, I will not listen, for your hands are covered with the blood of innocent victims.

God is not into religion. He sees the dangerous trap it can be in making us feel like we have it together and that we are impressing God with our religious activities. Even acts like prayer, reading the Bible, church attendance, and putting Christian bumper stickers on our cars are meaningless if our hearts are not engaged. These people knew how to follow the rules. What they lacked was a relationship with God. Many today find themselves in the same predicament.

Knowledge of God must be accompanied by a real experience with God. He is a relational being and made us to be like Him. God want you to do more than just learn about Him, He wants to reveal Himself in intimate prayer and solitude. He wants to speak to you through His Word.

> They will act religiously but reject the power that could make them godly. Stay away from people like that! 2 Tim. 3:5

Religion can deceive us into thinking we are right because of what we believe or what we do for God. Here is a question I would pose to help you determine whether your relationship with God is religious or relational. Would you describe your prayer life as more of a monologue or dialogue? In other words, do you listen and wait for God to respond, or do you present all your needs without listening for God to react or even direct your prayers?

God knows our hearts. It is best to be transparent and come humbly to receive. Value listening more than talking.

> Don't make rash promises, and don't be hasty in bringing matters before God. After all, God is in heaven, and you are here on earth. So let your words be few. Ecclesiastes 5:2

DAY 5

Isaiah 1:16-17

> Wash yourselves and be clean! Get your sins out of my sight. Give up your evil ways. 17 Learn to do good. Seek justice. Help the oppressed. Defend the cause of orphans. Fight for the rights of widows.

If we want to impress God, His interests are to take our attention off ourselves and place it on Him.

"Humility is not thinking less of yourself, it's thinking of yourself less." — CS Lewis

This is demonstrated in caring for those who cannot care for themselves and thus represent God in loving the poor.

> Pure and genuine religion in the sight of God the Father means caring for orphans and widows in their distress and refusing to let the world corrupt you. James 1:27

A pathway to restored righteousness is loving others. Do something good for oppressed people who cannot pay back. This is the heart of God, who loves us unconditionally. We love this way as we give back what God gives us. That is what we are doing in seeking justice for others. We are taking from God's deposit in us and sharing it, thus sharing God with others.

It might not be sin that is holding you back from receiving God's love or giving it to others. There may be past trauma and emotional wounds that have kept you distanced from God and people. If this is your situation come before God humbly and ask Him to fill you with His love. Sometimes gratitude can be a way to get our minds off of pain and refocused on God's love.

God is generous and provides "seed to the sower ".

Another metaphor would be to picture ourselves as a water hose focused on a plant that needs water. The life-sustaining water must come from God all we can offer is far less that what God can do through someone open to allowing His love to flow through them.

Prayer: Father, help me see where you want to flow and where I can be a conduit of your love. Show me specific ways and incidents to show justice and kindness, especially to the oppressed.

DAY 6
Isaiah 1:18-20

Come now, let's settle this," says the LORD. "Though your sins are like scarlet, I will make them as white as snow. Though they are red like crimson, I will make them as white as wool. If you will only obey me, you will have plenty to eat. 20 But if you turn away and refuse to listen, you will be devoured by the sword of your enemies. I, the LORD, have spoken!"

Here is one of the most beautiful passages in all of scripture. The God of all creation says, I understand; your brain is limited, and you can't grasp my grace fully. But, come to me, and let's reason this out together. I'll make it as simple as it needs to be. Your sins were a bloody stain on your soul, and I am going to make it pure white. In addition, you will have plenty to eat. I will take care of you. But rebellion has consequences.

These people are beaten down, sick, and overrun by their enemies; their crops are failing, and God sees their offerings as detestable. Jerusalem, the once great city of David and Solomon, is now in ruins.

But with our God, there is always grace. Even in the Old Testament, we see a God of mercy, compassion, and unfailing love throughout the pages, always offering hope.

What if you've not received much grace in your life. You've had to work for every honor or word of appreciation? It is difficult for many to embrace the idea that God loves them unconditionally and nothing they do or don't do can affect God's love for them. Until we can believe and trust in this truth we can never really grasp God's love to the extent He wants us to.

> But God showed his great love for us by sending Christ to die for us while we were still sinners. Romans 5:8

God offers you and me today the same grace in our rebellion. He cannot be anything but loving and full of grace while also being holy and perfect. You will see how these qualities contrast and complement each other throughout Isaiah.

DAY 7
Isaiah 1:21-31

See how Jerusalem, once so faithful, has become a prostitute. Once the home of justice and righteousness, she is now filled with murderers. 22 Once like pure silver, you have become like worthless slag. Once so pure, you are now like watered-down wine. 23 Your leaders are rebels, the companions of thieves. All of them love bribes and demand payoffs but they refuse to defend the cause of orphans or fight for the rights of widows.

God indicts the Israelites, further referring to them as prostitutes. This a picture God uses throughout the Old Testament, such as in the book of Hosea. The people have given their allegiance and worship to foreign gods. The God of Heaven sees us in an eternal covenant of marriage, which is not to be broken or violated. God is perfect in keeping His part of the constant; it is we who fail and turn our affection and devotion to idols.

We see how God can love us unconditionally while calling out sin because He is holy. There is no conflict between God's love and holiness. God is merciful and just. We can approach Him regardless of sin in our lives because we are appealing to His love and under the New Covenant Jesus instituted, we come based on His shed blood. While Isaiah will speak often of judgment there is always grace for those who turn toward Him. We must always keep this in mind as we read the Old Testament.

Therefore, the Lord, the LORD of Heaven's Armies, the Mighty One of Israel, says, "I will take revenge on my enemies and pay back my foes! 25 I will raise my fist against you. I will melt you down and skim off your slag. I will remove all your impurities. 26 Then I will give you good judges again and wise counselors like you used to have. Then Jerusalem will again be called the Home of Justice and the Faithful City." 27 Zion will be restored by justice; those who repent will be revived by righteousness. 28 But rebels and sinners will be completely destroyed, and those who desert the LORD will be consumed. 29 You will be ashamed of your idol worship in groves of sacred oaks. You will blush because you worshiped in gardens dedicated to idols. 30 You will be like a great tree with withered leaves, like a garden without water. 31 The strongest among you will disappear like straw; their evil deeds will be the spark that sets it on fire. They and their evil works will burn up together, and no one will be able to put out the fire.

The people of God become the enemies of God, whom He must fight and subdue. God shares with them the outcome of fighting against God: total annihilation.

DAY 8

Isaiah 2:1-4

This is a vision that Isaiah son of Amoz saw concerning Judah and Jerusalem: 2 In the last days, the mountain of the LORD's house will be the highest of all— the most important place on earth. It will be raised above the other hills, and people from all over the world will stream there to worship. 3 People from many nations will come and say, "Come, let us go up to the mountain of the LORD, to the house of Jacob's God. There he will teach us his ways, and we will walk in his paths." For the LORD's teaching will go out from Zion; his word will go out from Jerusalem. 4 The LORD will mediate between nations and will settle international disputes. They will hammer their swords into plowshares and their spears into pruning hooks. Nation will no longer fight against nation, nor train for war anymore.

From their humble circumstances, God paints a picture of God's ultimate victory before Isaiah. Knowing these words will not apply to Israel. Still, to the New Covenant and the New Heavens established when Jesus returns to rule the earth for eternity, we get this beautiful glimpse and connect the Old Testament promises and the New Testament fulfillment—a link between Isaiah's vision and John's Revelation.

There will be no place for man's rebellion because every desire will be fulfilled in the presence of Jesus, our King. We will move away from a soldier mentality, always on guard, ready to defend ourselves from danger. Instead, we will be at peace as farmers cultivating the soil, growing and producing in a peaceful environment.

All that we need will be provided in extravagance. This is too wonderful for us even to imagine. Later, Isaiah will expand on this theme, and the Apostle will quote him in his first letter to Corinth.

"No eye has seen, no ear has heard and no mind has imagine what God has prepare for those who love him." 1 Corinthians 2:9

DAY 9

Isaiah 2:5-17

Come, descendants of Jacob, let us walk in the light of the LORD! 6 For the LORD has rejected his people, the descendants of Jacob, because they have filled their land with practices from the East and with sorcerers, as the Philistines do. They have made alliances with pagans. 7 Israel is full of silver and gold; there is no end to its treasures. Their land is full of warhorses; there is no end to its chariots. 8 Their land is full of idols; the people worship things they have made with their own hands. 9 So now they will be humbled, and all will be brought low— do not forgive them. 10 Crawl into caves in the rocks. Hide in the dust from the terror of the LORD and the glory of his majesty. 11 Human pride will be brought down, and human arrogance will be humbled. Only the LORD will be exalted on that day of judgment.

God is calling the people back to Himself. He is reminding them that the true treasure is in God. He has more gold and silver than the Philistines and other nations and gods can offer them. Again, God is reasoning with the people. He is not demanding or appealing to them. Everything they have gained through human strength is about to be lost. This is precisely what happened when foreign enemies, including Babylon, destroyed the city of Jerusalem and carried the people off into captivity.

God accuses the people of pride and arrogance. Pride is the result of the human spirit who was not fed encouragement, so it fed itself. Humility is always the correct posture before the Lord, not because we are to grovel to impress Him, but because God is worthy of all honor and worship we give to Him.

For the LORD of Heaven's Armies has a day of reckoning. He will punish the proud and mighty and bring down everything that is exalted. 13 He will cut down the tall cedars of Lebanon and all the mighty oaks of Bashan. 14 He will level all the high mountains and all the lofty hills. 15 He will break down every high tower and every fortified wall. 16 He will destroy all the great trading ships and every magnificent vessel. 17 Human pride will be humbled, and human arrogance will be brought down. Only the LORD will be exalted on that day of judgment.

Here, we see an example of prophecy speaking to two time periods, the coming destruction of Jerusalem and the future destruction of the Babylonian kingdom described by John in Revelation. These are the "days of reckoning," Isaiah describes.

DAY 10
Isaiah 2:18-22

Idols will completely disappear. 19 When the LORD rises to shake the earth, his enemies will crawl into holes in the ground. They will hide in caves in the rocks from the terror of the LORD and the glory of his majesty. 20 On that day of judgment they will abandon the gold and silver idols they made for themselves to worship. They will leave their gods to the rodents and bats, 21 while they crawl away into caverns and hide among the jagged rocks in the cliffs. They will try to escape the terror of the LORD and the glory of his majesty as he rises to shake the earth. 22 Don't put your trust in mere humans. They are as frail as breath. What good are they?

Isaiah repeats this picture of the Israelites hiding in the caves and rocks. All of their collected wealth is gone, and their worship of foreign gods has only brought destruction and living in fear in the shadows.

Man's life is fragile and temporary. His breath is in his nostrils, ready to stop at any moment. With all our boastings, ingenuity, and marvelous inventions, man is but a poor, vain creature. In all our littleness and helplessness, we must turn away from men's answers and ask for God's breath.

We are just one breath away from not existing. Everything we are doing or need to get done stops at that point. All our plans cease. Life that we lived for is over. All of our plans cease. Life that we lived for is over.

The ultimate contrast occurs between those who know God and have devoted their lives to Him versus those who have lived for themselves.

A moment, a choice that moved us down a path either toward God or away, will determine our eternity. It will be our choice. How often when faced with the choice of trusting in man, including ourselves, or God we choose man. Isaiah described people as "frail". This is why you need strong people around you. Find a church, find a people of faith who can challenge and encouragement you and always point you to God.

DAY 11
Isaiah 3:1-9

The Lord, the LORD of Heaven's Armies, will take away from Jerusalem and Judah everything they depend on: every bit of bread and every drop of water, 2 all their heroes and soldiers, judges and prophets, fortune-tellers and elders, 3 army officers and high officials, advisers, skilled sorcerers, and astrologers. 4 I will make boys their leaders, and toddlers their rulers. 5 People will oppress each other— man against man, neighbor against neighbor. Young people will insult their elders, and vulgar people will sneer at the honorable. 6 In those days a man will say to his brother, "Since you have a coat, you be our leader! Take charge of this heap of ruins!" 7 But he will reply, "No! I can't help. I don't have any extra food or clothes. Don't put me in charge!" 8 For Jerusalem will stumble, and Judah will fall, because they speak out against the LORD and refuse to obey him. They provoke him to his face. 9 The very look on their faces gives them away. They display their sin like the people of Sodom and don't even try to hide it. They are doomed! They have brought destruction upon themselves.

Isaiah sees the issue very clearly. We either depend on God or we put our trust in man. Whether we trust ourselves or others, nothing goes before God. Whatever we place there, God will compassionately remove. It is uncomfortable to feel things slipping our fingers we have trusted in. Maybe it is a job, an investment, or a relationship. Anything that becomes an idol, God separates from us. Of course, we cannot see this value at the time, but we will see it one day and thank God for His intervention.

We find ourselves in a similar climate today. The people and rulers we have trusted to lead our nation, tell us the truth in the media, and advocate for us through institutions all seem to be abandoning us. The people who lead seem to lack integrity and are motivated only by their gain. Never before have we needed to trust in God over man.

YHWH is the supreme ruler overall. We cannot abandon our trust in Father God or place anyone before Him. We are children, sheep, and we need someone to care for us. I embrace this idea and hold in tension the view that God is empowering and working through me. Humility and faith walk hand in hand.

DAY 12

Isaiah 3:10-26

Tell the godly that all will be well for them. They will enjoy the rich reward they have earned! 11 But the wicked are doomed, for they will get exactly what they deserve. 12 Childish leaders oppress my people, and women rule over them. O my people, your leaders mislead you; they send you down the wrong road. 13 The LORD takes his place in court and presents his case against his people. 14 The LORD comes forward to pronounce judgment on the elders and rulers of his people: "You have ruined Israel, my vineyard. Your houses are filled with things stolen from the poor. 15 How dare you crush my people, grinding the faces of the poor into the dust?" demands the Lord, the LORD of Heaven's Armies. 16 The LORD says, "Beautiful Zion is haughty: craning her elegant neck, flirting with her eyes, walking with dainty steps, tinkling her ankle bracelets. 17 So the Lord will send scabs on her head; the LORD will make beautiful Zion bald." 18 On that day of judgment the Lord will strip away everything that makes her beautiful: ornaments, headbands, crescent necklaces, 19 earrings, bracelets, and veils; 20 scarves, ankle bracelets, sashes, perfumes, and charms; 21 rings, jewels, 22 party clothes, gowns, capes, and purses; 23 mirrors, fine linen garments, head ornaments, and shawls. 24 Instead of smelling of sweet perfume, she will stink. She will wear a rope for a sash, and her elegant hair will fall out. She will wear rough burlap instead of rich robes. Shame will replace her beauty. 25 The men of the city will be killed with the sword, and her warriors will die in battle. 26 The gates of Zion will weep and mourn. The city will be like a ravaged woman, huddled on the ground.

God is removing all that the people value, including gold, silver, jewelry, fine linens, and garments, and all the luxuries similar to what we hold as precious today. This once beautiful woman representing God's beauty is being destroyed by sin. God is taking away everything that defines them and leaving them bare.

It should not surprise us when we pursue these things today. God removes them from becoming idols and distracts us from what is essential.

Imagine God's perspective as Isaiah describes Jerusalem, the City of God, Zion, as a woman who has been molested and left in the street. We forget what sin does to the heart of God and how he grieves over sin and the brokenness and destruction it brings.

DAY 13
Isaiah 4:1-6

In that day so few men will be left that seven women will fight for each man, saying, "Let us all marry you! We will provide our own food and clothing. Only let us take your name so we won't be mocked as old maids." 2 But in that day, the branch of the LORD will be beautiful and glorious; the fruit of the land will be the pride and glory of all who survive in Israel. 3 All who remain in Zion will be a holy people—those who survive the destruction of Jerusalem and are recorded among the living. 4 The Lord will wash the filth from beautiful Zion and cleanse Jerusalem of its bloodstains with the hot breath of fiery judgment. 5 Then the LORD will provide shade for Mount Zion and all who assemble there. He will provide a canopy of cloud during the day and smoke and flaming fire at night, covering the glorious land. 6 It will be a shelter from daytime heat and a hiding place from storms and rain.

Chapter 4 should be viewed as a continuation of chapter three regarding the women of Zion. The women of Zion can also be a metaphor for the church. There is coming a day when the church will become so destitute of answers that she will turn to the one, the Lord Jesus, and take hold of him.

Jesus becomes our Kinsman-Redeemer, also described in the book of Ruth. He redeems us, and we become His bride. He cleanses us and the world in which we will live for eternity. Isaiah refers back to the exodus when God provided a cloud by day and a fire by night to the Israelites. The clouds during the day provided shade from the desert heat, and the fire at night provided warmth. These two manifestations also provided direction for when they moved, the Israelites were to break camp and move.

DAY 14
Isaiah 5:1-7

Now I will sing for the one I love a song about his vineyard: My beloved had a vineyard on a rich and fertile hill. 2 He plowed the land, cleared its stones, and planted it with the best vines. In the middle he built a watchtower and carved a winepress in the nearby rocks. Then he waited for a harvest of sweet grapes, but the grapes that grew were bitter. 3 Now, you people of Jerusalem and Judah, you judge between me and my vineyard. 4 What more could I have done for my vineyard that I have not already done? When I expected sweet grapes, why did my vineyard give me bitter grapes? 5 Now let me tell you what I will do to my vineyard: I will tear down its hedges and let it be destroyed. I will break down its walls and let the animals trample it. 6 I will make it a wild place where the vines are not pruned and the ground is not hoed, a place overgrown with briers and thorns. I will command the clouds to drop no rain on it. 7 The nation of Israel is the vineyard of the LORD of Heaven's Armies. The people of Judah are his pleasant garden. He expected a crop of justice, but instead he found oppression. He expected to find righteousness, but instead he heard cries of violence.

God now uses the metaphor of a vineyard to show Israel what He did for them. A vineyard and a wine press were treasured and challenging to build. All the rock had to be dug out and shaped to accommodate the harvest of grapes and to process them into wine. The wine was more than just a drink for celebrating; it had medicinal purposes. In this case, God built everything perfectly to provide a harvest of the best wine, representing the happiness of the people of Israel. What should have been perfect vines became weeds and wild bushes with thorns. God will tear it all up and even stop the rain from nourishing what has become weeds and briars.

God once again relates Israel's rebellion to injustice for the poor. We don't tend to connect this theme to the extent God seems to.

DAY 15

Isaiah 5:8-30

What sorrow for you who buy up house after house and field after field, until everyone is evicted and you live alone in the land. 9 But I have heard the LORD of Heaven's Armies swear a solemn oath: "Many houses will stand deserted; even beautiful mansions will be empty. 10 Ten acres of vineyard will not produce even six gallons of wine. Ten baskets of seed will yield only one basket of grain." 11 What sorrow for those who get up early in the morning looking for a drink of alcohol and spend long evenings drinking wine to make themselves flaming drunk. 12 They furnish wine and lovely music at their grand parties— lyre and harp, tambourine and flute— but they never think about the LORD or notice what he is doing. 13 So my people will go into exile far away because they do not know me. Those who are great and honored will starve, and the common people will die of thirst. 14 The graved is licking its lips in anticipation, opening its mouth wide. The great and the lowly and all the drunken mob will be swallowed up. 15 Humanity will be destroyed, and people brought down; even the arrogant will lower their eyes in humiliation. 16 But the LORD of Heaven's Armies will be exalted by his justice. The holiness of God will be displayed by his righteousness. 17 In that day, lambs will find good pastures, and fattened sheep and young goats will feed among the ruins. 18 What sorrow for those who drag their sins behind them with ropes made of lies, who drag wickedness behind them like a cart! 19 They even mock God and say, "Hurry up and do something! We want to see what you can do. Let the Holy One of Israel carry out his plan, for we want to know what it is."

20 What sorrow for those who say that evil is good and good is evil, that dark is light and light is dark, that bitter is sweet and sweet

is bitter. 21 What sorrow for those who are wise in their own eyes and think themselves so clever. 22 What sorrow for those who are heroes at drinking wine and boast about all the alcohol they can hold. 23 They take bribes to let the wicked go free, and they punish the innocent. 24 Therefore, just as fire licks up stubble and dry grass shrivels in the flame, so their roots will rot and their flowers wither. For they have rejected the law of the LORD of Heaven's Armies; they have despised the word of the Holy One of Israel. 25 That is why the LORD's anger burns against his people, and why he has raised his fist to crush them. The mountains tremble, and the corpses of his people litter the streets like garbage. But even then the LORD's anger is not satisfied. His fist is still poised to strike!

Here, Isaiah calls out the sins of selfishness, pride, drunkenness, and gluttony. They have descended to such a low moral place that dark "is light and light is dark, that bitter is sweet and sweet is bitter." He uses the word "sorrow" over and over to describe what they will face. Though they seem to be on top of the world right now, they soon will face God's judgment and be crushed.

26 He will send a signal to distant nations far away and whistle to those at the ends of the earth. They will come racing toward Jerusalem. 27 They will not get tired or stumble. They will not stop for rest or sleep. Not a belt will be loose, not a sandal strap broken. 28 Their arrows will be sharp and their bows ready for battle. Sparks will fly from their horses' hooves, and the wheels of their chariots will spin like a whirlwind. 29 They will roar like lions, like the strongest of lions. Growling, they will pounce on their victims and carry them off, and no one will be there to rescue them. 30 They will roar over their victims on that day of destruction like the roaring of the sea. If someone looks across the land, only darkness and distress will be seen; even the light will be darkened by clouds.

When God takes His hand of protection off His people, neighboring kingdoms throughout the region are ready to pounce until, eventually, the great army of Babylonia will run them over and destroy Jerusalem.

The same thing happens in our lives. God warned Cain in Gen. 4 that "You will be accepted if you do what is right. But if you refuse to do what is right, then watch out! Sin is crouching at the door, eager to control you. But you must subdue it and be its master."

Every step you take away from God there will be someone there telling you that you are doing the right thing. There will also be someone there to take advantage of you. It is better to be humble before God than celebrated among sinners.

DAY 16
Isaiah 6:1-8

It was in the year King Uzziah died that I saw the Lord. He was sitting on a lofty throne, and the train of his robe filled the Temple. 2 Attending him were mighty seraphim, each having six wings. With two wings they covered their faces, with two they covered their feet, and with two they flew. 3 They were calling out to each other,"Holy, holy, holy is the LORD of Heaven's Armies! The whole earth is filled with his glory!" 4 Their voices shook the Temple to its foundations, and the entire building was filled with smoke.

King Uzziah died in 740 B.C., so we have a reference to a specific time that helps us date Isaiah's writing.

One of the most beautiful passages in Isaiah is the vision of his calling. He has already obeyed God and faithfully delivered messages to the nations of Israel and Judah. The description of the throneroom of God parallels that of Joghn's vision in Revelation, from the angels and creatures around the throne who worship God continually. When Isaiah starts to take all of this in, he realizes his humanity is no match for the holiness of God's presence.

5 Then I said, "It's all over! I am doomed, for I am a sinful man. I have filthy lips, and I live among a people with filthy lips. Yet I have seen the King, the LORD of Heaven's Armies." 6 Then one of the seraphim flew to me with a burning coal he had taken from the altar with a pair of tongs. 7 He touched my lips with it and said, "See, this coal has touched your lips. Now your guilt is removed, and your sins are forgiven." 8 Then I heard the Lord asking, "Whom should I send as a messenger to this people? Who will go for us?" I said, "Here I am. Send me."

Isaiah becomes the first person to experience saving grace. His sins are forgiven for these marvelous moments so he can stand in God's presence. This, too, could have been just a vision, as he might not have literally seen God or been transported to Heaven. Either way, his vision was similar to that of the Apostle Paul, who would not even attempt to describe what he experienced. John only shared his vision of Heaven and the end of time because he was instructed to write.

In response to this vision, Isaiah quickly volunteers and devotes his life to serving God and speaking on his behalf.

Note the seven requirements of the Divine call:

(1) a revelation of God, high and lifted up (vv. 1–4),

(2) a revelation of holiness (vv. 1–4),

(3) a revelation of our uncleanness (v. 5),

(4) Divine cleansing (vv. 6–7),

(5) a personal call—the voice of the Lord (v. 8),

(6) abandonment to God (v. 8), and

(7) divine commissioning (vv. 9–13).

Each one of us has a calling first to be a child of God. We are called into the family of God and are adopted trough surrendering our life to Christ. This is the basis of our identity. There is nothing in life more important than our decision to follow Christ and to embrace our identity as a child of God. This revelation alone can provide a direction for many struggling with mental health issues. Insecurity, fear, anxiety, hopelessness and more can be overcome when we understand how much God loves us and what He has done for us.

DAY 17

Isaiah 6:9-13

And he said, "Yes, go, and say to this people, 'Listen carefully, but do not understand. Watch closely, but learn nothing.' 10 Harden the hearts of these people. Plug their ears and shut their eyes. That way, they will not see with their eyes, nor hear with their ears, nor understand with their hearts and turn to me for healing." 11 Then I said, "Lord, how long will this go on?" And he replied, "Until their towns are empty, their houses are deserted, and the whole country is a wasteland; 12 until the LORD has sent everyone away, and the entire land of Israel lies deserted. 13 If even a tenth—a remnant—survive, it will be invaded again and burned. But as a terebinth or oak tree leaves a stump when it is cut down, so Israel's stump will be a holy seed."

God knows that they will reject his message when Isaiah speaks to the people. They will not be able to comprehend what God is going to do. This is not God's desire; it is the choice of the people who refuse to listen and obey. The people had many years and prophets whom God sent to call them to repentance.

Interestingly, the last line, "Israel's stump will be a holy seed." Jesus later describes His sacrifice as a seed that must be sown into the ground to bear fruit. The holy seed in the stump is the remnant of the covenant God made with Abraham.

This is why I emphasis praying as we open scripture. We ask the Holy Spirit to reveal what God is wanting to communicate to us each day through His Word. The writer of Hebrews calls the Bible, *"living and active".* As the Words of God, the Bible text is more than just history it is means of current communication. God speaks to us what He wants us to know as He reveals truth.

"It exposes our innermost thoughts and desires" (Heb. 4:12). The Word of God helps us discern what God wants for us. It cuts or distinguishes our mind from our heart.

DAY 18
Isaiah 7:1-6

When Ahaz, son of Jotham and grandson of Uzziah, was king of Judah, King Rezin of Syria and Pekah son of Remaliah, the king of Israel, set out to attack Jerusalem. However, they were unable to carry out their plan. 2 The news had come to the royal court of Judah: "Syria is allied with Israel against us!" So the hearts of the king and his people trembled with fear, like trees shaking in a storm.

3 Then the LORD said to Isaiah, "Take your son Shear-jashub and go out to meet King Ahaz. You will find him at the end of the aqueduct that feeds water into the upper pool, near the road leading to the field where cloth is washed. 4 Tell him to stop worrying. Tell him he doesn't need to fear the fierce anger of those two burned-out embers, King Rezin of Syria and Pekah son of Remaliah. 5 Yes, the kings of Syria and Israel are plotting against him, saying, 6 'We will attack Judah and capture it for ourselves. Then we will install the son of Tabeel as Judah's king.'

I love how real and confident God communicates to the King through Isaiah. First, God knows exactly where the King is and where Isaiah can find him. God is going to do His part, and all the King has to do is, 'Stay calm! Be quiet and guard your heart! Don't panic or be discouraged.

These words all point to the source of our calmness, quietness, and peace. We are not "encouraged" because our circumstances change. Before we see anything, hear any news, or anticipate something happening, good or bad, we know our God, The God, is in control. We look to Him, and our faces are radiant.

Those who look to him for help will be radiant with joy; no shadow of shame will darken their faces. Psa. 34:5

DAY 19

Isaiah 7:7-9

> But this is what the Sovereign LORD says: "This invasion will never happen; it will never take place; 8 for Syria is no stronger than its capital, Damascus, and Damascus is no stronger than its king, Rezin. As for Israel, within sixty-five years it will be crushed and completely destroyed. 9 Israel is no stronger than its capital, Samaria, and Samaria is no stronger than its king, Pekah son of Remaliah. Unless your faith is firm, I cannot make you stand firm."

Faith is the only sure foundation—faith in God's nature and character. Jesus told the parable of two houses; one built on sand and the other on rock. I want my life built upon confidence in God rather than myself or trusting in man.

Paul tells us to put on the whole armor of God so that we can stand and keep standing.

What is the alternative to standing? Falling.

Falling for lies, moving away from our confidence in God. Moving toward the sandy beach house that we think will make us happy.

Amazingly, people build homes near the ocean, only to potentially risk everything in a hurricane. They love the sand and the view that much but ignore the wisdom of building on a more solid foundation.

Why do people rebuild houses in hurricane zones instead of moving away?

- Because someone will pay for it. The federal government and many insurance companies.

- Because the properties are valuable.

- Because they weren't killed or even seriously injured.

- Because no one will stop them.

- Because people never learn.

The house built on the rock may not give us the pleasure of looking outside and seeing the ocean, but we rest well knowing our house will stand.

You can also build your house to look less fashionable with 12-foot stairs you must climb daily to lessen the impact. But you will never make soft ground hard compared to rock.

In the same way, building my life on God may mean giving up some momentary pleasures of sin, but it is well worth knowing that my life and eternity are secure in Jesus, who loves me. It is not like I'm suffering. I can live in anticipation of Jesus' promise of abundant life.

Isaiah 30:18 describes our hearts as *"entwined with God's"* so that we are *"overwhelmed with bliss".*

All day long...I'll put my hope in you!

DAY 20
Isaiah 7:10-16

Later, the LORD sent this message to King Ahaz: 11"Ask the LORD your God for a sign of confirmation, Ahaz. Make it as difficult as you want—as high as heaven or as deep as the place of the dead." 12 But the king refused. "No," he said, "I will not test the LORD like that." 13 Then Isaiah said, "Listen well, you royal family of David! Isn't it enough to exhaust human patience? Must you exhaust the patience of my God as well?

Isaiah shares that God is eager to confirm His promise, but the King sees this as presumptuous. People always misinterpret God because they do not know Him personally.

14 All right then, the Lord himself will give you the sign. Look! The virgin will conceive a child! She will give birth to a son and will call him Immanuel (which means 'God is with us'). 15 By the time this child is old enough to choose what is right and reject what is wrong, he will be eating yogurt and honey. 16 For before the child is that old, the lands of the two kings you fear so much will both be deserted.

The sign God did send ultimately skips this King and his descendants. God addresses the family and lineage of David because this will fulfill God's promise to David of someone to sit upon his throne. It points to the only time in human history that a virgin conceived and brought forth a son. Mary becomes the mother of Jesus and fulfills this 700+ year prophecy.

Immanuel, "God with us." What a beautiful statement to describe Jesus's coming to earth. He not only came to fulfill His mission to die and redeem mankind, but He also came to reveal the nature and character of His Father.

We also learn here that Jesus had an age in which He matured to discern between right and wrong and be responsible for his choices, just like we do today.

DAY 21
Isaiah 7:17-25

"Then the LORD will bring things on you, your nation, and your family unlike anything since Israel broke away from Judah. He will bring the king of Assyria upon you!" 18 In that day the LORD will whistle for the army of southern Egypt and for the army of Assyria. They will swarm around you like flies and bees. 19 They will come in vast hordes and settle in the fertile areas and also in the desolate valleys, caves, and thorny places. 20 In that day the Lord will hire a "razor" from beyond the Euphrates Riverh—the king of Assyria—and use it to shave off everything: your land, your crops, and your people. 21 In that day a farmer will be fortunate to have a cow and two sheep or goats left. 22 Nevertheless, there will be enough milk for everyone because so few people will be left in the land. They will eat their fill of yogurt and honey. 23 In that day the lush vineyards, now worth 1,000 pieces of silver, will become patches of briers and thorns. 24 The entire land will become a vast expanse of briers and thorns, a hunting ground overrun by wildlife. 25 No one will go to the fertile hillsides where the gardens once grew, for briers and thorns will cover them. Cattle, sheep, and goats will graze there.

What we don't weed and feed in our lives deteriorates into a useless existence. Vineyards represent life and joy-giving resources—a person who brings happiness and encouragement and inspires spiritual growth in others. We feed off the gift of God in them.

But when our lives with God are untested, we become just another voice outdoors echoing the complaints of people around us. Trampling and being trampled as victims and judges of others so much so people don't want to be around us.

Prayer: Father, help me to cultivate the Vineyard you have planted in my life. Make it fruitful so that others can receive from You through me.

May people be drawn to us rather than repelled just as they were to Jesus.

DAY 22
Isaiah 8:1-10

Then the LORD said to me, "Make a large signboard and clearly write this name on it: Maher-shalal-hash-baz." 2 I asked Uriah the priest and Zechariah son of Jeberekiah, both known as honest men, to witness my doing this. 3 Then I slept with my wife, and she became pregnant and gave birth to a son. And the LORD said, "Call him Maher-shalal-hash-baz. 4 For before this child is old enough to say 'Papa' or 'Mama,' the king of Assyria will carry away both the abundance of Damascus and the riches of Samaria." 5 Then the LORD spoke to me again and said, 6 "My care for the people of Judah is like the gently flowing waters of Shiloah, but they have rejected it. They are rejoicing over what will happen to King Rezin and King Pekah. 7 Therefore, the Lord will overwhelm them with a mighty flood from the Euphrates River—the king of Assyria and all his glory. This flood will overflow all its channels 8 and sweep into Judah until it is chin deep. It will spread its wings, submerging your land from one end to the other, O Immanuel. 9 "Huddle together, you nations, and be terrified. Listen, all you distant lands. Prepare for battle, but you will be crushed! Yes, prepare for battle, but you will be crushed! 10 Call your councils of war, but they will be worthless. Develop your strategies, but they will not succeed. For God is with us!"

Maher-shalal-hash-baz means *"Swift to plunder and quick to carry away."* God often uses these prophetic acts to reinforce His message to His people. Here, Isaiah makes a sign to describe how swift judgment is coming. In addition, he has a son whom God has him call by the same name. This child's life will be a timeline toward prophetic fulfillment.

God will send a flood, meaning an invading army from Assyria. Their take-over of the land of Judah will be complete and thorough. In other words, there would be no escape for the Israelites celebrating what had happened to two different kingdoms. They can "prepare for battle, but they will be crushed" is repeated twice. You see this practice of speaking the exact phrase twice throughout the Bible. This is because there were no exclamation points, bold, or caps in their written language. To emphasize something important, you would repeat it twice. For example, Jesus would say, "Verily verily, I say unto you." He uses verily twice to add importance.

DAY 23
Isaiah 8:11-17

The LORD has given me a strong warning not to think like everyone else does. He said, 12 "Don't call everything a conspiracy, like they do, and don't live in dread of what frightens them. 13 Make the LORD of Heaven's Armies holy in your life. He is the one you should fear. He is the one who should make you tremble. 14 He will keep you safe. But to Israel and Judah he will be a stone that makes people stumble, a rock that makes them fall. And for the people of Jerusalem he will be a trap and a snare. 15 Many will stumble and fall, never to rise again. They will be snared and captured." 16 Preserve the teaching of God; entrust his instructions to those who follow me. 17 I will wait for the LORD, who has turned away from the descendants of Jacob. I will put my hope in him.

I can not think of a timelier message for us today. Don't chase conspiracies; don't be afraid. We live in a world filled with fear and the worst speculation. Establish God as holy and all-powerful in your life. He is our hope and our safety.

This prophetic passage also points toward Jesus, who will come as a stumbling block and rock over which they will trip. In other words, Jesus is going to perplex the Jews in how He comes, not as a conquering military hero they are anticipating, but as a sacrificial lamb to launch an eternal spiritual Kingdom access for everyone who believes.

I heard someone say, "you can polish Him all you want but Jesus will still be a stumbling block." In other words, You can emphasize the gentleness, kindness and love of Jesus but you cannot hide His holiness and His unwillingness to ignore sin.

DAY 24
Isaiah 8:18-22

I and the children the LORD has given me serve as signs and warnings to Israel from the LORD of Heaven's Armies who dwells in his Temple on Mount Zion. 19 Someone may say to you, "Let's ask the mediums and those who consult the spirits of the dead. With their whisperings and mutterings, they will tell us what to do." But shouldn't people ask God for guidance? Should the living seek guidance from the dead? 20 Look to God's instructions and teachings! People who contradict his word are completely in the dark. 21 They will go from one place to another, weary and hungry. And because they are hungry, they will rage and curse their king and their God. They will look up to heaven 22 and down at the earth, but wherever they look, there will be trouble and anguish and dark despair. They will be thrown out into the darkness.

We are to give this response to those who consult the dead through mediums, tarot cards, palm readings, etc. These mystical portals do put us in contact with the supernatural, but it is demonic.

These sources will return a message full of lies and deception to lead us away from God. We can subtly open ourselves by "rolling the dice" or "flipping a coin." We are asking something to direct our course outside of the indwelling Holy Spirit.

This is how we respond to those who think checking their horoscope is just curiosity or entertainment. We are to direct them to the teachings of God's Word for truth, especially if they start saying things unaligned with the Bible.

These people risk the danger of going dark and losing any connection with the One True God and exchanging it for darkness and deception.

Light refers to revelation. We cannot chase revelation and truth from two opposing sources. There is only one truth, though today we like to say there are many versions. We must have our own. I gave up my truth in exchange for God's. My thoughts are now His thoughts.

We must trust God to guide us continually.

DAY 25
Isaiah 9:1-7

Nevertheless, that time of darkness and despair will not go on forever. The land of Zebulun and Naphtali will be humbled, but there will be a time in the future when Galilee of the Gentiles, which lies along the road that runs between the Jordan and the sea, will be filled with glory.

Isaiah presents one of the most beautiful prophetic songs about Jesus's coming. Jesus spent much of his life and ministry in Galilee. The Israelites, especially the Bible scholars of Jesus' day, had to look at the passage repeatedly when He began to fulfill all of these promises of what His coming would mean.

2 The people who walk in darkness will see a great light. For those who live in a land of deep darkness, a light will shine. 3 You will enlarge the nation of Israel, and its people will rejoice. They will rejoice before you as people rejoice at the harvest and like warriors dividing the plunder. 4 For you will break the yoke of their slavery and lift the heavy burden from their shoulders. You will break the oppressor's rod, just as you did when you destroyed the army of Midian. 5 The boots of the warrior and the uniforms bloodstained by war will all be burned. They will be fuel for the fire. 6 For a child is born to us, a son is given to us. The government will rest on his shoulders. And he will be called: Wonderful Counselor, Mighty God, Everlasting Father, Prince of Peace. 7 His government and its peace will never end. He will rule with fairness and justice from the throne of his ancestor David for all eternity. The passionate commitment of the LORD of Heaven's Armies will make this happen!

What a beautiful prophetic tribute to Jesus. I wonder if Isaiah just got the words, a vision, a mental picture of Jesus coming to fulfill all the prophetic promises.

The yoke of slavery and freedom Jesus described was a spiritual yoke, not the oppression of the Roman Empire. He offers His yoke, which is easy and light compared to the harsh reality of living under an occupying army. The statements applying to rulership are not the earthly governments but rulership in people's hearts. Jesus becomes our Wonderful Counselor, Mighty God, Everlasting Father, and Prince of Peace. When you think of these qualities, they cover everything we need in life and eternity. If Jesus rules our hearts and decisions, we will live in complete peace.

DAY 26
Isaiah 9:8-21

The Lord has spoken out against Jacob; his judgment has fallen upon Israel. 9 And the people of Israel and Samaria, who spoke with such pride and arrogance, will soon know it. 10 They said, "We will replace the broken bricks of our ruins with finished stone, and replant the felled sycamore-fig trees with cedars."

Confidence is only a good thing when it is placed in God. We love entrepreneurs and people who are "self-made." They "pull themselves up by their bootstraps," as we like to say.

But if our trust is only in our wisdom and strength and we arrogantly ignore the God who gives us the ability to make wealth or become successful in any endeavor (Deut. 8:18).

The Israelites had rejected God, and now they were facing his judgment through the armies that were attacking them. Their response was humanistic: "We will build back better."

The proper response would have been to humble themselves and ask God for forgiveness and grace to follow him.

The apostle Paul had it right when he said, *I can do all things through Christ who strengthens me* (Phil. 4:13).

He had confidence in himself to the extent that he trusted he was walking with God, who was directing him and empowering him. This was bravado about who God was to him.

This is the life that glorifies God and walks in His blessing—humble, childlike dependence because of God's greatness and love for us.

11 But the LORD will bring Rezin's enemies against Israel and stir up all their foes. 12 The Syrians from the east and the Philistines from the west will bare their fangs and devour Israel. But even then the LORD's anger will not be satisfied. His fist is still poised to strike. 13 For after all this punishment, the people will still not repent. They will not seek the LORD of Heaven's Armies. 14 Therefore, in a single day the LORD will destroy both the head and the tail, the noble palm branch and the lowly reed.

God is often accused of being cruel and quick to judge. You can draw this conclusion by isolating a verse or two and pulling it from its context. When you see the greater context, you see people who are rebellious and choose to resist God. Even in judgment, God calls them to repent, allowing them to stop judgment and receive mercy. God would instead display mercy to His children and the heir of Abraham's covenant.

15 The leaders of Israel are the head, and the lying prophets are the tail. 16 For the leaders of the people have misled them. They have led them down the path of destruction. 17 That is why the Lord takes no pleasure in the young men and shows no mercy even to the widows and orphans. For they are all wicked hypocrites, and they all speak foolishness. But even then the LORD's anger will not be satisfied. His fist is still poised to strike. 18 This wickedness is like a brushfire. It burns not only briers and thorns but also sets the forests ablaze. Its burning sends up clouds of smoke. 19 The land will be blackened by the fury of the LORD of Heaven's Armies. The people will be fuel for the fire, and no one will spare even his own brother. 20 They will attack their neighbor on the right but will still be hungry. They will devour their neighbor on the left but will not be satisfied. In the end they will even eat their own children. 21 Manasseh will feed on Ephraim, Ephraim will feed on Manasseh, and both will devour Judah. But even then the LORD's anger will not be satisfied. His fist is still poised to strike.

What a picture. You have the people being led away from God by their Kings and prophets behind them telling them this is the right direction. This is why God judges leaders with stronger judgment. They are responsible for hearing from God and following Him so that the people follow.

Finally, when people become so hard of heart, they devour everyone around them. Bitterness makes us caustic to those around us. Sin is an insatiable appetite that is never satisfied. The only way we overcome sin and temptation is to be filled with the Spirit of God. Our brains desire dopamine and it doesn't care about the source. We can find ourselves battling our own brain, not giving it what it wants. The only way to win this fight is to learn how to feed godly sources of dopamine to the brain. We can get the same release of the hormone through worship, prayer, meditation, stillness, gratitude, and fellowship with another believer.

DAY 27

Isaiah 10:1-4

What sorrow awaits the unjust judges and those who issue unfair laws. 2 They deprive the poor of justice and deny the rights of the needy among my people. They prey on widows and take advantage of orphans. 3 What will you do when I punish you, when I send disaster upon you from a distant land? To whom will you turn for help? Where will your treasures be safe? 4 You will stumble along as prisoners or lie among the dead. But even then the LORD's anger will not be satisfied. His fist is still poised to strike.

In the end, God settles all accounts. All of the injustices, all of the sorrow and pain caused to another person, will be judged by the perfect Judge of all creation.

Before we get too excited about our brother or sister being judged, remember Jesus's words, who warned us that the measure of judgment we use, or desire toward others is the same level we will receive.

I am grateful that the God of mercy and grace is the one who will judge righteously with compassion. He is also the perfectly holy God, and only the perfect sacrifice can wash away our sins.

In our day, we tend to focus primarily on God's mercy and grace, forgetting that He is the Holy Judge who will refuse to overlook sin and rebellion. He still knows how to make a fist that is ready to strike.

Walking in love means we cover over sins by letting God deal with those issues. Yes, there are times when I am discipling someone and they ask me to point out things or they want to confess and find help overcoming a sin I will help. Without this permission I seldom say something or hold something in my heart. What I want to be there is love. Any kind of bitterness or grudge I hold against someone only hurts me and any possible relationship where I could help them. If I love well this will provide a better opportunity for God to work through our relationship to bring freedom to the other person.

DAY 28
Isaiah 10:5-11

"What sorrow awaits Assyria, the rod of my anger. I use it as a club to express my anger. 6 I am sending Assyria against a godless nation, against a people with whom I am angry. Assyria will plunder them, trampling them like dirt beneath its feet. 7 But the king of Assyria will not understand that he is my tool; his mind does not work that way. His plan is simply to destroy, to cut down nation after nation. 8 He will say, 'Each of my princes will soon be a king. 9 We destroyed Calno just as we did Carchemish. Hamath fell before us as Arpad did. And we destroyed Samaria just as we did Damascus. 10 Yes, we have finished off many a kingdom whose gods were greater than those in Jerusalem and Samaria. 11 So we will defeat Jerusalem and her gods, just as we destroyed Samaria with hers.'"

In verse five in the New King James Bible the words "rod" and "club" are translated "rod and staff" which reminds us of David's words in Psalm23, *"Thy rod and Thy staff they comfort me."* Here rather than comfort God is using a foreign nation to administer justice on Israel for their rebellion against God. This again points to God's grave and His holiness which both must be regarded. Thankfully, Jesus took our punishment and died for our rebellion, and we are now God's children. We are not waiting for some impending judgment but instead we rejoice and take comfort in the fact that our sins are forgiven, and we are children of God.

I wonder if the Assyrian king believed his own press. Did he believe he was accomplishing all of these victories over the Israelites on his own?

Confidence is only a good thing when it is placed in God. We love to celebrate entrepreneurs and people who we call "self-made." They "pulled themselves up by their bootstraps," as we like to say.

But if our trust is only in our own wisdom and strength and we arrogantly ignore the God who gives us the ability to make wealth or become successful in any endeavor (Deut. 8:18).

The Israelites had rejected God, and now they were facing his judgment through the armies that were attacking them. Their response was a humanistic approach: "We will build back better".

The proper response would have been to humble themselves and ask God for forgiveness and grace to follow him.

> The apostle Paul had it right when he said, *I can do all things through Christ who strengthens me* (Phil. 4:13).

He had confidence in himself to the extent he trusted he was walking with God, who was directing him and empowering him. It was bravado about who God was to him.

This is the life that glorifies God and walks in His blessing. It is humble, childlike dependence because of God's greatness and love for us.

DAY 29
Isaiah 10:12-19

After the Lord has used the king of Assyria to accomplish his purposes on Mount Zion and in Jerusalem, he will turn against the king of Assyria and punish him—for he is proud and arrogant. 13 He boasts, "By my own powerful arm I have done this. With my own shrewd wisdom I planned it. I have broken down the defenses of nations and carried off their treasures. I have knocked down their kings like a bull. 14 I have robbed their nests of riches and gathered up kingdoms as a farmer gathers eggs. No one can even flap a wing against me or utter a peep of protest." 15 But can the ax boast greater power than the person who uses it? Is the saw greater than the person who saws? Can a rod strike unless a hand moves it? Can a wooden cane walk by itself? 16 Therefore, the Lord, the LORD of Heaven's Armies, will send a plague among Assyria's proud troops, and a flaming fire will consume its glory. 17 The LORD, the Light of Israel, will be a fire; the Holy One will be a flame. He will devour the thorns and briers with fire, burning up the enemy in a single night. 18 The LORD will consume Assyria's glory like a fire consumes a forest in a fruitful land; it will waste away like sick people in a plague. 19 Of all that glorious forest, only a few trees will survive— so few that a child could count them!

God is using them as a tool to bring judgment to Israel. Yet, they think it is their wisdom, strategy, and power that is winning these victories on the battlefields. Isaiah uses a couple of illustrations of tools who can take no credit for what they do. They only succeed by the hand that controls them.

We don't look at a beautiful painting and celebrate the brush or the paint. It is the artist that deserves honor. It is the same with us. Anything excellent or fruitful in our lives is from God. This is why Paul describes to the Galatians what he calls the fruit of the Spirit (Gal. 5:22-23). The Holy Spirit inspires and leads us so that good things are accomplished through us. In the end, we redirect any applause to God.

Never take credit for what God has done. He will not share the spotlight or allow us to trick others into believing we accomplished something on our own. God has a way of exposing this disregard for His work and taking what is due Him.

DAY 30
Isaiah 10:20-27

In that day the remnant left in Israel, the survivors in the house of Jacob, will no longer depend on allies who seek to destroy them. But they will faithfully trust the LORD, the Holy One of Israel. 21 A remnant will return; yes, the remnant of Jacob will return to the Mighty God. 22 But though the people of Israel are as numerous as the sand of the seashore, only a remnant of them will return. The LORD has rightly decided to destroy his people. 23 Yes, the Lord, the LORD of Heaven's Armies, has already decided to destroy the entire land. 24 So this is what the Lord, the LORD of Heaven's Armies, says: "O my people in Zion, do not be afraid of the Assyrians when they oppress you with rod and club as the Egyptians did long ago. 25 In a little while my anger against you will end, and then my anger will rise up to destroy them." 26 The LORD of Heaven's Armies will lash them with his whip, as he did when Gideon triumphed over the Midianites at the rock of Oreb, or when the LORD's staff was raised to drown the Egyptian army in the sea. 27 In that day the LORD will end the bondage of his people. He will break the yoke of slavery and lift it from their shoulders.

Israel had allied with Egypt to help them against Assyria, which was threatening to attack them. The Jewish nation has come full circle. They were freed from slavery in Egypt through Moses. They conquered and reigned in their Promised Land for hundreds of years. Now they see returning to the one who held them captive, who abused them, as a source of help rather than God.

We have short memories and become desperate when driven by fear. We will run to unhealthy sources or seek to escape our pain by the old means we thought we had put behind us.

"Yes, the credit card interest is 20%, but I need or want this thing, and I see no other way to get it. God could have intervened sooner, but He didn't. Now it's up to me and my resources because no one will help." This is the lie we believe that puts us in bondage to debt, abusive relationships, drugs, pornography, and so on, all in the pursuit of pleasure and security.

What an insult this must have been to God, the Israelites turning to Egypt for help. God has always protected His people when they turn to Him. Unfortunately, the moment's stress kept the Israelites and us from stilling ourselves long enough to hear God's voice.

There is good news. God's love and faithfulness exceed our sinfulness and lack of remembering the God we serve.

He will break the yoke of slavery and lift it from their shoulders.

The King James Version says, *"The yoke will be destroyed because of the anointing."* God wants to fill their lives to such an extent that nothing oppressive can rule over them. Neither Assyria currently nor Egypt in the past is stronger than God's anointing.

Anointing here represents the anointing oil poured upon the priests to designate them exclusive to God. In the New Testament, the Apostle John tells us,

> But the wonderful anointing you have received from God is much greater than their deception and now lives in you. 1 John 2:27a

The Holy Spirit fulfills God's promise of always being with us, just as Jesus promised His disciples.

Isaiah pictures the presence of God so significant that it breaks all oppression. A power more fantastic than any type of spiritual, emotional, and physical bondage is within us.

DAY 31

Isaiah 10:28-34

Look, the Assyrians are now at Aiath. They are passing through Migron and are storing their equipment at Micmash. 29 They are crossing the pass and are camping at Geba. Fear strikes the town of Ramah. All the people of Gibeah, the hometown of Saul, are running for their lives. 30 Scream in terror, you people of Gallim! Shout out a warning to Laishah. Oh, poor Anathoth! 31 There go the people of Madmenah, all fleeing. The citizens of Gebim are trying to hide. 32 The enemy stops at Nob for the rest of that day. He shakes his fist at beautiful Mount Zion, the mountain of Jerusalem. 33 But look! The Lord, the LORD of Heaven's Armies, will chop down the mighty tree of Assyria with great power! He will cut down the proud. That lofty tree will be brought down. 34 He will cut down the forest trees with an ax. Lebanon will fall to the Mighty One.

No matter what things look like in the natural realm, we always must consider what God is doing in the supernatural realm.

> So, we don't look at the troubles we can see now; instead, we fix our gaze on things that cannot be seen. The things we see now will soon be gone, but the things we cannot see will last forever.
> 2 Corinthians 4:18

God is never late, but He sure passes up a lot of opportunities to be early. When He has the choice between making us comfortable or making us happy, God always chooses character over comfort.

A wonderful faith practice is to simply stop in the midst of a difficult circumstance, ask God what He is doing, and allow yourself to see your situation from His perspective. What parent doesn't want to share insights with their children? We are honored when our children show that much confidence in us. I believe God is the perfect Father who feels the same way when we place our trust in Him.

Access to God's thoughts and direction is one of the incredible benefits of knowing God.

> If you need wisdom, ask our generous God, and he will give it to you. He will not rebuke you for asking (James 1:5).

DAY 32:

Isaiah 11:1-5

Out of the stump of David's family will grow a shoot— yes, a new Branch bearing fruit from the old root. 2 And the Spirit of the LORD will rest on him— the Spirit of wisdom and understanding, the Spirit of counsel and might, the Spirit of knowledge and the fear of the LORD. 3 He will delight in obeying the LORD. He will not judge by appearance nor make a decision based on hearsay. 4 He will give justice to the poor and make fair decisions for the exploited. The earth will shake at the force of his word, and one breath from his mouth will destroy the wicked. 5 He will wear righteousness like a belt and truth like an undergarment.

Isaiah paints a picture of the coming Messiah. Though King Hezekiah could have fit the description the prophetic nature of Isaiah's writing and the passages that point forward seem to guide us to see this as a prophecy of Jesus. It is an apt description of His character and empowerment.

Notice that each statement begins with "the Spirit." This same Holy Spirit is also our source of wisdom, power, and insight.

We desperately need to live in close communion with the Spirit of God to live a life that is beyond the ordinary.

> He will find his delight in living by the Spirit of the Fear of the Lord. He will neither judge by appearances nor make his decisions based on rumors. 4 With righteousness, he will uphold justice for the poor and defend the lowly of the earth. Isaiah 11:3-4

Walking in step and allowing the Holy Spirit has the same impact on us and through us that it had on Jesus. The Holy Spirit reveals the heart of God, so we stand in awe of Him and reflect His love for others, especially the oppressed.

DAY 33
Isaiah 11:6-9

In that day the wolf and the lamb will live together; the leopard will lie down with the baby goat. The calf and the yearling will be safe with the lion, and a little child will lead them all. 7 The cow will graze near the bear. The cub and the calf will lie down together. The lion will eat hay like a cow. 8 The baby will play safely near the hole of a cobra. Yes, a little child will put its hand in a nest of deadly snakes without harm. 9 Nothing will hurt or destroy in all my holy mountain, for as the waters fill the sea, so the earth will be filled with people who know the LORD.

What a beautiful picture of restoration to how things were when God first created the earth. All will be reconciled in all realms. The world and even the animal kingdom will be restored to its original intention before sin, disease, and death through the curse caused by Adam's sin. Imagine fierce carnivores becoming herbivores, lions grazing in a field next to their former prey. Animal instincts to attack and protect their young will be rewired. This kind of world is hard to imagine after thousands of years of man's destruction of the planet and one another.

All of this because people who inhabit the earth "know the Lord." What if those of us who know the Lord today got a headstart and started treating one another and animals with respect and love? What if we cared for God's planet, not to be worshipped as "Mother Earth," but in a way that honored God?

DAY 34

Isaiah 11:10-16

In that day the heir to David's throne will be a banner of salvation to all the world. The nations will rally to him, and the land where he lives will be a glorious place. 11 In that day the Lord will reach out his hand a second time to bring back the remnant of his people— those who remain in Assyria and northern Egypt; in southern Egypt, Ethiopia, and Elam; in Babylonia, Hamath, and all the distant coastlands. 12 He will raise a flag among the nations and assemble the exiles of Israel. He will gather the scattered people of Judah from the ends of the earth. 13 Then at last the jealousy between Israel and Judah will end. They will not be rivals anymore. 14 They will join forces to swoop down on Philistia to the west. Together they will attack and plunder the nations to the east. They will occupy the lands of Edom and Moab, and Ammon will obey them. 15 The LORD will make a dry path through the gulf of the Red Sea. He will wave his hand over the Euphrates River, sending a mighty wind to divide it into seven streams so it can easily be crossed on foot. 16 He will make a highway for the remnant of his people, the remnant coming from Assyria, just as he did for Israel long ago when they returned from Egypt.

You have a repeated theme throughout Isaiah's writing of seeing two time periods. Isaiah is given a vision of the restoration period under Nehemiah and Ezra when the people return from captivity in Babylon. He is also witnessing a prophetic vision of the restoration of all things when Jesus returns.

Of course, it is no secret who the heir to David's throne is—Jesus Christ. This describes the period when Jesus comes back to establish His Kingdom rule and reign over the earth that is restored to its former glory, which began in the Garden of Eden. The world will still need to be cultivated, and dominion will still be the mandate for man.

There is a wonderful message at the end of this passage about God's refusal to give up on His people even though they abandoned Him. Knowing that man will again rebel against God, this cannot stop God from being who He is, the God who originated love.

DAY 35

Isaiah 12:2-3

In that day you will sing: "I will praise you, O LORD! You were angry with me, but not anymore. Now you comfort me. 2 See, God has come to save me. I will trust in him and not be afraid. The LORD God is my strength and my song; he has given me victory." 3 With joy, you will drink deeply from the fountain of salvation! Isaiah 12:2-3

What would it look like to live life every day confident and unafraid? Confident in who God made you to be. Unafraid of people or their opinions? Not worried about financial crises, job insecurity, health, the stock market, or our kids' future.

Here, Isaiah gives us a great way to measure our spiritual health: how much do we sing? Do you break into worship throughout the day? Are there particular songs that redirect you from worry to worship? If we can sing in a crisis, we will stay connected to God and experience joy amid adverse circumstances.

Never forget that we have "wells of salvation" within us, an unending supply to fill us up and pour out to others. In ancient times, we sang,

"I've got a river of life flowing out of me,

It makes the lame to walk and the blind to see,

It opens prison doors and sets the captive free,

I've got a river of life flowing out of me

Spring up O well with my soul,

Spring up O well and make me whole,

Spring up O well, and give to me, that life abundantly."

Then on the most important day of the feast, the last day, Jesus stood and shouted out to the crowds—"All you thirsty ones, come to me! Come to me and drink! Believe in me so that rivers of living water will burst out from within you, flowing from your innermost being, just like the Scripture says!" John 7:37-38

DAY 36

Isaiah 12:4-6

With joy you will drink deeply from the fountain of salvation! 4 In that wonderful day you will sing: "Thank the LORD! Praise his name! Tell the nations what he has done. Let them know how mighty he is! 5 Sing to the LORD, for he has done wonderful things. Make known his praise around the world. 6 Let all the people of Jerusalem shout his praise with joy! For great is the Holy One of Israel who lives among you."

This is one of twelve songs in Isaiah. It celebrates that God will someday free the people of Israel from captivity.

This is also my song celebrating my deliverance from spiritual death. It is also your song and everyone's song who places their trust in God.

I like how Isaiah emphasizes that giving thanks provokes greater faith and belief in God for even greater things. "Give thanks to the Lord and ask him for more!"

We have a more remarkable story as God does more in our lives. Worship and gratitude are the two most significant ways to connect with God.

Did you know neuroscience research has established that gratitude is the fastest way to regulate our emotions and return to a state of peace and job when we have been upset.

At Helping Others Heal we teach the people we serve how to establish big gratitude memories they can go to in a moment of stress or anxiety and calm themselves.

Take a moment and sing this song of praise to the One who is worthy, Jesus!

DAY 37
Isaiah 13:1-12

Isaiah son of Amoz received this message concerning the destruction of Babylon: 2 "Raise a signal flag on a bare hilltop. Call up an army against Babylon. Wave your hand to encourage them as they march into the palaces of the high and mighty. 3 I, the LORD, have dedicated these soldiers for this task. Yes, I have called mighty warriors to express my anger, and they will rejoice when I am exalted." 4 Hear the noise on the mountains! Listen, as the vast armies march! It is the noise and shouting of many nations. The LORD of Heaven's Armies has called this army together. 5 They come from distant countries, from beyond the farthest horizons. They are the LORD's weapons to carry out his anger. With them he will destroy the whole land. 6 Scream in terror, for the day of the LORD has arrived— the time for the Almighty to destroy. 7 Every arm is paralyzed with fear. Every heart melts, 8 and people are terrified. Pangs of anguish grip them, like those of a woman in labor. They look helplessly at one another, their faces aflame with fear. 9 For see, the day of the LORD is coming – the terrible day of his fury and fierce anger. The land will be made desolate, and all the sinners destroyed with it. 10 The heavens will be black above them; the stars will give no light. The sun will be dark when it rises, and the moon will provide no light. 11 "I, the LORD, will punish the world for its evil and the wicked for their sin. I will crush the arrogance of the proud and humble the pride of the mighty. 12 I will make people scarcer than gold— more rare than the fine gold of Ophir.

This next section of Isaiah prophetically declares the outcome of several nations, starting with Babylon. Babylon was the nation God allowed Babylon to overrun and take the Israelites captive. The word in verse 1, "message" is better translated "burden" or a heavy message. The message is less for Babylon and more for the people of God to know He takes care of His children and the unrighteous will not escape punishment.

DAY 37

This prophecy against Babylon was spoken by Isaiah approximately 174 years before Babylon fell in 536 BC. Babylon becomes a metaphor for the world's political and religious system in the book of Revelation. (See also Isa. 46–47; Rev. 18).

So once again, the prophet points to the overthrow of ancient Babylon and the end of time when Jesus returns to establish His Kingdom throne on earth.

Side note: Every generation believes they are the last. We love to discuss the end times. Of course, this is true. We are in the last days because we only get to live one life, one generation, so yes, we live in our last days.

Someday, the clock will strike twelve on God's clock, and Jesus will return and make all things new (Rev. 21:5). Notice, though, that it is God who judges the nations, not us. Our job is to trust God through all difficulties, love people, and share God's truth about eternity.

Don't get lost in the weeds of predicting seasons and dates for a timetable that only God is privileged to know. Instead, focus on the fact that the light of Christ shines brightest in the darkness. God will be with His children and reveal Himself in any circumstances we face.

DAY 38
Isaiah 13:13-22

For I will shake the heavens. The earth will move from its place when the LORD of Heaven's Armies displays his wrath in the day of his fierce anger." 14 Everyone in Babylon will run about like a hunted gazelle, like sheep without a shepherd. They will try to find their own people and flee to their own land. 15 Anyone who is captured will be cut down— run through with a sword. 16 Their little children will be dashed to death before their eyes. Their homes will be sacked, and their wives will be raped. 17 "Look, I will stir up the Medes against Babylon. They cannot be tempted by silver or bribed with gold. 18 The attacking armies will shoot down the young men with arrows. They will have no mercy on helpless babies and will show no compassion for children." 19 Babylon, the most glorious of kingdoms, the flower of Chaldean pride, will be devastated like Sodom and Gomorrah when God destroyed them. 20 Babylon will never be inhabited again. It will remain empty for generation after generation. Nomads will refuse to camp there, and shepherds will not bed down their sheep. 21 Desert animals will move into the ruined city, and the houses will be haunted by howling creatures. Owls will live among the ruins, and wild goats will go there to dance. 22 Hyenas will howl in its fortresses, and jackals will make dens in its luxurious palaces. Babylon's days are numbered; its time of destruction will soon arrive.

Isaiah continues his vision of the horrific end of the nation of Babylone both in ancient times and in the future time. The setting and people will be different, but the hearts of men will not change over time. The same greed, lust, and desires have captured men's hearts and turned them from God since the begging and will do so until the end.

In verse 14, we recognize a statement Jesus will later quote before His triumphal entry into Jerusalem. He describes the people as *"sheep without a shepherd."* The crowds in Jerusalem were quick to celebrate Jesus as the Messiah one day and be all for His crucifixion the next. People in these last days will act in the same way by declaring God on Sunday but then run to every source other God all week.

DAY 39
Isaiah 14:1-11

But the Lord will have mercy on the descendants of Jacob. He will choose Israel as his special people once again. He will bring them back to settle once again in their own land. And people from many different nations will come and join them there and unite with the people of Israel. 2 The nations of the world will help the people of Israel to return, and those who come to live in the Lord's land will serve them. Those who captured Israel will themselves be captured, and Israel will rule over its enemies. 3 In that wonderful day when the Lord gives his people rest from sorrow and fear, from slavery and chains, 4 you will taunt the king of Babylon. You will say, "The mighty man has been destroyed. Yes, your insolence is ended. 5 For the Lord has crushed your wicked power and broken your evil rule. 6 You struck the people with endless blows of rage and held the nations in your angry grip with unrelenting tyranny. 7 But finally the earth is at rest and quiet. Now it can sing again! 8 Even the trees of the forest— the cypress trees and the cedars of Lebanon— sing out this joyous song: 'Since you have been cut down, no one will come now to cut us down!' 9 "In the place of the dead there is excitement over your arrival. The spirits of world leaders and mighty kings long dead stand up to see you. 10 With one voice they all cry out, 'Now you are as weak as we are. 11 Your might and power were buried with you. The sound of the harp in your palace has ceased. Now maggots are your sheet, and worms your blanket.'

I guess the NFL Taunting Penalty does not apply to wicked kings. The Israelites went through all the pain and suffering, even though it was their fault for turning away from God to other gods and idols. The believers who were persecuted or didn't enjoy the finest things in life will have the last laugh. All pain and troubles are past, and it will be affirmed that every sacrifice by faithful followers of Jesus was worth it.

DAY 39

That day refers to the Day of the Lord. The Day of the Lord always points to a day of judgment. Usually, it refers to the Great White Throne Judgment John describes in Revelation 20:11-5. This is when everything will make way for Jesus' return and put the world in order under His rulership. In every nation, the leader will surrender to the true King. All the controlling economic and financial systems will be destroyed. Only God's Kingdom will prevail.

This is a day of rejoicing for believers and a day of terror for those who trusted in the systems just mentioned. If these people don't want Jesus to rule in their life now, they won't like it then. This is where Jesus described how He would separate the sheep from the goat. The submitted and humble sheep enter paradise, and the rebellious goat enters judgment.

DAY 40
Isaiah 14:12-23

"How you are fallen from heaven, O shining star, son of the morning! You have been thrown down to the earth, you who destroyed the nations of the world. 13 For you said to yourself, 'I will ascend to heaven and set my throne above God's stars. I will preside on the mountain of the gods far away in the north. 14 I will climb to the highest heavens and be like the Most High.' 15 Instead, you will be brought down to the place of the dead, down to its lowest depths. 16 Everyone there will stare at you and ask, 'Can this be the one who shook the earth and made the kingdoms of the world tremble? 17 Is this the one who destroyed the world and made it into a wasteland? Is this the king who demolished the world's greatest cities and had no mercy on his prisoners?' 18 "The kings of the nations lie in stately glory, each in his own tomb, 19 but you will be thrown out of your grave like a worthless branch. Like a corpse trampled underfoot, you will be dumped into a mass grave with those killed in battle. You will descend to the pit. 20 You will not be given a proper burial for you have destroyed your nation and slaughtered your people. The descendants of such an evil person will never again receive honor. 21 Kill this man's children! Let them die because of their father's sins! They must not rise and conquer the earth, filling the world with their cities." 22 This is what the Lord of Heaven's Armies says: "I, myself, have risen against Babylon! I will destroy its children and its children's children," says the Lord. 23 "I will make Babylon a desolate place of owls, filled with swamps and marshes. I will sweep the land with the broom of destruction. I, the Lord of Heaven's Armies, have spoken!"

Tertullian, Justin, and Origen were probably some of the first Christian writers to identify the king of Babylon as the devil. Debate goes on today among theologians about whether this is a human king, a form of government and fallen society, or Satan himself. If Isaiah is describing the origin of Satan, then he is giving us the background and one of the most explicit descriptions of Satan before and after his fall and his ultimate demise. I believe you can hold either view within orthodoxy or Biblical view.

Satan certainly qualifies for the description of his deception and fall for trying to usurp God's throne. His eternal place is described as the pit, whereas John's description in Revelation 20:10 is a fiery lake.

Regardless of whether this is Satan or a world system he has created and imposed to oppose God's Kingdom, it doesn't matter. The destruction of humanity aligns with Satan and everyone he influences with a desire to undermine God's people.

Satan and all of his followers will share in the judgment for rejecting God. Whether they be kings or gods or people who served themselves as their god, all will be separated from the Holy God for eternity.

DAY 41
Isaiah 15:1-9

This message came to me concerning Moab: In one night the town of Ar will be leveled, and the city of Kir will be destroyed.

2 Your people will go to their temple in Dibon to mourn. They will go to their sacred shrines to weep. They will wail for the fate of Nebo and Medeba, shaving their heads in sorrow and cutting off their beards.

3 They will wear burlap as they wander the streets. From every home and public square will come the sound of wailing.

4 The people of Heshbon and Elealeh will cry out; their voices will be heard as far away as Jahaz!

The bravest warriors of Moab will cry out in utter terror. They will be helpless with fear. 5 My heart weeps for Moab. Its people flee to Zoar and Eglath-shelishiyah. Weeping, they climb the road to Luhith. Their cries of distress can be heard all along the road to Horonaim.

6 Even the waters of Nimrim are dried up! The grassy banks are scorched. The tender plants are gone; nothing green remains.

7 The people grab their possessions and carry them across the Ravine of Willows.

8 A cry of distress echoes through the land of Moab from one end to the other- from Eglaim to Beer- eli.

9 The stream near Dibon runs red with blood, but I am still not finished with Dibon! Lions will hunt down the survivors—both those who try to escape and those who remain behind.

Moab was a neighboring country to the southeast of Israel in the current region of southern Jordan. They were often at odds with Israel. Moab also represents the name given to describe all who are enemies of God and His people.

Typically, an invading army would conquer an entire region. All the cities and nations would be leveled and laid waste with resources being taken. All the cities of Moab will be destroyed and though the people run to their temples and cry out to their gods they will not be saved.

Beyond the conquering army, you see the judgment of God in the natural disasters of water resources drying up and crops failing. What invaders don't destroy and what natural disasters don't take away hungry animals will finish.

With all this destruction we must remember that these nations surrounding Israel and Judah knew about the God they served. They could have turned to God and He would forgive and heal them. Unfortunately, the Israelites were in a period of rebellion, so they were not much of a witness as they were undergoing their season of judgment.

DAY 42
Isaiah 16:1-13

Send lambs from Sela as tribute to the ruler of the land. Send them through the deserto the mountain of beautiful Zion.

2 The women of Moab are left like homeless birds at the shallow crossings of the Arnon River.

3 "Help us," they cry. "Defend us against our enemies. Protect us from their relentless attack. Do not betray us now that we have escaped.

4 Let our refugees stay among you. Hide them from our enemies until the terror is past.

When oppression and destruction have ended and enemy raiders have disappeared, 5 then God will establish one of David's descendants as king. He will rule with mercy and truth. He will always do what is just and be eager to do what is right.

6 We have heard about proud Moab—about its pride and arrogance and rage. But all that boasting has disappeared.

7 The entire land of Moab weeps. Yes, everyone in Moab mourns for the cakes of raisins from Kir-hareseth. They are all gone now.

8 The farms of Heshbon are abandoned; the vineyards at Sibmah are deserted.

The rulers of the nations have broken down Moab— that beautiful grapevine.

Its tendrils spread north as far as the town of Jazer and trailed eastward into the wilderness.

Its shoots reached so far west that they crossed over the Dead Sea.

9 So now I weep for Jazer and the vineyards of Sibmah; my tears will flow for Heshbon and Elealeh.

There are no more shouts of joy over your summer fruits and harvest.

10 Gone now is the gladness, gone the joy of harvest.

> There will be no singing in the vineyards, no more happy shouts, no treading of grapes in the winepresses. I have ended all their harvest joys.
>
> 11 My heart's cry for Moab is like a lament on a harp. I am filled with anguish for Kir-hareseth.
>
> 12 The people of Moab will worship at their pagan shrines, but it will do them no good. They will cry to the gods in their temples, but no one will be able to save them.
>
> 13 The Lord has already said these things about Moab in the past. 14 But now the Lord says, "Within three years, counting each day, the glory of Moab will be ended. From its great population, only a feeble few will be left alive."

Here again, Isaiah is lamenting Israel's neighbor Moab for the destruction that has come through invaders and God's judgment for their rebellion. Isaiah understands the cause behind the disaster, but he cannot help but think about better times when the two nations traded supplies and resources, such as the wine from Moab's vineyards. Wine always speaks of abundance and celebration. There is nothing to celebrate; a luxury crop like grapes cannot be tended to without food.

According to the last verses, Moab's fate is sealed. Isaiah is being shown what will happen, and there is no changing course. Moab was conquered by the Babylonians in 582 BC when the Moabites disappeared from history just as Isaiah prophesied. God's word is always true and never fails. What He promises will always come to pass, whether judgment on a nation or a promise to care for us as His children.

DAY 43
Isaiah 17:1-6

This message came to me concerning Damascus "Look, the city of Damascus will disappear! It will become a heap of ruins.

2 The towns of Aroer will be deserted. Flocks will graze in the streets and lie down undisturbed, with no one to chase them away.

3 The fortified towns of Israel will also be destroyed, and the royal power of Damascus will end.

All that remains of Syria will share the fate of Israel's departed glory," declares the Lord of Heaven's Armies.

4 "In that day Israel's glory will grow dim; its robust body will waste away.

5 The whole land will look like a grainfield after the harvesters have gathered the grain.

> It will be desolate, like the fields in the valley of Rephaim after the harvest.

> 6 Only a few of its people will be left, like stray olives left on a tree after the harvest. Only two or three remain in the highest branches, four or five scattered here and there on the limbs," declares the Lord, the God of Israel.

After Moab, Isaiah turns his attention from Israel's neighbor to the north. Damascus was the principal city of the northern tribes of Israel, which was defeated and absorbed into Syria. Even Syria will eventually be conquered by Babylon.

"That day" refers to the Day the people come face to face with the reality that God is God and they are not. All their attempts to build human kingdoms and religious efforts have failed. They thought they were better at running their lives than submitting to God. Though they would never speak these thoughts out loud, it was how they lived and cost them the better life they could have had, along with their influence and legacy.

The Good News is that we can awaken like the Israelites before our world collapses. We can set our gaze toward our Creator. To gaze means to contemplate God's greatness, express gratitude for what He's done, and worship Him for who He is.

This is a sobering message to each of us. Do we just talk a good game and mentally ascribe to the right doctrines, or do we live in such a way that people observe we are deeply in love with Jesus? As Christians we say we trust God with our eternity, but do we trust Him day to day? Our transition to Jesus' rulership when He returns should be just a material reality of what we have already been experiencing in this inaugural period where we see the Kingdom operating but not fulfilled. Our goal should be live everyday with God as our source rather than building our own kingdom and having to wrestle it from our grip when Jesus returns.

DAY 44

Isaiah 17:7-14

7 Then at last the people will look to their Creator and turn their eyes to the Holy One of Israel.

8 They will no longer look to their idols for help or worship what their own hands have made.

They will never again bow down to their Asherah poles or worship at the pagan shrines they have built.

9 Their largest cities will be like a deserted forest, like the land the Hivites and Amorites abandon when the Israelites came here so long ago. It will be utterly desolate.

10 Why? Because you have turned from the God who can save you.

You have forgotten the Rock who can hide you. So you may plant the finest grapevines and import the most expensive seedlings.

11 They may sprout on the day you set them out; Yes, they may blossom on the very morning you plant them, but you will never pick any grapes from them. Your only harvest will be a load of grief and unrelieved pain.

12 Listen! The armies of many nations roar like the roaring of the sea.

Hear the thunder of the mighty forces as they rush forward like thundering waves.

13 But though they thunder like breakers on a beach God will silence them, and they will run away.

They will flee like chaff scattered by the wind, like a tumbleweed whirling before a storm.

14 In the evening Israel waits in terror, but by dawn its enemies are dead. This is the just reward of those who plunder us, a fitting end for those who destroy us.

In verse 7, Isaiah declares, "At last they will look to their Creator." How low do we have to get? How far from God do we run before we realize we cannot outrun His love? When will we realize that the idols of financial security, even the love and support of people, or accomplishments will not sustain us? Only God can fulfill every area of our lives.

God will not allow us contentment without Him. He will not allow distractions and temporary comforts to fill the spaces in our lives that belong to Him. This may seem disappointing, but God's grace is shepherding us toward our eternity.

Isaiah ends this portion by reminding the Israelites that all the conquering enemies who have attacked them will pay the price as these are still God's covenant people. God will never abandon His covenant.

DAY 45
Isaiah 18:1-7

Listen, Ethiopia—land of fluttering sails that lies at the headwaters of the Nile, 2 that sends ambassadors in swift boats down the river. Go, swift messengers!

Take a message to a tall, smooth-skinned people, who are feared far and wide for their conquests and destruction, and whose land is divided by rivers.

3 All you people of the world, everyone who lives on the earth when I raise my battle flag on the mountain, look! When I blow the ram's horn, listen!

4 For the Lord has told me this: "I will watch quietly from my dwelling place— as quietly as the heat rises on a summer day, or as the morning dew forms during the harvest."

5 Even before you begin your attack, while your plans are ripening like grapes, the Lord will cut off your new growth with pruning shears. He will snip off and discard your spreading branches.

6 Your mighty army will be left dead in the fields for the mountain vultures and wild animals. The vultures will tear at the corpses all summer. The wild animals will gnaw at the bones all winter.

7 At that time the Lord of Heaven's Armies will receive gifts from this land divided by river from this tall, smooth-skinned people, who are feared far and wide for their conquests and destruction. They will bring the gifts to Jerusalem, where the Lord of Heaven's Armies dwells.

Isaiah extends his message again to a southern kingdom farther away, Ethiopia. This thriving nation to the south and east of Egypt had a large group of exiled Jews living among them. You hear of people from Ethiopia both in the Old and New Testaments. God will also conquer them and draw the people to come and worship Him in Jerusalem.

DAY 46

Isaiah 19:1-10

This message came to me concerning Egypt: Look! The Lord is advancing against Egypt, riding on a swift cloud.

The idols of Egypt tremble. The hearts of the Egyptians melt with fear.

2 "I will make Egyptian fight against Egyptian— brother against brother, neighbor against neighbor, city against city, province against province.

3 The Egyptians will lose heart, and I will confuse their plans.

They will plead with their idols for wisdom and call on spirits, mediums, and those who consult the spirits of the dead.

4 I will hand Egypt over to a hard, cruel master.

A fierce king will rule them," says the Lord, the Lord of Heaven's Armies.

5 The waters of the Nile will fail to rise and flood the fields. The riverbed will be parched and dry.

6 The canals of the Nile will dry up, and the streams of Egypt will stink with rotting reeds and rushes.

7 All the greenery along the riverbank and all the crops along the river will dry up and blow away.

8 The fishermen will lament for lack of work.

Those who cast hooks into the Nile will groan, and those who use nets will lose heart.

9 There will be no flax for the harvesters, no thread for the weavers.

10 They will be in despair, and all the workers will be sick at heart. Israel and Egypt have a long history. From the days of Joseph and his sons to Moses and the Exodus, Egypt played a strong role in the formation of the Israelites' history. In later years, they would go to Egypt for help, which was a slap in the face of God, who had delivered them from bondage there.

God defeated Egypt the first time by sending plagues to confront each of the gods whom the Egyptians trusted. The time again, God showed His power over nature and the gods worshipped by the Egyptians. God will send foreign armies like the Babylonians and natural disasters to bring Egypt to a place of repentance. Even the mighty Nile, their water source, irrigation, fishing, and transportation, is under God's judgment.

I have served thousands of people in personal coaching and counseling sessions over the years. I have watched God allow tragedy to come into the lives of people of those rebelling against God. I have also seen as Jesus said, "the rain falls on the just as well as the unjust." For those who turned to God in these crises in marked a life change. Some resisted and ever grew angrier with God. Everything in life draws us to God or away from God. St. Ignatius called this consolation, things that bring us closer to God, and desolation, things that move us further from God. We are to seek those things that are consolation and avoid desolation. This is not always easy living in a broken world full of desolation to find consolation and sources of peace.

DAY 47
Isaiah 20:1-6

In the year when King Sargon of Assyria sent his commander in chief to capture the Philistine city of Ashdod, 2 the Lord told Isaiah son of Amoz, "Take off the burlap you have been wearing, and remove your sandals." Isaiah did as he was told and walked around naked and barefoot.

3 Then the Lord said, "My servant Isaiah has been walking around naked and barefoot for the last three years. This is a sign—a symbol of the terrible troubles I will bring upon Egypt and Ethiopia. 4 For the king of Assyria will take away the Egyptians and Ethiopians as prisoners. He will make them walk naked and barefoot, both young and old, their buttocks bared, to the shame of Egypt. 5 Then the Philistines will be thrown into panic, for they counted on the power of Ethiopia and boasted of their allies in Egypt! 6 They will say, 'If this can happen to Egypt, what chance do we have? We were counting on Egypt to protect us from the king of Assyria.'"

What affected one area of the Middle East kingdoms affected them all? God is pulling out each leg on which they are trusting. The Philistines trust in the Egyptians and Assyria for protection, but they are being defeated. Who can they trust? This all happens so that the unsettling inability to trust in any man or nation will drive the people both in Israel and in the surrounding territories to the one true God.

God visual illustration in Isaiah's nakedness was to say to the people we are naked and shameful without God. How obvious does God have to be? Anyone could receive the message unless their hearts were so hard they missed the clear sign from Isaiah for three years!

I think back of times I ignored God and thought I was sufficient on my own. It was looking back when I realized how blind, deaf and spiritually naked I was. This was the same accusation God brought against the Church at Laodicea.

You say, 'I am rich. I have everything I want. I don't need a thing!' And you don't realize that you are wretched and miserable and poor and blind and naked. Rev. 3:17

DAY 48
Isaiah 21:1-10

This message came to me concerning Babylon—the desert by the sea: Disaster is roaring down on you from the desert, like a whirlwind sweeping in from the Negev.

2 I see a terrifying vision: I see the betrayer betraying, the destroyer destroying. Go ahead, you Elamites and Mede attack and lay siege. I will make an end to all the groaning Babylon caused.

3 My stomach aches and burns with pain. Sharp pangs of anguish are upon me, like those of a woman in labor. I grow faint when I hear what God is planning; I am too afraid to look.

4 My mind reels, and my heart races I longed for evening to come, but now I am terrified of the dark.

5 Look! They are preparing a great feast. They are spreading rugs for people to sit on. Everyone is eating and drinking. But quick! Grab your shields and prepare for battle. You are being attacked!

6 Meanwhile, the Lord said to me, "Put a watchman on the city wall. Let him shout out what he sees.

7 He should look for chariots drawn by pairs of horses, and for riders on donkeys and camels. Let the watchman be fully alert."

8 Then the watchman called out, "Day after day I have stood on the watchtower, my lord. Night after night I have remained at my post.

9 Now at last—look! Here comes a man in a chariot with a pair of horses!" Then the watchman said, "Babylon is fallen, fallen! All the idols of Babylon lie broken on the ground!"

10 O my people, threshed and winnowed, I have told you everything the Lord of Heaven's Armies has said, everything the God of Israel has told me.

Finally, judgment comes to the nation of Babylon, which has inflicted so much hurt on the nations it has conquered. Every kingdom of man falls. No one can stand very long if they are opposed to God. This time, God uses the Medes and Persians to overthrow Babylon.

The lesson over and over is not to put your trust in man. This is a lesson every generation and people must learn. Even if a kingdom lasts a lifetime, it is nothing compared to eternity. Many live luxurious lives only to face an eternity of spiritual poverty and ruin. Others who suffer but keep their hope in God inherit His Kingdom.

Isaiah is so sure about God's faithfulness to His word that he posts a watchman to stand on the wall and watch for the news that Babylon has fallen. This is such a wonderful sign to the Israelites. It means an end to bondage and a new freedom that will come under the Persian Empire of Cyrus. It is a chance to return and rebuild Jerusalem and once again worship God in Israel.

Later in Revelation 18 we see the Kingdoms and systems of this world that have operated against God referred to as Babylon. In the last times before Jesus returns Babylon the woman falls never to recover and those who lived under her system wept.

DAY 49
Isaiah 21:11-17

This message came to me concerning Edom: Someone from Edom keeps calling to me, "Watchman, how much longer until morning? When will the night be over?"

12 The watchman replies, "Morning is coming, but night will soon return. If you wish to ask again, then come back and ask."

13 This message came to me concerning Arabia: O caravans from Dedan, hide in the deserts of Arabia.

14 O people of Tema, bring water to these thirsty people, food to these weary refugees.

15 They have fled from the sword, from the drawn sword, from the bent bow and the terrors of battle.

16 The Lord said to me, "Within a year, counting each day, all the glory of Kedar will come to an end. 17 Only a few of its courageous archers will survive. I, the Lord, the God of Israel, have spoken!"

Isaiah hears the prophetic voice of someone representing Edom. They ask when this night or season of warfare and invasion will be over. Isaiah tells him the morning is coming, but there will be more nights. There will always be "wars and rumors of war," as Jesus said. Mankind cannot get along because we are selfish by nature.

The sentry stood at their post and watched to see any threat at a distance so they could warn the people. Knowing when to signal the people of danger was an important role and great discernment.

Today's spiritual equivalent would be the intercessor who spends time in God's Word and prayer, watching for threats to God's people, the church.

It seems an increasing number of people are running and declaring all kinds of end-time conspiracies. These are not the watchmen of the Bible or the intercessors. These fear-filled people are blown about by every new wind (Eph. 4:14). They yell warnings more to be heard than to speak for God.

The true intercessor sees a potential crisis or attack spiritually coming and first listens to the Father about how to pray. Most times, they will not need to sound a warning but simply pray alone, with no public fanfare, just to please God and be obedient to their calling.

All the nations oppressed by Babylon are now free. They need to know it was God orchestrating their deliverance from Babylon. War has devastated the area. The people are hungry and lack protection. Isaiah offers them security in the God who controls the nations and oversees their success or destruction down to specific dates and times.

DAY 50
Isaiah 22:1-14

This message came to me concerning Jerusalem—the Valley of Vision: What is happening? Why is everyone running to the rooftops?

2 The whole city is in a terrible uproar. What do I see in this reveling city?

Bodies are lying everywhere killed not in battle but by famine and disease.

3 All your leaders have fled. They surrendered without resistance.

The people tried to slip away but they were captured, too.

4 That's why I said, "Leave me alone to weep do not try to comfort me.

Let me cry for my people as I watch them being destroyed."

5 Oh, what a day of crushing defeat! What a day of confusion and terror brought by the Lord, the Lord of Heaven's Armies upon the Valley of Vision!

The walls of Jerusalem have been broken, and cries of death echo from the mountainsides.

6 Elamites are the archers, with their chariots and charioteers. The men of Kir hold up the shields.

7 Chariots fill your beautiful valleys and charioteers storm your gates.

8 Judah's defenses have been stripped away. You run to the armory for your weapons.

9 You inspect the breaks in the walls of Jerusalem. You store up water in the lower pool.

10 You survey the houses and tear some down for stone to strengthen the walls.

11 Between the city walls, you build a reservoir for water from the old pool. But you never ask for help from the One who did all this. You never considered the One who planned this long ago.

12 At that time the Lord, the Lord of Heaven's Armies, called you to weep and mourn.

He told you to shave your heads in sorrow for your sin and to wear clothes of burlap to show your remorse.

13 But instead, you dance and play; you slaughter cattle and kill sheep. You feast on meat and drink wine. You say, "Let's feast and drink for tomorrow we die!"

14 The Lord of Heaven's Armies has revealed this to me: "Till the day you die, you will never be forgiven for this sin." That is the judgment of the Lord, the Lord of Heaven's Armies.

Isaiah brings his focus back to Judah and Jerusalem.

Jerusalem tried to fortify itself against invaders. The people busied themselves and worked hard, but their efforts were futile because they never turned to God.

What a great lesson and reminder that our most significant source is the Creator of all things. We have a Father in Heaven who loves us and who also happened to make the world in which we live. He knows exactly what we need. He has the storehouse of Heaven from which to resource us. All we have to do is remember to ask and trust.

The people of Jerusalem lament and weep over their situation. They should have and expressed their emotions to God. He made us emotional being, like God Himself. We see God display all kinds of emotions from joy to sadness to anger and rage. Yet no emotions changes God's character. He is consistent and nothing exceeds His perfect love.

DAY 51

Isaiah 22:15-25

This is what the Lord, the Lord of Heaven's Armies, said to me: "Confront Shebna, the palace administrator, and give him this message:

16 "Who do you think you are and what are you doing here, building a beautiful tomb for yourself— a monument high up in the rock?

17 For the Lord is about to hurl you away, mighty man. He is going to grab you, 18 crumple you into a ball, and toss you away into a distant, barren land.

There you will die and your glorious chariots will be broken and useless. You are a disgrace to your master!

19 "Yes, I will drive you out of office," says the Lord. "I will pull you down from your high position. 20 And then I will call my servant Eliakim son of Hilkiah to replace you. 21 I will dress him in your royal robes and will give him your title and your authority. And he will be a father to the people of Jerusalem and Judah. 22 I will give him the key to the house of David—the highest position in the royal court. When he opens doors, no one will be able to close them;

DAY 51

when he closes doors, no one will be able to open them. 23 He will bring honor to his family name, for I will drive him firmly in place like a nail in the wall. 24 They will give him great responsibility, and he will bring honor to even the lowliest members of his family."

25 But the Lord of Heaven's Armies also says: "The time will come when I will pull out the nail that seemed so firm. It will come out and fall to the ground. Everything it supports will fall with it. I, the Lord, have spoken!"

This is God's politics. Isaiah prophesies that God will remove those who force their way into leadership and replace them with His choice. Maybe if we, as God's people, trusted God to do what only He can do instead of feeling helpless and angry about a given political situation. We would pray, and God would release His will. Yes, our prayers matter that much.

This passage is also a prophecy about Jesus, who will come in about 700 years, take up the Throne of David, and initiate His Kingdom.

We see this same language used by John in the Book of Revelation, chapter 3:7, who quotes Isaiah's prophecy to encourage a church that feels overwhelmed by the culture around them.

Bottom line: Jesus reminds Isaiah, the people of Israel, the Church at Philadelphia, and us as His people today that He is in control and we can trust Him.

DAY 52
Isaiah 23:1-17

This message came to me concerning Tyre: Wail, you trading ships of Tarshish, for the harbor and houses of Tyre are gone! The rumors you heard in Cyprus are all true.

2 Mourn in silence, you people of the coast and you merchants of Sidon. Your traders crossed the sea, 3 sailing over deep waters. They brought you grain from Egypt and harvests from along the Nile. You were the marketplace of the world.

4 But now you are put to shame, city of Sidon, for Tyre, the fortress of the sea, says, "Now I am childless; I have no sons or daughters."

5 When Egypt hears the news about Tyre, there will be great sorrow.

6 Send word now to Tarshish! Wail, you people who live in distant lands!

7 Is this silent ruin all that is left of your once joyous city? What a long history was yours! Think of all the colonists you sent to distant

places. I feel like this is a word spoken from the heart of God to me. I want to be a laborer. I want to see supernatural births of sons and daughters being born again into Your kingdom. I long to see sons and daughters, disciples and reproducing their lives in others.

I want our leaders to be soul-winners. I know this is your heart as well, Father. You want to see your church healthy and growing by making disciples. Help us see what stands in the way, in me, or in my schedule. Draw me to where you are preparing people. Inspire and equip me to love and train them well.

8 Who has brought this disaster on Tyre, that great creator of kingdoms? Her traders were all princes, her merchants were nobles.

9 The Lord of Heaven's Armies has done it to destroy your pride and bring low all earth's nobility.

10 Come, people of Tarshish, sweep over the land like the flooding Nile, for Tyre is defenseless.

11 The Lord held out his hand over the sea and shook the kingdoms of the earth. He has spoken out against Phoenicia, ordering that her fortresses be destroyed.

12 He says, "Never again will you rejoice, O daughter of Sidon, for you have been crushed. Even if you flee to Cyprus, you will find no rest."

13 Look at the land of Babylonia— the people of that land are gone!

The Assyrians have handed Babylon over to the wild animals of the desert. They have built siege ramps against its walls, torn down its palaces, and turned it to a heap of rubble.

14 Wail, you ships of Tarshish, for your harbor is destroyed!

15 For seventy years, the length of a king's life, Tyre will be forgotten. But then the city will come back to life as in the song about the prostitute:

16 Take a harp and walk the streets, you forgotten harlot. Make sweet melody and sing your songs so you will be remembered again.

17 Yes, after seventy years the Lord will revive Tyre. But she will be no different than she was before. She will again be a prostitute to all kingdoms around the world. 18 But in the end her profits will be given to the Lord. Her wealth will not be hoarded but will provide good food and fine clothing for the Lord's priests.

God compares nations such as Tyre to prostitutes because they are violating their marriage covenant. Their choosing to worship other gods provokes God's jealousy for His people. He will not tolerate our pursuit of idols and other means of fulfillment and pleasure.

In the end, all the wealth that has been gathered by evil devices such as idol worship will fall, and their resources will go to help the poor and the church. I'm praying this happens today as well.

DAY 53
Isaiah 24:1-13

Look! The Lord is about to destroy the earth and make it a vast wasteland. He devastates the surface of the earth and scatters the people.

2 Priests and laypeople, servants and masters, maids and mistresses, buyers and sellers, lenders and borrowers, bankers and debtors—none will be spared.

3 The earth will be completely emptied and looted. The Lord has spoken!

This destruction of the earth is the culmination of all the judgments pronounced over the last several chapters. It will not be a literal destruction of mankind, but it will seem that way with fewer people left from the wars and conquering armies that have come through.

There are several contrasts between the poor and wealthy, the successful and those who fail; priests and lay people will all experience God's judgment.

4 The earth mourns and dries up, and the land wastes away and withers Even the greatest people on earth waste away.

5 The earth suffers for the sins of its people, for they have twisted God's instructions, violated his laws, and broken his everlasting covenant.

6 Therefore, a curse consumes the earth. Its people must pay the price for their sin. They are destroyed by fire, and only a few are left alive.

7 The grapevines waste away, and there is no new wine. All the merrymakers sigh and mourn.

8 The cheerful sound of tambourines is stilled; the happy cries of celebration are heard no more. The melodious chords of the harp are silent.

9 Gone are the joys of wine and song; alcoholic drink turns bitter in the mouth.

10 The city writhes in chaos; every home is locked to keep out intruders.

11 Mobs gather in the streets, crying out for wine. Joy has turned to gloom. Gladness has been banished from the land.

12 The city is left in ruins, its gates battered down.

13 Throughout the earth the story is the same— only a remnant is left, like the stray olives left on the tree or the few grapes left on the vine after harvest.

The cities and nations left in ruins are compared to vineyards. People want life to go on and the wine to keep flowing, but there is an accounting before God that all people must face. All the parties will end, and it is time to face God. What a scary thought, to ignore God and now face Him under the weight and the consequences of all our sins.

By contrast imagine standing before God without any sin attached to us thank to Jesus' sacrifice for us on the Cross. We may still feel unworthy but that doesn't disqualify us.

DAY 54
Isaiah 24:14-23

But all who are left shout and sing for joy. Those in the west praise the Lord's majesty.

15 In eastern lands, give glory to the Lord. In the lands beyond the sea, praise the name of the Lord, the God of Israel.

16 We hear songs of praise from the ends of the earth, songs that give glory to the Righteous One!

But my heart is heavy with grief. Weep for me, for I wither away. Deceit still prevails, and treachery is everywhere.

17 Terror and traps and snares will be your lot, you people of the earth.

18 Those who flee in terror will fall into a trap, and those who escape the trap will be caught in a snare. Destruction falls like rain from the heavens; the foundations of the earth shake.

19 The earth has broken up. It has utterly collapsed; it is violently shaken.

20 The earth staggers like a drunk. It trembles like a tent in a storm. It falls and will not rise again, for the guilt of its rebellion is very heavy.

21 In that day the Lord will punish the gods in the heavens and the proud rulers of the nations on earth.

22 They will be rounded up and put in prison. They will be shut up in prison and will finally be punished.

23 Then the glory of the moon will wane, and the brightness of the sun will fade, for the Lord of Heaven's Armies will rule on Mount Zion. He will rule in great glory in Jerusalem, in the sight of all the leaders of his people.

Isaiah records his apocalyptic vision in chapters 24-26, which parallels portions of the Book of Revelation. Without getting deep into eschatology, here is how two groups of people respond to extremely difficult circumstances.

The first group (verses 11-13) has lost all sense of security and happiness. The security they found in their nation's strength and resources is gone. Everything they have trusted in has failed them. They are vulnerable, empty, and in despair.

The next group (verses 14-16) lives in the same world under the same circumstances. They have chosen not to look to the government or any human resources. Their focus is on the God of Heaven.

This "remnant" experiences the same crisis, but they respond in worship. They know God will take care of them, and this shaking will humble the proud, who will hopefully turn to God.

Isaiah feels God's pain for the people of the earth who have brought judgment and destruction upon themselves. The closer we get to the Father, the more we feel what He feels. God is a relational being. If all we know of God is what we've read in the Bible, we do have a relationship, just knowledge. We can admire someone from a distance, but our God wants a relationship with His children.

Eventually, Isaiah knows God will win. He will establish His throne on the earth and be a light to everyone. Those who have opposed His rule will be locked up and unable to stir rebellion in the people who worship God.

DAY 55
Isaiah 25:1-12

O Lord, I will honor and praise your name, for you are my God. You do such wonderful things! You planned them long ago, and now you have accomplished them.

2 You turn mighty cities into heaps of ruins. Cities with strong walls are turned to rubble.

Beautiful palaces in distant lands disappear and will never be rebuilt.

3 Therefore, strong nations will declare your glory; ruthless nations will fear you.

Previously, we looked at how Isaiah drew closer to God's heart and felt His pain over His people's rebellion. In response, Isaiah worships God for His plans and wisdom in bringing judgment to some and grace to others where it is deserved.

4 But you are a tower of refuge to the poor, O Lord, a tower of refuge to the needy in distress.

You are a refuge from the storm and a shelter from the heat. For the oppressive acts of ruthless people are like a storm beating against a wall, 5 or like the relentless heat of the desert. But you silence the roar of foreign nations. As the shade of a cloud cools relentless heat, so the boastful songs of ruthless people are stilled.

6 In Jerusalem, the Lord of Heaven's Armies will spread a wonderful feast for all the people of the world. It will be a delicious banquet with clear, well-aged wine and choice meat.

7 There he will remove the cloud of gloom, the shadow of death that hangs over the earth.

8 He will swallow up death forever! The Sovereign Lord will wipe away all tears.

He will remove forever all insults and mockery against his land and people.

The Lord has spoken!

9 In that day the people will proclaim, "This is our God! We trusted in him, and he saved us!

This is the Lord, in whom we trusted. Let us rejoice in the salvation he brings!"

10 For the Lord's hand of blessing will rest on Jerusalem. But Moab will be crushed. It will be like straw trampled down and left to rot.

11 God will push down Moab's people as a swimmer pushes down water with his hands. He will end their pride and all their evil works.

12 The high walls of Moab will be demolished. They will be brought down to the ground, down into the dust.

The thought of death hangs over every person. It may only arise to the surface of our thoughts at the news of someone's passing or when we attend funerals, but our mortality is ever before us. Jesus takes this concern away. We don't fear eternity because we know it is the ultimate victory for everyone who follows Christ. At the moment of death, Jesus wipes every tear of regret from our eyes. He will remove fear, anxiety, shame, and any sense of unworthiness or disgrace. He perfects us and embraces us.

Isaiah uses this picture of eternity to encourage us to draw close to God now and trust Him. Every sacrifice will be worth it. Every denial of some momentary pleasure to choose holy intimacy with God instead will be worth it. He is worth waiting for, no matter the cost or time.

We have a glorious Kingdom of peace and God's presence to look forward to. Our eternity starts with a magnificent banquet in which we will feast as the bride of Christ at the Marriage Supper of the Lamb. Any suffering or sacrifice will be worth it as we celebrate with Jesus and His armies carry out final vengeance and justice on those who have opposed God and His people.

DAY 56
Isaiah 26:1-21

In that day, everyone in the land of Judah will sing this song: Our city is strong! We are surrounded by the walls of God's salvation.

2 Open the gates to all who are righteous; allow the faithful to enter.

3 You will keep in perfect peace all who trust in you, all whose thoughts are fixed on you!

In the original Hebrew text, "perfect peace" is actually "shalom shalom." Shalom means more than peace of mind; it means feeling secure, having my needs met, and being made whole. The Hebrew language repetition communicates intensity. It isn't just shalom; it is "shalom shalom", "perfect absolute peace".

It is an excellent choice for our focus. At any time, we can place our thoughts on God and how wonderful He is. We can remember His faithfulness throughout the Bible, throughout human history, and to us personally. This brings us peace, fires our imagination, and builds faith. This is how we stay secure on the ageless solid Rock.

In my book, "No Longer Stuck," I feature a gratitude lab resource that helps restores us to joy and peace in any circumstance. I encourage you to check it out.

4 Trust in the Lord always, for the Lord God is the eternal Rock.

5 He humbles the proud and brings down the arrogant city. He brings it down to the dust.

6 The poor and oppressed trample it underfoot, and the needy walk all over it.

7 But for those who are righteous, the way is not steep and rough.

You are a God who does what is right, and you smooth out the path ahead of them.

8 Lord, we show our trust in you by obeying your laws; our heart's desire is to glorify your name.

9 In the night I search for you; in the morning I earnestly seek you. For only when you come to judge the earth will people learn what is right.

10 Your kindness to the wicked does not make them do good. Although others do right, the wicked keep doing wrong and take no notice of the Lord's majesty.

11 O Lord, they pay no attention to your upraised fist. Show them your eagerness to defend your people.

Then they will be ashamed. Let your fire consume your enemies.

If the road we are traveling through life seems full of potholes, detours, and darkness, maybe we are not on God's road but one we are trying to blaze on our own.

I know we live in a messed-up world, and being a follower of Jesus doesn't exempt us from problems. But I believe that if we yearn for God and reach out to Him like Isaiah every morning, our path through life will become more meaningful and clearer. This is God's promise; why not believe it?

This starts with choosing to follow God's ways, receive God's love, and know that my heart is entwined with His. In other words, I want what God wants. I want to please Him, to return in worship and obedience, just a comparatively tiny portion of what He has given me. According to Isaiah, our highest motive is to bring honor to His name.

> 12 Lord, you will grant us peace; all we have accomplished is really from you.

> 13 O Lord our God, others have ruled us, but you alone are the one we worship.

> 14 Those we served before are dead and gone. Their departed spirits will never return!

> You attacked them and destroyed them, and they are long forgotten.

> 15 O Lord, you have made our nation great; yes, you have made us great.

> You have extended our borders, and we give you the glory!

16 Lord, in distress we searched for you. We prayed beneath the burden of your discipline.

17 Just as a pregnant woman writhes and cries out in pain as she gives birth, so were we in your presence, Lord.

18 We, too, writhe in agony, but nothing comes of our suffering.

We have not given salvation to the earth, nor brought life into the world.

19 But those who die in the Lord will live; their bodies will rise again!

Those who sleep in the earth will rise up and sing for joy!

For your life-giving light will fall like dew on your people in the place of the dead! 20 Go home, my people, and lock your doors!

Hide yourselves for a little while until the Lord's anger has passed.

21 Look! The Lord is coming from heaven to punish the people of the earth for their sins.

The earth will no longer hide those who have been killed. They will be brought out for all to see.

DAY 57
Isaiah 27:1-6

In that day the Lord will take his terrible, swift sword and punish Leviathan, the swiftly moving serpent, the coiling, writhing serpent. He will kill the dragon of the sea.

2 "In that day sing about the fruitful vineyard.

3 I, the Lord, will watch over it, watering it carefully. Day and night I will watch so no one can harm it.

4 My anger will be gone. If I find briers and thorns growing, I will attack them; I will burn them up— 5 unless they turn to me for help. Let them make peace with me; yes, let them make peace with me."

This is one of my favorite Bible passages. The Father conveys His heart for us through the words of Isaiah.

We are God's "delight," not a burden or a bother. Every moment of our lives, God watered, refreshed, and protected us. Stop and meditate on a God who is attentive to the children He loves.

This kind of unconditional love goes after sin and weakness, like weeds and thorns, that can hurt the vine and reduce the fruit it can produce.

Yesterday, the picture was "entwined our hearts with God." Today, the metaphor is branches clinging to the vigorous vine for stability and protection.

Verse 5 presents a challenge or invitation from our Father. We can make "true peace" with God by submitting to His love, or "Surrender to Love," as David Benner titled his book I highly recommend.

Finally, we choose to "friend" God. What would it look like to have God as your closest friend? Pause for a moment and allow that thought to paint pictures in your head of how different your life could be by walking with God throughout the day.

> 6 The time is coming when Jacob's descendants will take root.
> Israel will bud and blossom and fill the whole earth with fruit!

Jacob was a deceiver, a con man who victimized his brother Esau to gain his inheritance. God confronts Jacob and wrestles him until he submits and surrenders control of his life. God wants control so He can bless Jacob.

"Your name will no longer be Jacob," the man told him.

> "From now on you will be called Israel, because you have fought
> with God and with men and have won." Genesis 32:28

Jacob goes from the identity of a deceiver to Israel, which means "God fights." He wins by yielding to God.

Jacob dies of his self-centeredness and is buried in his old life. As a result, he rises as a new man who is entirely God's. God can now work through the new Israel and bless the world through it.

This is a beautiful picture of Jesus' death and resurrection on our behalf so that we can be raised to a new life in which God dwells within us and leads us to bless the world around us.

DAY 58
Isaiah 27:7-13

7 Has the Lord struck Israel as he struck her enemies? Has he punished her as he punished them?

8 No, but he exiled Israel to call her to account. She was exiled from her land as though blown away in a storm from the east.

9 The Lord did this to purge Israel's wickedness, to take away all her sin. As a result, all the pagan altars will be crushed to dust. No Asherah pole or pagan shrine will be left standing.

10 The fortified towns will be silent and empt the houses abandoned, the streets overgrown with weeds. Calves will graze there, chewing on twigs and branches.

11 The people are like the dead branches of a tree, broken off and used for kindling beneath the cooking pots. Israel is a foolish and stupid nation, for its people have turned away from God. Therefore, the one who made them will show them no pity or mercy.

God's forgiveness costs us nothing except surrender to Him. We accept the gift of His new life in exchange for our old sinful one—the best offer in all eternity.

But, we will not experience this abundant new life, as Jesus called it, until we do some house cleaning. We must remove the thought patterns and human instincts we have followed. Idols of self-centeredness and self-preservation come to mind.

> The Apostle Paul said, *We destroy arguments and every lofty opinion raised against the knowledge of God and take every thought captive to obey Christ* (2 Cor. 10:5).

We ask God to show us what false ideas we have trusted in can hear and obey His will. One of the keys to growing in spiritual maturity is to identify the lies we believe to be the truth. If Satan can get you to believe a lie is true you will destroy yourself. How many people God loves have been convinced God is mad at them and won't hear their prayers. If we don't confront this lie we will not pray and have connection with God. The only way to defeat a lie is to expose it God's light and replace it with God's truth.

> 12 Yet the time will come when the Lord will gather them together like handpicked grain. One by one, he will gather them—from the Euphrates River in the east to the Brook of Egypt in the west. 13 In that day, the great trumpet will sound. Many who died in exile in Assyria and Egypt will return to Jerusalem to worship the Lord on his holy mountain.

Throughout the Old Testament, people seemed to suffer for the sins of their leaders, either through war, famine, or direct judgment. At the final judgment, each person will stand before God individually, and we will only be responsible for our lives.

DAY 59

Isaiah 28:1-19

What sorrow awaits the proud city of Samaria— the glorious crown of the drunks of Israel.

It sits at the head of a fertile valley, but its glorious beauty will fade like a flower. It is the pride of a people brought down by wine.

2 For the Lord will send a mighty army against it. Like a mighty hailstorm and a torrential rain, they will burst upon it like a surging flood and smash it to the ground.

3 The proud city of Samaria— the glorious crown of the drunks of Israel— will be trampled beneath its enemies' feet.

4 It sits at the head of a fertile valley, but its glorious beauty will fade like a flower. Whoever sees it will snatch it as an early fig is quickly picked and eaten.

5 Then at last the Lord of Heaven's Armies will himself be Israel's glorious crown. He will be the pride and joy of the remnant of his people.

6 He will give a longing for justice to their judges. He will give great courage to their warriors who stand at the gates.

7 Now, however, Israel is led by drunks who reel with wine and stagger with alcohol. The priests and prophets stagger with alcohol and lose themselves in wine. They reel when they see visions and stagger as they render decisions.

8 Their tables are covered with vo filth is everywhere.

9 "Who does the Lord think we are?" they ask. "Why does he speak to us like this? Are we little children just recently weaned?

10 He tells us everything over and over—one line at a time, one line at a time, a little here and a little there!"

11 So now God will have to speak to his people through foreign oppressors who speak a strange language!

12 God has told his people, "Here is a place of rest; let the weary rest here. This is a place of quiet rest. But they would not listen.

13 So the Lord will spell out his message for them again, one line at a time, one line at a time, a little here, and a little there,

so that they will stumble and fall. They will be injured, trapped, and captured.

14 Therefore, listen to this message from the Lord, you scoffing rulers in Jerusalem.

15 You boast, "We have struck a bargain to cheat death and have made a deal to dodge the grave.

The coming destruction can never touch us, for we have built a strong refuge made of lies and deception."

16 Therefore, this is what the Sovereign Lord says: "Look! I am placing a foundation stone in Jerusalem, a firm and tested stone. It is a precious cornerstone that is safe to build on. Whoever believes need never be shaken.

17 I will test you with the measuring line of justice and the plumb line of righteousness.

Since your refuge is made of lies, a hailstorm will knock it down. Since it is made of deception, a flood will sweep it away.

18 I will cancel the bargain you made to cheat death, and I will overturn your deal to dodge the grave.

When the terrible enemy sweeps through, you will be trampled into the ground.

19 Again and again that flood will come, morning after morning, day and night, until you are carried away."

Isaiah is attacking alignments that Israel has made with Assyria and Egypt to protect them rather than God. They have lied to themselves and one another. God responds in judgment to break this pact that will destroy their lives. Lies were my refuge to make myself look better or to tell myself I was a success.

This passage is very personal to me. In 1991, I found myself with years of ministry under my belt but no real depth of relationship with God. I loved God and believed the truth about God, but I trusted in my strength and ability, even in life and ministry. I knew what to say and how to plan and manage. I thought I was benefiting God's Kingdom. It was all lies to myself and others around me to make myself look good and feed my insecurity.

Through these words of Isaiah, God began to tear down my wall of lies. Through some faithful brothers and times alone with God, a conviction would wash over me like a storm passing through me. Humility, brokenness, and tears of repentance helped me see that God loved me so deeply. Day after day, I let God do His work and invited Him to go even deeper into the roots of my insecurity and fears. It was as if I was born again, again. I'll share more of this part of my journey tomorrow.

DAY 60
Isaiah 28:20-26

This message will bring terror to your people.

20 The bed you have made is too short to lie on. The blankets are too narrow to cover you.

21 The Lord will come as he did against the Philistines at Mount Perazim and against the Amorites at Gibeon.

He will come to do a strange thing; he will come to do an unusual deed:

22 For the Lord, the Lord of Heaven's Armies, has plainly said that he is determined to crush the whole land.

So scoff no more, or your punishment will be even greater. 23 Listen to me; listen, and pay close attention.

24 Does a farmer always plow and never sow? Is he forever cultivating the soil and never planting?

25 Does he not finally plant his seeds— black cumin, cumin, wheat, barley, and emmer wheat—each in its proper way, and each in its proper place?d

26 The farmer knows just what to do, for God has given him understanding.

In the last few days, I've shared a little of my journey through brokenness and repentance as God healed issues from my past that hindered me from knowing and following Him.

Here, Isaiah brings a comforting parable of God's love and the other side of brokenness.

Plowing has a purpose. Turning over the hard soil makes the ground ready for planting so fruit can be born, which is the purpose of the land.

> 'Plant the good seeds of righteousness, and you will harvest a crop of love. Plow up the hard ground of your hearts, for now, is the time to seek the Lord, that he may come and shower righteousness upon you.' Hosea 10:12

Jesus discussed this in His parable of the sower or soils, Matthew 13:1–23, Mark 4:1–20, and Luke 8:4–15.

In John 15, Jesus reminds his disciples that He wants them to bear fruit.

Brokenness and repentance are not just penance for our wrongs. This is how we humbly accept Jesus as Lord and Leader of our lives.

> So get rid of all the filth and evil in your lives, and humbly accept the word God has planted in your hearts, for it has the power to save your souls. James 1:21

DAY 61
Isaiah 28:27-29

27 A heavy sledge is never used to thresh black cumin; rather, it is beaten with a light stick. A threshing wheel is never rolled on cumin; instead, it is beaten lightly with a flail.

28 Grain for bread is easily crushed, so he doesn't keep on pounding it. He threshes it under the wheels of a cart, but he doesn't pulverize it.

29 The Lord of Heaven's Armies is a wonderful teacher, and he gives the farmer great wisdom.

Isaiah continues his farming metaphor with a picture to help us understand God's discipline. He shows how each type of grain is harvested and separated from its shell. There is a perfect tool for each seed to be released. Larger, tougher grains require stronger force and bigger tools, while smaller grains and spices require a more delicate touch.

Sometimes, God requires a strong shaking in our lives to get our attention and turn us away from sin that has hardened our hearts. His goal is not to crush us and destroy us. He uses the perfect amount of force to open us up. The seed inside us is the fruit of the Holy Spirit (Gal. 5:22-23), waiting to be ripened.

There are also smaller issues, Adjustments God wants to make to smooth rough edges like our speech and maintain integrity in the little things.

If we humble ourselves, God will guide us and show us what He is doing in us. He will provide wisdom to understand and cooperate, knowing His desire is love and growing us to fulfillment and fruitfulness.

DAY 62

Isaiah 29:1-14

"What sorrow awaits Ariel, the City of David. Year after year you celebrate your feasts.

2 Yet I will bring disaster upon you, and there will be much weeping and sorrow. For Jerusalem will become what her name Ariel means— an altar covered with blood.

3 I will be your enemy, surrounding Jerusalem and attacking its walls. I will build siege towers and destroy it.

4 Then deep from the earth you will speak; from low in the dust your words will come. Your voice will whisper from the ground like a ghost conjured up from the grave.

5 "But suddenly, your ruthless enemies will be crushed like the finest of dust. Your many attackers will be driven away like chaff before the wind. Suddenly, in an instant, 6 I, the Lord of Heaven's Armies, will act for you with thunder and earthquake and great noise, with whirlwind and storm and consuming fire.

7 All the nations fighting against Jerusalem will vanish like a dream! Those who are attacking her walls will vanish like a vision in the night.

8 A hungry person dreams of eating but wakes up still hungry. A thirsty person dreams of drinking but is still faint from thirst when morning comes. So it will be with your enemies, with those who attack Mount Zion."

9 Are you amazed and incredulous? Don't you believe it?

Then go ahead and be blind. You are stupid, but not from wine! You stagger, but not from liquor!

10 For the Lord has poured out on you a spirit of deep sleep. He has closed the eyes of your prophets and visionaries.

11 All the future events in this vision are like a sealed book to them. When you give it to those who can read, they will say, "We can't read it because it is sealed." 12 When you give it to those who cannot read, they will say, "We don't know how to read."

13 And so the Lord says, "These people say they are mine. They honor me with their lips, but their hearts are far from me. And their worship of me is nothing but man-made rules learned by rote.

14 Because of this, I will once again astound these hypocrites with amazing wonders. The wisdom of the wise will pass away, and the intelligence of the intelligent will disappear."

We adapt to whatever becomes normalized in our lives. If we install faucets in our kitchen backward, we adapt to the new wrong direction rather than taking everything apart. It is the same way in our spiritual life. We adapt if the church and our relationship with God become routine or dull. We go to church when it's convenient, arriving at the last minute, half-heartedly worshiping, and maybe picking something from the message to think about applying later. We've done our duty, and God should be impressed with our effort.

But what if God is not satisfied and longs for more? What if He suddenly breaks through? What if He shows up in a chapel service in a small Kentucky Seminary and shakes the student body? What if this spreads across the nation as people come and experience God's presence in such a casual way normal is no longer enough? What if people get a taste of God's presence, and this creates a hunger for more?

I hope to see and experience that today as I travel to Wilmore, KY, and join thousands who suddenly feel drawn to be where God is showing up uniquely.

Some critics want to hold back, wait, and judge. I would instead come hungry, humble, and in faith and believe I will meet God.

Afterword: We made the trip to Kentucky and did wonderfully experience God. It was not dynamic in the sense of emotional and exuberant mortality but more of a sensing of God being near. As we pressed into worship, God met us in that chapel in Kentucky the way He met tens of thousands during that season of revival.

DAY 63
Isaiah 29:15-24

15 What sorrow awaits those who try to hide their plans from the Lord, who do their evil deeds in the dark!

"The Lord can't see us," they say. "He doesn't know what's going on!"

16 How foolish can you be? He is the Potter, and he is certainly greater than you, the clay! Should the created thing say of the one who made it, "He didn't make me"? Does a jar ever say, "The potter who made me is stupid"?

17 Soon—and it will not be very long— the forests of Lebanon will become a fertile field, and the fertile field will yield bountiful crops.

18 In that day the deaf will hear words read from a book, and the blind will see through the gloom and darkness.

19 The humble will be filled with fresh joy from the Lord. The poor will rejoice in the Holy One of Israel.

Life can be going in a bad direction. We can feel hopeless, and our circumstances can be overwhelming, but in a moment, God can break in. He first works inside us at the heart level and invites us to respond with humility and trust.

As we open ourselves to God's truth, spiritual blindness, and deafness give way to deeper communion and communication with God. Though our situation may not change immediately, the change within our hearts and our closeness and confidence in our Father lift our perspective. Joy and worship replace fear and anxiety.

We can be that fruitful field, someone who lives confidently and optimistically because we know our God.

> 20 The scoffer will be gone, the arrogant will disappear, and those who plot evil will be killed.

> 21 Those who convict the innocent by their false testimony will disappear. A similar fate awaits those who use trickery to pervert justice and who tell lies to destroy the innocent.

> 22 That is why the Lord, who redeemed Abraham, says to the people of Israel, "My people will no longer be ashamed or turn pale with fear. 23 For when they see their many children and all the blessings I have given them, they will recognize the holiness of the Holy One of Jacob. They will stand in awe of the God of Israel.

> 24 Then the wayward will gain understanding, and complainers will accept instruction.

We adapt to whatever becomes normalized in our lives. If we install faucets in our kitchen backward, we adapt to the new wrong direction rather than take everything apart. It is the same way in our spiritual life. We adapt if the church and our relationship with God become routine or boring. We go to church, arriving at the last minute, half-heartedly worshipping, and picking one or two things from a message we might remember. We've done our duty, and God should be impressed with our effort.

But what if God suddenly breaks through? What if He shows up in a chapel service in a small Kentucky Seminary and shakes the student body? What if this spreads across the nation as people come and experience God's presence in such a tangible way normal is no longer enough? What if people have a taste of God's presence that awakens them and creates a hunger for more? I hope to see and experience that today as I travel to Wilmore, KY, and join thousands who suddenly feel the sense of drawing to be where God is showing up uniquely.

Some critics want to hold back, wait, and judge. I would instead come humbly and humble and, in faith, believe I will meet God.

DAY 64

Isaiah 30:1-5

"What sorrow awaits my rebellious children," says the Lord.

"You make plans that are contrary to mine. You make alliances not directed by my Spirit, thus piling up your sins.

2 For without consulting me, you have gone down to Egypt for help.

You have put your trust in Pharaoh's protection. You have tried to hide in his shade. 3 But by trusting Pharaoh, you will be humiliated, and by depending on him, you will be disgraced.4 For though his power extends to Zoan and his officials have arrived in Hanes,5 all who trust in him will be ashamed. He will not help you. Instead, he will disgrace you."

Whenever God speaks to us directly or through a messenger, and His first word is "Woe," you can be assured something not so good is following.

In this case, the Israelites were feeling pressure from a nearby nation on the verge of attacking them. Rather than trusting God, they run to Egypt for help. Imagine how God views this situation. Hundreds of years earlier, God delivered His people from Egypt through Moses. Now, they are coming full circle and making alliances with the ones who held them in bondage.

Egypt was not the problem. The problem was not consulting God first. God calls this rebellion. We think we can make our plans and then pray a token prayer or assume God is blessing whatever we want to do. This is choosing my wisdom over God's, not humility, and not acknowledging the power and protection of God. It is saying, I can do this without you.

We need to humble ourselves or risk rebellion, leading to our shame and disaster.

Prayer: Father, you are my source of wisdom and everything I need to live a fulfilling life. Lead me in your paths. Be my strength and protection.

DAY 65
Isaiah 30:8-11

Now go and write down these words. Write them in a book.

They will stand until the end of time as a witness

9 that these people are stubborn rebel who refuse to pay attention to the Lord's instructions.

10 They tell the seers, "Stop seeing visions!"

They tell the prophets, "Don't tell us what is right.

Tell us nice things. Tell us lies.

11 Forget all this gloom. Get off your narrow path.

Stop telling us about your 'Holy One of Israel.'"

Isaiah is witnessing a generation of young people turning away from God. Sound familiar?

A few weeks ago, I'd settled into the belief that the pendulum had swung too far in our time among Gen Z. I watch the indoctrination of students on college campuses to a worldview that is opposed to those of their parents, their communities and their churches. I see young people leaving churches and deconstructing their faith. Every generation has to come to their values and beliefs. The challenge is that the pull away from God is so strong.

As I settled into the idea, I realized that this is just the way things are, and we can only do our best to love the young people who hang around and reach out in love to those opposed.

Then, news came of God breaking through at Asbury University and many other campuses.

These are not just nice Bible studies by a few young Christians. This is a revival marked by repentance and the open confession of sin. Young people passionately worship God for hours on end. They say yes to following Jesus to tell others of His grace.

My hope has been renewed, and my response to what is happening is to intercede for this generation and for them to experience God in their way.

Pray with me that revival will spread and ignite holy fires on college campuses and churches nationwide.

DAY 66
Isaiah 30:12-17

This is the reply of the Holy One of Israel:

"Because you despise what I tell you and trust instead in oppression and lies, 13 calamity will come upon you suddenly— like a bulging wall that bursts and falls. In an instant it will collapse and come crashing down.

14 You will be smashed like a piece of pottery— shattered so completely that there won't be a piece big enough to carry coals from a fireplace or a little water from the well." 15 This is what the Sovereign Lord, the Holy One of Israel, says:"Only in returning to me and resting in me will you be saved.In quietness and confidence is your strength. But you would have none of it. 16 You said, 'No, we will get our help from Egypt. They will give us swift horses for riding into battle.'But the only swiftness you are going to see is the swiftness of your enemies chasing you. 17 One of them will chase a thousand of you. Five of them will make all of you flee.You will be left like a lonely flagpole on a hill or a tattered banner on a distant mountaintop."

The God of the Old Testament can appear harsh and judgmental. Many who only glance at scripture come to this conclusion. The truth is that the Holy, perfect God and Creator of Heaven and Earth, desperately desires a relationship with sin-stained humanity.

Yet, like kids who have played in the mud, God has a way of cleansing and redeeming us because we cannot carry sin into a perfect Heaven. God offers His own Son to sacrifice for our sins. He offers us cleansing at no cost beyond the control of our lives, submitting our will to His.

This is God's invitation through Isaiah: Return to God, rest in His control, and we will be saved from sin's pain. Calming ourselves and seeking God's wisdom and power to work on our behalf strengthens us.

The amazing thing is that people have still responded to this offer throughout human history by being unwilling to give up control of their lives. They refuse God's offer because the pain they experience is all they know. The cap on their capacity for real peace, true joy, and unconditional love has blinded them to the fact that there can be more.

Today, come back to God. Give Him your life, offer Him control, and be made strong.

DAY 67
Isaiah 30:18-22

So the Lord must wait for you to come to him so he can show you his love and compassion. For the Lord is a faithful God. Blessed are those who wait for his help.

It is so difficult for a parent or teacher to be patient while a child learns to do something independently, like tying their shoes. We want to get in there and help, especially when we see them struggling. Our offers of help are often rejected as the child wants to do it on their own.

How patient and graciously our Father waits for us to finally turn to Him in trust when we face an overwhelming challenge. God waits to be wanted and is anxious to pour out His peace and wisdom. Nothing should stop us from coming to Him.

> So, let us come boldly to the throne of our gracious God. There, we will receive his mercy and find grace to help us when we need it most. Hebrews 4:16 NLT

Do not wait; talk to God right now; draw so close that, as Isaiah describes, your heart is "entwined in Him" so that you can be "overwhelmed with bliss," which means joy and peace magnified.

How amazing and accessible is the love of God!

> 19 O people of Zion, who live in Jerusalem, you will weep no more. He will be gracious if you ask for help. He will surely respond to the sound of your cries. 20 Though the Lord gave you adversity for food and suffering for drink, he will still be with you to teach you.

You will see your teacher with your own eyes. 21 Your own ears will hear him. Right behind you a voice will say, "This is the way you should whether to the right or to the left. 22 Then you will destroy all your silver idols and your precious gold images. You will throw them out like filthy rags, saying to them, "Good riddance!"

We forget we are trained and equipped for something beyond existence and comfort in this life and into eternity. Without this knowledge, we will resist God's teaching and shaping us into His image.

Notice that even in the tough seasons, our Father promises to be there with us. Not just available but right there in the circumstances of life. In these times, the Holy Spirit is directing us if we listen.

Rather than chasing our solutions, we still ourselves and listen for that voice, that sensing: pray this, say that, go here, avoid that, all guiding us to safety and happiness and deeper devotion and obedience to God.

This is a fulfilling life.

DAY 68
Isaiah 30:23-33

Then the Lord will bless you with rain at planting time. There will be wonderful harvests and plenty of pastureland for your livestock. 24 The oxen and donkeys that till the ground will eat good grain, its chaff blown away by the wind. 25 In that day, when your enemies are slaughtered and the towers fall, there will be streams of water flowing down every mountain and hill. 26 The moon will be as bright as the sun, and the sun will be seven times brighter—like the light of seven days in one! So it will be when the Lord begins to heal his people and cure the wounds he gave them.

In the previous verses we looked at yesterday, God offers to guide His people with His voice. We see the world more clearly when we hear and follow His leading. Things in which we've placed our trust are shown to be weak or vile and not worth the devotion we have given them.

With fresh clarity, we see the idols to which we've sacrificed our time, money, and energy. Something may feel right in the darkness, but when the lights are turned on, we see it for what it truly is.

Following God and getting free from these distractions creates space in our thinking and resource capacity, which God can now fill with creativity, peace, and fruitfulness.

We plant the seeds with this newfound time to invest in God's presence in prayer, worship, and listening as the Word of God speaks to us. The results are that God pours into our lives, and a harvest naturally follows.

27 Look! The Lord is coming from far away, burning with anger, surrounded by thick, rising smoke. His lips are filled with fury; his

words consume like fire. 28 His hot breath pours out like a flood up to the neck of his enemies. He will sift out the proud nations for destruction. He will bridle them and lead them away to ruin. 29 But the people of God will sing a song of joy, like the songs at the holy festivals. You will be filled with joy, as when a flutist leads a group of pilgrims to Jerusalem, the mountain of the Lord— to the Rock of Israel. 30 And the Lord will make his majestic voice heard. He will display the strength of his mighty arm. It will descend with devouring flames, with cloudbursts, thunderstorms, and huge hailstones. 31 At the Lord's command, the Assyrians will be shattered. He will strike them down with his royal scepter. 32 And as the Lord strikes them with his rod of punishment, his people will celebrate with tambourines and harps. Lifting his mighty arm, he will fight the Assyrians. 33 Topheth—the place of burning— has long been ready for the Assyrian king; the pyre is piled high with wood.

The Father promises simultaneously joyous feasting for His followers as He comes with judgment for those who reject Him and go their own way. In the end, no one will doubt God's majesty and worthiness.

He promises a song in the night to chase away the attacks of anxiety and fear. Rather than stress, the Holy Spirit will lead us into a feast. Feasts are celebrations of victory with plenty of food, music, and joy.

As God reveals Himself today to His children, we do not have to wait to begin the celebration. We can dance up the mountain (what an incredible picture) and into God's presence. There, we will hear His voice, and He will open our eyes to see His power and glory.

What a contrast. What a simple but profound choice. Choose God over foolish rebellion that brings sorrow and, ultimately, destruction. Come feast, come dance, and celebrate our God.

DAY 69
Isaiah 31:1-5

What sorrow awaits those who look to Egypt for help, trusting their horses, chariots, and charioteers and depending on the strength of human armies instead of looking to the Lord, the Holy One of Israel. 2 In his wisdom, the Lord will send great disaster; he will not change his mind. He will rise against the wicked and against their helpers. 3 For these Egyptians are mere humans, not God! Their horses are puny flesh, not mighty spirits! When the Lord raises his fist against them, those who help will stumble, and those being helped will fall. They will all fall down and die together. 4 But this is what the Lord has told me: "When a strong young lion stands growling over a sheep it has killed, it is not frightened by the shouts and noise of a whole crowd of shepherds. In the same way, the Lord of Heaven's Armies will come down and fight on Mount Zion.

5 The Lord of Heaven's Armies will hover over Jerusalem and protect it like a bird protecting its nest. He will defend and save the city; he will pass over it and rescue it."

The Devil knows us. He knows our power is not in human strength, ingenuity, or bonds of love. We can unite, but we still are not enough to overcome this spiritual foe.

But if we gather in Christ, place Him at the center, and unify around Him, God will take on our battles and win for us.

Mount Zion represents God's presence, and Jerusalem represents the church, us, and God's people. We abide by the safety of God's promise to protect us, deliver us, spare us, and rescue us.

Take a moment and step into this picture. What would it look like today to be protected, delivered, spared, and rescued by God? Where does Jesus particularly want to bring freedom to me today? We must ask that question and then embrace God's answer with faith.

DAY 70
Isaiah 31:6-9

Though you are such wicked rebels, my people, come and return to the Lord. 7 I know the glorious day will come when each of you will throw away the gold idols and silver images your sinful hands have made. 8 "The Assyrians will be destroyed, but not by the swords of men.The sword of God will strike them, and they will panic and flee.The strong young Assyrians will be taken away as captives. 9 Even the strongest will quake with terror, and princes will flee when they see your battle flags,"says the Lord, whose fire burns in Zion, whose flame blazes from Jerusalem.

The last phrase of this chapter caught my attention: "Whose flame blazes from Jerusalem?" A furnace is a place where an intense fire is created. The passage speaks of God dealing with the Assyrian enemy. He promises to remove anything that would stop Israel's sacrifices once he has restored them to their land.

Whenever we read of Jerusalem and Zion in Old Testament prophetic books, we also see a future promise and application for us. God wants to ignite a passion that burns within us. A consuming within that burns away anything that distracts us or pulls us away from Jesus. I can feed that furnace in worship, in prayer, and meditating on scripture. I can ask the wind of the Holy Spirit to blow across the embers and ignite a flame. I believe God is doing this in individual churches and college campuses.

Working as a Chaplain for the Fire Department, I've learned a little about Fire Science. There is a principle in fighting fires, especially forest fires, where embers from one location are blown by the wind and ignite new fires. When these fires gather, you get "Area Ignition". This becomes a firestorm that is almost impossible to contain.

What if enough of us embraced this time and pressed into God's presence more intently? What if the embers of God's presence blew into others? I mentioned a few days ago, Jesus challenged Jerusalem about how they had missed their time of visitation. Let's not miss ours.

> This is why I remind you to fan into flames the spiritual gift God gave you when I laid my hands on you. 2 Tim. 1:6

DAY 71

Isaiah 32:1-2

Look, a righteous king is coming!

And honest princes will rule under him.

2 Each one will be like a shelter from the wind

and a refuge from the storm,

like streams of water in the desert

and the shadow of a great rock in a parched land.

Bible commentators are divided on whether these verses describe the future King Hezekiah or if they are prophetically looking forward to us as children of God, princes, and princesses in God's Kingdom.

I believe God is giving Isaiah a view into the near and far future. As the writer of Hebrews tells us, "the Word of God is living" (Heb. 4:12). This means God can speak through this sacred text to ancient and modern generations from the same passage.

I believe Isaiah prophecies align with the New Testament truth about us. Jesus is certainly the reigning King over those in His Kingdom. You hear Him speak similar words recorded by John,

> On the last day, the climax of the festival, Jesus stood and shouted to the crowds, "Anyone who is thirsty may come to me! Anyone who believes in me may come and drink! For the Scriptures declare, 'Rivers of living water will flow from his heart.'" John 7:37-38 NLT

We are a refuge where hurting and troubled people can find Christ. We are steady rocks that point to Jesus in the storms of life. Through our words from the heart of God, we bring refreshing life.

Ask God to fill you to overflowing with His love right now. As you walk through a desert of empty people, pause often and ask God to use you to bring refreshing encouragement to dry and desperate lives.

DAY 72
Isaiah 32:3-20

Then everyone who has eyes will be able to see the truth, and everyone who has ears will be able to hear it.

4 Even the hotheads will be full of sense and understanding. Those who stammer will speak out plainly.

5 In that day ungodly fools will not be heroes. Scoundrels will not be respected.

6 For fools speak foolishness and make evil plans. They practice ungodliness and spread false teachings about the Lord. They deprive the hungry of food and give no water to the thirsty.

7 The smooth tricks of scoundrels are evil. They plot crooked schemes. They lie to convict the poor, even when the cause of the poor is just.

8 But generous people plan to do what is generous, and they stand firm in their generosity.

9 Listen, you women who lie around in ease.

Listen to me, you who are so smug.

10 In a short time—just a little more than a year— you careless ones will suddenly begin to care. For your fruit crops will fail, and the harvest will never take place.

11 Tremble, you women of ease; throw off your complacency. Strip off your pretty clothes, and put on burlap to show your grief.

12 Beat your breasts in sorrow for your bountiful farms, and your fruitful grapevines.

13 For your land will be overgrown with thorns and briers. Your joyful homes and happy towns will be gone.

14 The palace and the city will be deserted, and busy towns will be empty. Wild donkeys will frolic and flocks will graze in the empty forts and watchtowers

15 until at last the Spirit is poured out on us from heaven. Then the wilderness will become a fertile field, and the fertile field will yield bountiful crops.

16 Justice will rule in the wilderness and righteousness in the fertile field.

17 And this righteousness will bring peace.

Yes, it will bring quietness and confidence forever.

18 My people will live in safety, quietly at home. They will be at rest.

19 Even if the forest should be destroyed and the city torn down,

20 the Lord will greatly bless his people. Wherever they plant seed, bountiful crops will spring up. Their cattle and donkeys will graze freely.

When Jesus the King comes all will be made right, all things will be set in order. All unrighteousness, all injustice, and all kingdoms will bow to Jesus. Everyone who thought they could make it on their own will be gravely mistaken. They will finally bow their knees to the One true King.

DAY 73
Isaiah 33:1-6

This is a longer section of Isaiah today, but what a great passage. The multiple promises are for fruitfulness and peace, a life free from worry or fear regardless of circumstances or any calamity. All of this sounds like fantasy, but according to the first statement, it is possible to the degree the Spirit is poured out upon us, and we are willing to receive Him.

Happiness is never circumstantial to God's children. When God's presence fills our lives, and we are in communion with Him, our lives are regulated by what is happening inside us more than outside. Rather than pulling in from fear, we purposefully seek to sow seeds of kindness.

> What sorrow awaits you Assyrians, who have destroyed others but have never been destroyed yourselves.
>
> You betray others, but you have never been betrayed.
>
> When you are done destroying, you will be destroyed.
>
> When you are done betraying, you will be betrayed.
>
> 2 But Lord, be merciful to us, for we have waited for you.

Be our strong arm each day and our salvation in times of trouble.

3 The enemy runs at the sound of your voice. When you stand up, the nations flee!

4 Just as caterpillars and locusts strip the fields and vines, so the fallen army of Assyria will be stripped!

5 Though the Lord is very great and lives in heaven, he will make Jerusalem his home of justice and righteousness.

6 In that day he will be your sure foundation, providing a rich store of salvation, wisdom, and knowledge. The fear of the Lord will be your treasure.

Amazing promises! Love, salvation, wisdom, knowledge, and everything we need in life. Notice how these promises are framed in grasping just how powerful and holy and worthy God is of our devotion.

Isaiah tells us these treasures are accessed by acknowledging the greatness of our God. We revere His power, authority, and majesty in every realm.

It only makes sense that our inheriting these promises is tied to our humble submission to God.

Take a few moments and ask God to reveal more of Himself right now. Stay in His presence and worship until you gain new insights into who God is and who He wants to be to you.

Note: If you struggle focusing stop and take two quick breaths in through your mouth and then a long exhale through your nose. Repeat this three or four times until you sense yourself calming and able to focus.

DAY 74

Isaiah 33:7-16

But now your brave warriors weep in public. Your ambassadors of peace cry in bitter disappointment.

8 Your roads are deserted; no one travels them anymore. The Assyrians have broken their peace treaty and care nothing for the promises they made before witnesses. They have no respect for anyone.

9 The land of Israel wilts in mourning. Lebanon withers with shame. The plain of Sharon is now a wilderness. Bashan and Carmel have been plundered.

10 But the Lord says: "Now I will stand up. Now I will show my power and might.

11 You Assyrians produce nothing but dry grass and stubble. Your own breath will turn to fire and consume you.

12 Your people will be burned up completely, like thornbushes cut down and tossed in a fire.

13 Listen to what I have done, you nations far away! And you that are near, acknowledge my might!" The sinners in Jerusalem shake with fear.

Terror seizes the godless.

"Who can live with this devouring fire?" they cry.

"Who can survive this all-consuming fire?"

15 Those who are honest and fair, who refuse to profit by fraud, who stay far away from bribes, who refuse to listen to those who plot murder, who shut their eyes to all enticement to do wrong—

16 these are the ones who will dwell on high. The rocks of the mountains will be their fortress. Food will be supplied to them, and they will have water in abundance.

God is compassionate and longs for His children to come home and find grace in His arms. He is also Holy, and as Creator and Ruler, He determines how we should live.

Many who are far from God either think He does care or that He is angry and demanding. But God offers complete forgiveness and salvation to everyone who comes to Him and surrenders their life in exchange for new life.

Under the old covenant, closeness to God was based on man's ability to follow the Mosaic law. But Jesus came as a sacrifice for sin and made a way for us to be accepted as children of God.

The heart of God is still the same toward having integrity, caring for the poor, and abandoning evil. But now, God gives us new motives and reshapes our thinking. He makes us whole so we can be holy.

As our lives are guided by the Holy Spirit, we have all our needs met. We now focus on pleasing God and serving others because God cares for us.

> Jesus tells us, "So above all, constantly seek God's kingdom and righteousness, then all these less important things will be given to you abundantly. Matthew 6:33

DAY 75

Isaiah 33:17-24

Your eyes will see the king in all his splendor, and you will see a land that stretches into the distance.

18 You will think back to this time of terror, asking, "Where are the Assyrian officers who counted our towers? Where are the bookkeepers who recorded the plunder taken from our fallen city?"

19 You will no longer see these fierce, violent people with their strange, unknown language.

Israel had been overtaken by the Assyrians, who sent in assessors and bookkeepers to assess the value of resources and treasures they would be taking from the conquered kingdom. All the Israelis could do was watch others go through and take everything they owned and had worked for.

Think how demoralizing it would be to watch an enemy come in and take everything, and you have to stand and watch, defeated. This made a strong impact on the minds of the Jews. They also knew that it was their sin that caused this catastrophe. They had turned away from God to worship idols and foreign gods and found themselves distant from God when they needed Him.

In sharp contrast, Isaiah describes those who draw close to God. They will see their King and His Kingdom from this "high place." Though the Israelites are still on earth, as they draw close to God, they see His greatness and the vastness of His rule.

We, too, are invited to see God and our world from the perspective of a child who is close to the Father and sees from a high place seated next to Him.

> And He raised us up together with Him [when we believed], and seated us with Him in the heavenly places, [because we are] in Christ Jesus, Ephesians 2:6 Amp.

Don't get stuck focusing on what the enemy has taken. Instead, realize you are seated with Christ in a place of ultimate victory. Ask God to give you a glimpse of Him and His Kingdom from the high place.

> 20 Instead, you will see Zion as a place of holy festivals. You will see Jerusalem, a city quiet and secure. It will be like a tent whose ropes are taut and whose stakes are firmly fixed.

> 21 The Lord will be our Mighty One.

> He will be like a wide river of protection that no enemy can cross, that no enemy ship can sail upon.

> 22 For the Lord is our judge, our lawgiver, and our king. He will care for us and save us.

> 23 The enemies' sails hang loose on broken masts with useless tackle.

> Their treasure will be divided by the people of God. Even the lame will take their share!

24 The people of Israel will no longer say, "We are sick and helpless," for the Lord will forgive their sins.

God is taking us where the devil cannot follow. Here on earth, we faced his schemes and attacks each day. But a day is coming in which we will cross a wide river with our God and the enemy cannot follow. All that he has stolen will be returned to God's people who will all flourish under God's reign for eternity. That is some good news!

DAY 76
Isaiah 34:1-17

Come here and listen, O nations of the earth. Let the world and everything in it hear my words.

2 For the Lord is enraged against the nations. His fury is against all their armies. He will completely destroy them, dooming them to slaughter.

3 Their dead will be left unburied, and the stench of rotting bodies will fill the land. The mountains will flow with their blood.

4 The heavens above will melt away and disappear like a rolled-up scroll.

The stars will fall from the sky like withered leaves from a grapevine, or shriveled figs from a fig tree.

5 And when my sword has finished its work in the heavens, it will fall upon Edom, the nation I have marked for destruction.

6 The sword of the Lord is drenched with blood and covered with fat—with the blood of lambs and goats, with the fat of rams prepared for sacrifice.

Yes, the Lord will offer a sacrifice in the city of Bozrah. He will make a mighty slaughter in Edom.

7 Even men as strong as wild oxen will die— the young men alongside the veterans. The land will be soaked with blood and the soil enriched with fat.

8 For it is the day of the Lord's revenge, the year when Edom will be paid back for all it did to Israel.

9 The streams of Edom will be filled with burning pitch, and the ground will be covered with fire.

10 This judgment on Edom will never end; the smoke of its burning will rise forever. The land will lie deserted from generation to generation. No one will live there anymore.

11 It will be haunted by the desert owl and the screech owl, the great owl and the raven.

For God will measure that land carefully; he will measure it for chaos and destruction.

12 It will be called the Land of Nothing, and all its nobles will soon be gone.

13 Thorns will overrun its palaces; nettles and thistles will grow in its forts. The ruins will become a haunt for jackals and a home for owls.

14 Desert animals will mingle there with hyenas, their howls filling the night. Wild goats will bleat at one another among the ruins, and night creatures will come there to rest.

15 There the owl will make her nest and lay her eggs. She will hatch her young and cover them with her wings. And the buzzards will come, each one with its mate.

16 Search the book of the Lord, and see what he will do.

Not one of these birds and animals will be missing, and none will lack a mate, for the Lord has promised this. His Spirit will make it all come true.

17 He has surveyed and divided the land and deeded it over to those creatures. They will possess it forever, from generation to generation.

God is faithful to His promises, whether they are blessings or judgments. Nothing He speaks ever fails to come to pass. This is why we seek God in His Word. Through the Bible, God speaks to us.

> For the word of God is alive and powerful. It is sharper than the sharpest two-edged sword, cutting between soul and spirit, between joint and marrow. It exposes our innermost thoughts and desires. Hebrews 4:12 NLT

Through God's living word, He helps us separate what is of us (soul) from what is of God (spirit). This is why we prioritize reading the Bible and meditating on it to hear God's voice.

Isaiah describes God's unique destiny for each of us. Big dreams, places of fulfillment, and simple daily guidance may seem insignificant, but they lead us closer to that destiny through our obedience.

Because God leads us, and since He is worthy of our devotion, it only makes sense we prioritize seeking Him.

DAY 77
Isaiah 35:1-4

Even the wilderness and desert will be glad in those days.

The wasteland will rejoice and blossom with spring crocuses.

2 Yes, there will be an abundance of flowers and singing and joy!

The deserts will become as green as the mountains of Lebanon, as lovely as Mount Carmel or the plain of Sharon. There the Lord will display his glory, the splendor of our God.

3 With this news, strengthen those who have tired hands, and encourage those who have weak knees.

4 Say to those with fearful hearts, "Be strong, and do not fear, for your God is coming to destroy your enemies. He is coming to save you."

After all the darkness and upheaval, the people of God remember their Creator. The season of judgment is past, and now God is bringing His people into a time of restoration.

> We can't help but consider the prophetic call in 2 Chronicles 7:14, Then if my people who are called by my name will humble themselves, pray, seek my face, and turn from their wicked ways, I will hear from heaven, forgive their sins, and restore their land.

Isaiah 35 is God's response to His people's cry. God doesn't just revive His people; His grace pours into every institution. Cities are transformed. I believe we are seeing glimpses of this across the nation. I witnessed it in Wilmore, Kentucky, as the outpouring at Asbury impacted the entire community.

There is a rich history of awakening and revivals throughout our history. I am not speaking of some politically driven work of man. What Isaiah saw and what people have experienced in the past and are starting to see today is a sovereign act of God only He can do. Our challenge is to either embrace or reject what God may be doing in our day.

I believe this is the time for GenX and GenZ to have their encounter with God. They need to experience God's presence, and I want to do all I can to accommodate it and be where the Spirit is moving.

DAY 78

Isaiah 35:5-10

And when he comes, he will open the eyes of the blind and unplug the ears of the deaf.

6 The lame will leap like a deer, and those who cannot speak will sing for joy!

Springs will gush forth in the wilderness, and streams will water the wasteland.

7 The parched ground will become a pool, and springs of water will satisfy the thirsty land.

Marsh grass and reeds and rushes will flourish where desert jackals once lived.

Isaiah continues this theme of God's promised restoration of His children. There is a beautiful picture here of God coming to our aid and bringing help to others.

This is simultaneously a prayer for God to bless those who are discouraged and defeated and a challenge for us to bring God's presence to the hurting.

We carry a message of hope to people who feel overwhelmed. We announce that God is going to come through and bring victory. We are dispensers of hope to the hurting. Everyone needs a friend who can point them toward God.

> Then blind eyes will open and deaf ears will hear. Isaiah 35:5

Our task is to encourage people to turn to God. Then their eyes and ears will be open to God and they will find healing and freedom.

> 8 And a great road will go through that once deserted land. It will be named the Highway of Holiness.

Isaiah's vision spans all of human history. His message to the Israelites is that God will restore them to their land and freedom from Babylon. It will feel in some ways to them, like the Garden of Eden.

Though it would take rebuilding, God would be with His people, providing for and protecting them as they rebuilt under Nehemiah and Ezra.

In the same way, God walks us through this life, providing for and protecting us. This requires us to walk with God and follow His lead. The Sacred Way is God's direction, not the path we would always choose. But what if prayer guided us more than our plans? We may find ourselves on a highway of holiness and fulfillment in life.

Isaiah also refers to the future when Jesus returns when the earth will be renewed and restored to its original pre-sinful state. Jesus' rule will extend into all eternity.

Why not allow Him to be the King of our lives now and make our daily walk through life a sacred journey?

Evil-minded people will never travel on it.

It will be only for those who walk in God's ways; fools will never walk there.

> 9 Lions will not lurk along its course, nor any other ferocious beasts. There will be no other dangers. Only the redeemed will walk on it.

> 10 Those who have been ransomed by the Lord will return. They will enter Jerusalem singing, crowned with everlasting joy. Sorrow

and mourning will disappear, and they will be filled with joy and gladness.

Isaiah continues to describe two time periods: the return of the Israelites from Babylonian captivity and the time when Jesus returns to rule from the exact location, Zion. It is as if he is looking across a mountain range and seeing magnificent peaks. These are two times when God will restore His people.

The description of Jesus' reign reveals that there is no more lion (Satan) or demonic activity. Joy will be the characteristic that best describes life into eternity. There will be no more weariness or grief, no more pain, physically or emotionally, no more broken relationships or danger to fear, and complete and absolute freedom.

Here's some good news: You don't have to wait to experience these qualities in the future of the Kingdom. Jesus came to declare His kingdom had come. He inaugurated the rule of God, which He will someday complete. Until then, Jesus tells us to pray that His Kingdom will continue to come and that He will be done on earth just as He rules in Heaven.

This reign begins in you and me. When we surrender and are born into God's Kingdom, we can access the joy described above. We also carry out Jesus' mandate to tell others and demonstrate that the Kingdom of God is here.

DAY 79
Isaiah 36:1-22

In the fourteenth year of King Hezekiah's reign, King Sennacherib of Assyria came to attack the fortified towns of Judah and conquered them. 2 Then the king of Assyria sent his chief of staff from Lachish with a huge army to confront King Hezekiah in Jerusalem. The Assyrians took up a position beside the aqueduct that feeds water into the upper pool, near the road leading to the field where cloth is washed.

3 These are the officials who went out to meet with them: Eliakim son of Hilkiah, the palace administrator; Shebna the court secretary; and Joah son of Asaph, the royal historian.

Sennacherib Threatens Jerusalem

4 Then the Assyrian king's chief of staff told them to give this message to Hezekiah:

"This is what the great king of Assyria says: What are you trusting in that makes you so confident? 5 Do you think that mere words can substitute for military skill and strength? Who are you counting on, that you have rebelled against me? 6 On Egypt? If you lean on Egypt, it will be like a reed that splinters beneath your weight and pierces your hand. Pharaoh, the king of Egypt, is completely unreliable!

7 "But perhaps you will say to me, 'We are trusting in the Lord our God!' But isn't he the one who was insulted by Hezekiah? Didn't Hezekiah tear down his shrines and altars and make everyone in Judah and Jerusalem worship only at the altar here in Jerusalem?

8 "I'll tell you what! Strike a bargain with my master, the king of Assyria. I will give you 2,000 horses if you can find that many men to ride on them! 9 With your tiny army, how can you think of challenging even the weakest contingent of my master's troops, even with the help of Egypt's chariots and charioteers? 10 What's more, do you think we have invaded your land without the Lord's direction? The Lord himself told us, 'Attack this land and destroy it!'"

11 Then Eliakim, Shebna, and Joah said to the Assyrian chief of staff, "Please speak to us in Aramaic, for we understand it well. Don't speak in Hebrew, for the people on the wall will hear."

12 But Sennacherib's chief of staff replied, "Do you think my master sent this message only to you and your master? He wants all the people to hear it, for when we put this city under siege, they will suffer along with you. They will be so hungry and thirsty that they will eat their own dung and drink their own urine."

13 Then the chief of staff stood and shouted in Hebrew to the people on the wall, "Listen to this message from the great king of Assyria! 14 This is what the king says: Don't let Hezekiah deceive you. He will never be able to rescue you. 15 Don't let him fool you into trusting in the Lord by saying, 'The Lord will surely rescue us. This city will never fall into the hands of the Assyrian king!'

16 "Don't listen to Hezekiah! These are the terms the king of Assyria is offering: Make peace with me—open the gates and come out. Then each of you can continue eating from your own grapevine and fig tree and drinking from your own well. 17 Then I will arrange

to take you to another land like this one—a land of grain and new wine, bread and vineyards.

18 "Don't let Hezekiah mislead you by saying, 'The Lord will rescue us!' Have the gods of any other nations ever saved their people from the king of Assyria? 19 What happened to the gods of Hamath and Arpad? And what about the gods of Sepharvaim? Did any god rescue Samaria from my power? 20 What god of any nation has ever been able to save its people from my power? So what makes you think that the Lord can rescue Jerusalem from me?"

21 But the people were silent and did not utter a word because Hezekiah had commanded them, "Do not answer him."

22 Then Eliakim son of Hilkiah, the palace administrator; Shebna the court secretary; and Joah son of Asaph, the royal historian, went back to Hezekiah. They tore their clothes in despair, and they went in to see the king and told him what the Assyrian chief of staff had said.

Isaiah 36-39 could be called a tale of two kings. Hezekiah, the godly king of the Jews is being advanced upon by the Assyrians. The Assyrian King Sennacherib has sent an envoy to negotiate Israel's surrender. The goal is to undermine Hezekiah's leadership and to stir up fear in the people they will surrender.

Every day, we make a choice to make peace with and surrender to the enemy, the world, and our own former fallen desires, or to trust God.

The enemy promises you to live your own life. After all, you are the one most qualified to make all your own decisions. He even promises to take you to a land someday that is just like what is familiar. I would agree. It is a place of bondage for eternity. This king only makes you think you are in control.

But if you want a life that is fulfilling and meaningful, turn to the God King Hezekiah served, the God of Heaven.

The enemy always starts with a half-truth. In this case, he says, "Has any god ever saved someone from the King of Assyria?" This is true, but the Assyrian King had never faced a people who trusted in the one true God.

Don't believe the enemy's lies that God won't help you, you don't deserve it, or you've made too many mistakes. Jesus promises to receive all who come humbly to Him.

The question is, who will be your king?

DAY 80
Isaiah 37:1-29

When King Hezekiah heard their report, he tore his clothes and put on burlap and went into the Temple of the Lord. 2 And he sent Eliakim the palace administrator, Shebna the court secretary, and the leading priests, all dressed in burlap, to the prophet Isaiah son of Amoz. 3 They told him, "This is what King Hezekiah says: Today is a day of trouble, insults, and disgrace. It is like when a child is ready to be born, but the mother has no strength to deliver the baby. 4 But perhaps the Lord your God has heard the Assyrian chief of staff, sent by the king to defy the living God, and will punish him for his words. Oh, pray for those of us who are left!"

5 After King Hezekiah's officials delivered the king's message to Isaiah, 6 the prophet replied, "Say to your master, 'This is what the Lord says: Do not be disturbed by this blasphemous speech against me from the Assyrian king's messengers. 7 Listen! I myself will move against him, and the king will receive a message that he is needed at home. So he will return to his land, where I will have him killed with a sword.'"

8 Meanwhile, the Assyrian chief of staff left Jerusalem and went to consult the king of Assyria, who had left Lachish and was attacking Libnah.

9 Soon afterward King Sennacherib received word that King Tirhakah of Ethiopia was leading an army to fight against him. Before leaving to meet the attack, he sent messengers back to Hezekiah in Jerusalem with this message:

10 "This message is for King Hezekiah of Judah. Don't let your God, in whom you trust, deceive you with promises that Jerusalem will not be captured by the king of Assyria. 11 You know perfectly well what the kings of Assyria have done wherever they have gone. They have completely destroyed everyone who stood in their way! Why should you be any different? 12 Have the gods of other nations rescued them—such nations as Gozan, Haran, Rezeph, and the people of Eden who were in Tel-assar? My predecessors destroyed them all! 13 What happened to the king of Hamath and the king of Arpad? What happened to the kings of Sepharvaim, Hena, and Ivvah?"

Isaiah writes a history of the time King of Assyria threatened to attack Jerusalem. The Jewish King Hezekiah, first sends a delegation, who return in fear. There is another interaction, and this time, he goes to Isaiah as God's prophet and asks him to appeal to God and pray for him and the nation.

After further negotiations and threats from the Assyrian King, King Hezekiah is humbled and broken and goes to the Temple himself to seek God. No more human solutions, no more asking others to do the praying. Hezekiah cries out to God with complete vulnerability. The lesson is that God wants to hear from you personally. Rather than wasting time in worry, Jesus invites us to come to Him. He wants us to trust in His goodness, faithfulness, and power. Momma's prayers are wonderful, but God wants to hear from you, and you need to hear from Him.

14 After Hezekiah received the letter from the messengers and read it, he went up to the Lord's Temple and spread it out before the Lord. 15 And Hezekiah prayed this prayer before the Lord: 16 "O Lord of Heaven's Armies, God of Israel, you are enthroned between the mighty cherubim! You alone are God of all the kingdoms of the earth. You alone created the heavens and the earth. 17 Bend down, O Lord, and listen! Open your eyes, O Lord, and see! Listen to Sennacherib's words of defiance against the living God.

18 "It is true, Lord, that the kings of Assyria have destroyed all these nations. 19 And they have thrown the gods of these nations into the fire and burned them. But of course the Assyrians could destroy

them! They were not gods at all—only idols of wood and stone shaped by human hands. 20 Now, O Lord our God, rescue us from his power; then all the kingdoms of the earth will know that you alone, O Lord, are God."

This is what you do when faced with a challenge. King Hezekiah invites God into his situation. When was the last time you laid your bills and checkbook before the Lord and asked for his help? Because Hezekiah laid his circumstances down in the presence of God, look what happens next.

Isaiah Predicts Judah's Deliverance

21 Then Isaiah son of Amoz sent this message to Hezekiah: "This is what the Lord, the God of Israel, says: Because you prayed about King Sennacherib of Assyria, 22 the Lord has spoken this word against him:

"The virgin daughter of Zion despises you and laughs at you. The daughter of Jerusalem shakes her head in derision as you flee.

23 "Whom have you been defying and ridiculing? Against whom did you raise your voice? At whom did you look with such haughty eyes? It was the Holy One of Israel!

24 By your messengers you have defied the Lord. You have said, 'With my many chariots I have conquered the highest mountains— yes, the remotest peaks of Lebanon. I have cut down its tallest cedars and its finest cypress trees. I have reached its farthest heights and explored its deepest forests.

25 I have dug wells in many foreign lands and refreshed myself with their water. With the sole of my foot, I stopped up all the rivers of Egypt!'

26 "But have you not heard?

I decided this long ago. Long ago I planned it, and now I am making it happen. I planned for you to crush fortified cities into heaps of rubble.

27 That is why their people have so little power and are so frightened and confused. They are as weak as grass, as easily trampled as tender green shoots. They are like grass sprouting on a housetop, scorched before it can grow lush and tall.

28 "But I know you well—where you stay and when you come and go. I know the way you have raged against me.

29 And because of your raging against me and your arrogance, which I have heard for myself, I will put my hook in your nose and my bit in your mouth. I will make you return by the same road on which you came."

God took over the battle from Hezekiah. The king could watch and worship as God fought his battle. What a great reminder for us to open our hearts to the deepest issues we are facing and lay them at the feet of Jesus knowing He will bring about good on our behalf.

DAY 81
Isaiah 37:30-38

Then Isaiah said to Hezekiah, "Here is the proof that what I say is true: "This year you will eat only what grows up by itself, and next year you will eat what springs up from that. But in the third year you will plant crops and harvest them; you will tend vineyards and eat their fruit.

31 And you who are left in Judah, who have escaped the ravages of the siege, will put roots down in your own soil and grow up and flourish.

32 For a remnant of my people will spread out from Jerusalem, a group of survivors from Mount Zion. The passionate commitment of the Lord of Heaven's Armies will make this happen!

Hezekiah turns to God as an enemy army approaches. God responds with a promise of protection. It will take three years to get out of wartime and get life back to normal, but God will lead His people and restore them from this threat.

I think of Covid and its effect on so many lives. The virus itself and the controversy over the correct response. Then, the supply chain impact and economic problems. But God brought us through and will continue to be bigger than any circumstance we face.

33 "And this is what the Lord says about the king of Assyria: "'His armies will not enter Jerusalem. They will not even shoot an arrow at it. They will not march outside its gates with their shields nor build banks of earth against its walls.

34 The king will return to his own country by the same road on which he came. He will not enter this city,' says the Lord.

35 'For my own honor and for the sake of my servant David, I will defend this city and protect it.'"

36 That night the angel of the Lord went out to the Assyrian camp and killed 185,000 Assyrian soldiers. When the surviving Assyrians woke up the next morning, they found corpses everywhere. 37 Then King Sennacherib of Assyria broke camp and returned to his own land. He went home to his capital of Nineveh and stayed there.

38 One day while he was worshiping in the temple of his god Nisroch, his sons Adrammelech and Sharezer killed him with their swords. They then escaped to the land of Ararat, and another son, Esarhaddon, became the next king of Assyria.

Isaiah continues to declare God's promise to protect His people from impending doom. God is not going to defend it based on the devotion of the Israelites, the prayers they have prayed, or the offerings they have given.

God is going to protect His children for His honor and a covenant He made with David. A covenant is a binding forever agreement. In the same way, God protects us and cares for us according to the new covenant Jesus secured for us through His death on the cross.

I encourage you to read the rest of this chapter. You'll see just how faithful God is to his covenant. If He upheld His promises then He will uphold them now. He will care for us. When we come to Jesus with our needs our faith is not based on how good we are or what kind of offering we can bring, it is firmly rooted in His promise to keep covenant with us.

But now Jesus, our High Priest, has been given a ministry that is far superior to the old priesthood, for he is the one who mediates for us a far better covenant with God, based on better promises.
Hebrews 8:6

DAY 82
Isaiah 38:1-6

About that time Hezekiah became deathly ill, and the prophet Isaiah son of Amoz went to visit him. He gave the king this message: "This is what the Lord says: 'Set your affairs in order, for you are going to die. You will not recover from this illness.'"

2 When Hezekiah heard this, he turned his face to the wall and prayed to the Lord, 3 "Remember, O Lord, how I have always been faithful to you and have served you single-mindedly, always doing what pleases you." Then he broke down and wept bitterly.

4 Then this message came to Isaiah from the Lord: 5 "Go back to Hezekiah and tell him, 'This is what the Lord, the God of your ancestor David, says: I have heard your prayer and seen your tears. I will add fifteen years to your life, 6 and I will rescue you and this city from the king of Assyria. Yes, I will defend this city.

I remember my parents playing a song by Loretta Lynn, which was drawn from this passage titled, "Everybody Wants to God to Heaven, But Nobody Wants to Die." I think most of us can relate to this sentiment. We believe in the promise of Heaven, but this earth is all we know, and the fear of death and the possible pain involved is what we don't want to face.

Imagine having a prophet come in and tell you you're about to die. King Hezekiah's response does not come from a fear of death or a selfish motive. He seemed to have unfulfilled purposes for God. He may have known what would happen shortly to the nation of Israel and how important it was for them to have a leader who was devoted to God.

In those extra 15 years, Hezekiah accomplished good for the people and honored God with his life. I imagine he lived very intentionally and didn't waste any of this gift God gave him.

We don't want to wait until we're old and feeble and regret that we didn't live for God's honor and purpose. Ask God today to reveal any unfinished business He may want to accomplish through you. Or maybe it is words you've held back but need to express to someone as forgiveness or encouragement.

You may not be given an extra 15 years, but you have been given today, so make it count.

DAY 83

Isaiah 38:7-22

"'And this is the sign from the Lord to prove that he will do as he promised: **8** I will cause the sun's shadow to move ten steps backward on the sundial of Ahaz!'" So the shadow on the sundial moved backward ten steps.

Hezekiah's Poem of Praise

9 When King Hezekiah was well again, he wrote this poem:

10 I said, "In the prime of my life, must I now enter the place of the dead?   Am I to be robbed of the rest of my years?" **11** I said, "Never again will I see the Lord God while still in the land of the living. Never again will I see my friends or be with those who live in this world. **12** My life has been blown away like a shepherd's tent in a storm. It has been cut short, as when a weaver cuts cloth from a loom. Suddenly, my life was over. **13** I waited patiently all night, but I was torn apart as though by lions.   Suddenly, my life was over. **14** Delirious, I chattered like a swallow or a crane, and then I moaned like a mourning dove. My eyes grew tired of looking to heaven for help.   I am in trouble, Lord. Help me!"**15** But what could I say?   For he himself sent this sickness. Now I will walk humbly throughout my years because of this anguish I have felt. **16** Lord, your discipline is good, for it leads to life and health. You restore my health   and allow me to live! **17** Yes, this anguish was good for me, for you have rescued me from death   and forgiven all my sins. **18** For the dead cannot praise you; they cannot raise their voices in praise. Those who go down to the grave   can no longer hope in your faithfulness.

19 Only the living can praise you as I do today. Each generation tells of your faithfulness to the next. **20** Think of it—the Lord is ready to heal me! I will sing his praises with instruments every day of my life   in the Temple of the Lord.**21** Isaiah had said to Hezekiah's servants, "Make an ointment from figs and spread it over the boil, and Hezekiah will recover."**22** And Hezekiah had asked, "What sign will prove that I will go to the Temple of the Lord?"

God stacks signs on top of promises just to demonstrate His love for His people and King Hezekiah. It would be enough for God to promise deliverance from the Assyrians threatening to destroy Israel. In addition, God is going to heal Hezekiah and give him 15 more years of life. Now, to confirm even further God's faithfulness, He is going to cause the sun to move backward, just like the promises to give Hezekiah more time.

The Bible is full of promises God has made in this New Covenant in which we live. All of the miracles Jesus has done for others He can do for us. The challenge is aligning what I want Him to do with what His will is to do for me. I admit I do not know what is best for me. I have a limited view of the future. Knowing this, I place my life in God's hands to protect and guide me. This is always when life is at its best. I rest secure in God's lovingkindness because He made and kept the ultimate promise to me.

> **But God showed his great love for us by sending Christ to die for us while we were still sinners.** Romans 5:8 NLT

DAY 84
Isaiah 39:1-8

Soon after this, Merodach-baladan son of Baladan, king of Babylon, sent Hezekiah his best wishes and a gift. He had heard that Hezekiah had been very sick and that he had recovered. 2 Hezekiah was delighted with the Babylonian envoys and showed them everything in his treasure-houses—the silver, the gold, the spices, and the aromatic oils. He also took them to see his armory and showed them everything in his royal treasuries! There was nothing in his palace or kingdom that Hezekiah did not show them.

3 Then Isaiah the prophet went to King Hezekiah and asked him, "What did those men want? Where were they from?" Hezekiah replied, "They came from the distant land of Babylon."

4 "What did they see in your palace?" asked Isaiah. "They saw everything," Hezekiah replied. "I showed them everything I own—all my royal treasuries."

5 Then Isaiah said to Hezekiah, "Listen to this message from the Lord of Heaven's Armies: 6 'The time is coming when everything in your palace—all the treasures stored up by your ancestors until now—will be carried off to Babylon. Nothing will be left,' says the Lord. 7 'Some of your very own sons will be taken away into exile. They will become eunuchs who will serve in the palace of Babylon's king.'"

> 8 Then Hezekiah said to Isaiah, "This message you have given me from the Lord is good." For the king was thinking, "At least there will be peace and security during my lifetime."

Hezekiah wanted to impress an envoy from Babylon, so he showed them all of Israel's wealth and military capabilities. This, of course, was a mistake because trying to impress someone if we are successful just stirs jealousy and envy in them. News of this wealth would have been taken back to Babylon, and years later, it would be remembered that there was something to take from Israel.

Isaiah confronts Hezekiah over his irresponsible act of pride and Hezekiah agrees. Then Hezekiah reveals his shallowness and narrow-minded view. He knows Israel will pay a price someday for his mistake. All the wealth David and Solomon amassed, the security of his descendants, all at risk, and all Hezekiah can flippantly say is, well, at least I won't have to deal with it.

It is poor leadership to not think of future generations. Whether it is how we care for the environment, manage financial resources, or model character for our children and grandchildren, the inheritance we leave will either give them a start to a better life or create a mess with which they will be stuck.

> A good person leaves an inheritance for their children's children,
> but a sinner's wealth is stored up for the righteous. Proverbs 13:22

Let us leave an inheritance of trust in God, and good stewardship of our resources for generations to come.

DAY 85
Isaiah 40:1-5

"Comfort, comfort my people," says your God.

2 "Speak tenderly to Jerusalem.

Tell her that her sad days are gon and her sins are pardoned.

Yes, the Lord has punished her twice over for all her sins."

Isaiah seems to change direction and tone at the start of chapter 40. The first 39 chapters deal with sin, guilt, and judgment. The last 27 chapters of Isaiah emphasize grace and forgiveness. This corresponds to the Old Testament having 39 books while the New Testament contains 27. John the Baptist begins his ministry by quoting Isaiah 40 (see Mark 1:3).

"Their warfare is over, and her debt of sin is paid." What amazing words of comfort to the church. This is God's promise to everyone who trusts in Jesus. Isaiah now gets to bring good news—double the blessings for God's people. This is what they are told to expect. The promise still stands.

Listen! It's the voice of someone shouting, "Clear the way through the wilderness for the Lord! Make a straight highway through the wasteland for our God!

4 Fill in the valleys, and level the mountains and hills. Straighten the curves, and smooth out the rough places.

5 Then the glory of the Lord will be revealed, and all people will see it together. The Lord has spoken!"

Isaiah provides a link to John the Baptist hundreds of years in advance. He describes John's ministry mission to prepare the people hearts to receive Jesus.

By the time John the Baptist arrived on the scene, it had been at least 400 years since the Jews had heard from God. John would orient the people toward God. He answers the question, what would it be like if God were close to us again? How do we posture ourselves for God's coming?

We make space for God to teach us and lead us. We find times of quiet worship to still ourselves and make it easy for God to speak to us.

What barriers keep you from making space for God? Is it social media, news, sports, entertainment, gaming? Many things eat up our time and keep us from experiencing the "radiant glory" of God's presence. Make some smooth paths to your heart today by capturing moments to open yourself so the Holy Spirit can reveal Jesus to us.

DAY 86

Isaiah 40:6-11

A voice said, "Shout!"

I asked, "What should I shout?"

"Shout that people are like the grass.

Their beauty fades as quickly as the flowers in a field.

7 The grass withers and the flowers fade beneath the breath of the Lord.

And so it is with people.

8 The grass withers and the flowers fade, but the word of our God stands forever."

Isaiah is so true when he speaks God's Word about people being fragile and how quickly beauty, success, and feeling on top can fade. The influencer will lose their audience to someone more appealing. Success will peak, and those on top will find it impossible to stay there.

What does last forever? God's Word and His promises to be our Lord and rule our lives with kindness and grace. He promises to lead us in "paths of righteousness." God has never, and will never, break a promise.

Maybe, instead of envying someone else's temporary place at the top, we focus on the eternal stuff and God's promises and build our lives on that solid foundation rather than the sand of human success.

> 9 O Zion, messenger of good news, shout from the mountaintops!
>
> Shout it louder, O Jerusalem.
>
> Shout, and do not be afraid. Tell the towns of Judah,
>
> "Your God is coming!"
>
> 10 Yes, the Sovereign Lord is coming in power. He will rule with a powerful arm. See, he brings his reward with him as he comes.

We sense the closeness of Jesus and His Kingdom whenever we worship, and the veil between Heaven and Earth seems thinner. This is what thousands felt recently at Asbury University and why tens of thousands wanted to be there.

Jesus came to inaugurate a new covenant and a new Kingdom. He told us to pray that the realities of Heaven would break into this realm as His Kingdom comes.

We also experience the Kingdom whenever we read scripture, and the words leap off the page and challenge us.

The Kingdom is visibly in action when we pray and see God do a supernatural work of healing in someone's body.

Though we can experience Jesus in all these ways, it will not be until His return in the culmination of His Kingdom that every enemy will be defeated Heaven will envelop earth, and Jesus will reign overall. Until that day, we believe in times when Heaven breaks through, but we also live to carry the cry in our heart that has been shared with believers since the beginning of the church, Maranatha, come to Lord Jesus.

> 11 He will feed his flock like a shepherd.
>
> He will carry the lambs in his arms, holding them close to his heart.
>
> He will gently lead the mother sheep with their young.

It is easy to forget that God can be whatever He chooses. He could be a tyrannical despot demanding our sacrifice and servitude. He could be maniacal and watch us get what we deserve because of sinfulness. He could be aloof and distant because we ignored Him.

Instead, Jesus is a gentle Good Shepherd who carries us in His arms. Even in our rebellion and tendency to get ourselves in trouble, He still pursues us and draws us close to His heart.

If you have children today, pray this promise, asking Jesus to gently lead you. God wants to impart wisdom to you in how to love and care for your children. Let Him inspire you with words to communicate, a phone call or text to express your love.

The more we allow God to lead us, the better leaders of others we become.

DAY 87
Isaiah 40:12-25

Who else has held the oceans in his hand?

Who has measured off the heavens with his fingers?

Who else knows the weight of the earth or has weighed the mountains and hills on a scale?

13 Who is able to advise the Spirit of the Lord?

Who knows enough to give him advice or teach him?

14 Has the Lord ever needed anyone's advice?

Does he need instruction about what is good?

Did someone teach him what is right or show him the path of justice?

15 No, for all the nations of the world are but a drop in the bucket.

They are nothing more than dust on the scales.

He picks up the whole earth as though it were a grain of sand.

16 All the wood in Lebanon's forests and all Lebanon's animals would not be enough to make a burnt offering worthy of our God.

17 The nations of the world are worth nothing to him. In his eyes they count for less than nothing—mere emptiness and froth.

Isaiah reveals God's view of human government and the kingdoms of this world. Superpowers and third-world nations are insignificant compared to God. This is why we look to the Heavens and not to Washington as our source.

If everything in this world was completely dedicated to God He would still be worthy of more. If every tree was used to make a fire and every animal sacrificed it would still not be enough to give the honor due to Jesus.

So today when you head to church and the weather isn't perfect, or the coffee isn't just right, or they are not singing your favorite song, remember this passage and how much worship God deserves. Then humble yourself and offer everything to God because that is why we gather and that is what He deserves.

18 To whom can you compare God?

What image can you find to resemble him?

19 Can he be compared to an idol formed in a mold, overlaid with gold, and decorated with silver chains?

20 Or if people are too poor for that, they might at least choose wood that won't decay and a skilled craftsman to carve an image that won't fall down!

21 Haven't you heard? Don't you understand?

Are you deaf to the words of God—

the words he gave before the world began?

Are you so ignorant?

22 God sits above the circle of the earth.

The people below seem like grasshoppers to him!

He spreads out the heavens like a curtain and makes his tent from them.

23 He judges the great people of the world and brings them all to nothing.

24 They hardly get started, barely taking root,

when he blows on them and they wither.

The wind carries them off like chaff.

25-26 "To whom will you compare me?

Who is my equal?" asks the Holy One. Look up into the heavens.

Who created all the stars? He brings them out like an army, one after another, calling each by its name.

Because of his great power and incomparable strength, not a single one is missing.

27 O Jacob, how can you say the Lord does not see your troubles?

O Israel, how can you say God ignores your rights?

We fail to grasp God's magnitude and majesty. He is so vast and powerful that we could never comprehend His greatness. He works on a macro scale, creating the expanse of the Universe. At the same time, he cares about the micro details of our lives.

Isaiah reminds us that God not only created the stars, but He sustains them. In the same way, God didn't just cause us to be born He has invested in our lives. He calls us to Himself so He can fulfill His plans through us.

> For I know the plans I have for you," says the Lord. "They are plans for good and not for disaster, to give you a future and a hope. Jer. 29:11

Don't forget the greatest resource in your life is the God of all creation. He is infinitely interested in you. Never lose hope in the future God has for you.

DAY 88
Isaiah 41:1-7

"Listen in silence before me, you lands beyond the sea.

Bring your strongest arguments.

Come now and speak.

The court is ready for your case.

2 "Who has stirred up this king from the east, rightly calling him to God's service?

Who gives this man victory over many nations and permits him to trample their kings underfoot?

With his sword, he reduces armies to dust.

With his bow, he scatters them like chaff before the wind.

3 He chases them away and goes on safely, though he is walking over unfamiliar ground.

4 Who has done such mighty deeds, summoning each new generation from the beginning of time?

It is I, the Lord, the First and the Last. I alone am he."

As we have been hearing from Isaiah, there is no end to God's wisdom and greatness. He guides everything toward His desired end. A man may rebel or be confused and resist God's plans, creating havoc, but God will triumph.

Isaiah tells us to connect with God by stilling ourselves and listening. In silence, we sense God's closeness, receive His peace, hear His wisdom, and renew our strength.

Isn't it amazing that one of the easiest things we could do is also one of the most difficult? Our minds wander, we get distracted, and we feel this is unproductive. But in humble silence, we remember that this is the God who was at the beginning, will be there in the end, and is with us at this moment.

5 The lands beyond the sea watch in fear.

Remote lands tremble and mobilize for war.

6 The idol makers encourage one another, saying to each other, "Be strong!"

7 The carver encourages the goldsmith, and the molder helps at the anvil.

"Good," they say. "It's coming along fine." Carefully they join the parts together, then fasten the thing in place so it won't fall over.

By contrast, look at God's appeal to us.

Man creates false gods and then tries to say they are worthy of worship. Whether it is economic systems, government, political, or even religious leaders, they pat one another on the back and declare this will save them. But they have to protect their god and nail it down so the opposition can't take it down, which always happens.

Take a quick inventory of what you are currently trusting in. Maybe it is a political leader or party, your job, the market, what you've saved up, or your wisdom and abilities that have always gotten you by as long as you can stay nailed down and the opposition is not too great.

Now compare them to the Creator who offers to accept you, be near to you, be faithful, infuse you with strength, help you, and hold you securely.

It is that "servant" thing with which we struggle. To get these benefits, we must surrender our will and serve God. That is the cost to us. The question is, will we serve the God who created us in His image or the one we've made in our own?

DAY 89
Isaiah 41:8-14

"But as for you, Israel my servant, Jacob my chosen one,

descended from Abraham my friend,

9 I have called you back from the ends of the earth,

saying, 'You are my servant.'

For I have chosen you and will not throw you away.

10 Don't be afraid, for I am with you.

Don't be discouraged, for I am your God. I will strengthen you and help you.

I will hold you up with my victorious right hand.

11 "See, all your angry enemies lie there, confused and humiliated.

Anyone who opposes you will die

and come to nothing.

12 You will look in vain for those who tried to conquer you.

Those who attack you will come to nothing.

13 For I hold you by your right hand—

I, the Lord your God.

And I say to you, 'Don't be afraid. I am here to help you.

What an amazing statement God speaks to us through Isaiah. He is not just the Mighty God; He is your Mighty God. He is personally committed to you. He holds you personally by the hand and will never let go.

He whispers His love and protection. He whispers these words because He is so close to us that is all the volume necessary. We don't have to strain; we just need to draw close and listen. These words flow from God's heart to mine as I write them. I sense His love surrounding me. Thoughts, images, and memories of God's faithfulness flood my mind.

Fear has no place because my thoughts are filled with how amazing it is that the God of all creation would love me personally. I know I cannot focus on worries and worship at the same time, so I choose to worship. I chose to draw close to my Heavenly Father and allow the Holy Spirit to reveal more of Him to me.

> 14 Though you are a lowly worm, O Jacob, don't be afraid, people of Israel, for I will help you.

> I am the Lord, your Redeemer. I am the Holy One of Israel.'

Brian Simmons has some insightful notes to help us understand how we relate to grub worms and a Kinsman-Redeemer.

David used this term to point to Jesus as he was crucified prophetically. See Ps. 22:6. The Hebrew word is tola, which is a species of worm found in the Middle East (Coccus ilicus) that reproduces itself when the female fastens herself to a tree and lays eggs between her body and the tree. When the eggs hatch, the baby worms feed on her living body. When the eggs emerge, the blood remains on the tree as a crimson stain.

When Jesus died on the cross (tree), his blood left a crimson stain, and he gave birth to the church. He nourishes us and sustains us with His body and blood.

A kinsman-redeemer (go'el) is a male relative who was culturally responsible for acting on behalf of a relative who was in trouble or danger, needs to be redeemed from slavery, or needs rescue. He became a "savior" or "family protector" for his next of kin. Jesus, our next of kin, is our Kinsman-Redeemer.

The Hebrew verb ga'al ("to act as redeemer") is found more than one hundred times in the Hebrew Bible. See Ruth 2:20

DAY 90
Isaiah 41:15-29

You will be a new threshing instrument with many sharp teeth.

You will tear your enemies apart, making chaff of mountains.

16 You will toss them into the air, and the wind will blow them all away; a whirlwind will scatter them. Then you will rejoice in the Lord. You will glory in the Holy One of Israel.

17 "When the poor and needy search for water and there is none, and their tongues are parched from thirst, then I, the Lord, will answer them. I, the God of Israel, will never abandon them.

18 I will open up rivers for them on the high plateaus.

I will give them fountains of water in the valleys.

I will fill the desert with pools of water. Rivers fed by springs will flow across the parched ground.

19 I will plant trees in the barren desert— cedar, acacia, myrtle, olive, cypress, fir, and pine.

20 I am doing this so all who see this miracle will understand what it means— that it is the Lord who has done this, the Holy One of Israel who created it.

Long portion of Biblical text here but it completes an important thought. I hope you'll read it and grasp the wonderful truth Isaiah communicates to us.

The first portion describes how God works through us to break up the ground, remove weeds, and prepare for His planting. Here, I believe Isaiah is painting a picture of our prayers as we declare God's will. We play a role in God's plan to redeem mankind. Our prayers over our neighborhoods, schools, and workplaces are powerful, and they matter.

Yesterday we sent out teams to prayerwalk in our community. In prayerwalking, we are releasing in prayer what God wants to do in communities. It also softens the enemy's defenses for the work God wants to do.

Our part is to pray and rejoice. Rejoicing in Hebrew means to dance and twirl in worship. We aren't straining to convince God, we're simply declaring what He puts on our hearts to pray and rejoice that we get to have a role in His plan.

Next, God works in planting and providing resources in dry and barren places. What a beautiful picture of God establishing healthy churches where His presence is experienced and people are refreshed and renewed and the poor and the needy are made whole. When the church functions as God intended, people who are far from God are drawn to Him.

21 "Present the case for your idols," says the Lord.

"Let them show what they can do," says the King of Israel.

DAY 90

22 "Let them try to tell us what happened long ago so that we may consider the evidence. Or let them tell us what the future holds, so we can know what's going to happen.

23 Yes, tell us what will occur in the days ahead. Then we will know you are gods. In fact, do anything—good or bad! Do something that will amaze and frighten us.

24 But no! You are less than nothing and can do nothing at all. Those who choose you pollute themselves.

Our God is jealous for us. He does find it amusing or dismisses it as just a curiosity when we check our horoscope or have our palm read. He calls it a form of worship to seek any source other than Himself for insight about the future or direction for our lives.

The Apostle Paul saw the demonic roots in fortune-telling and knew how to respond to it.

One day as we were going down to the place of prayer, we met a slave girl who had a spirit that enabled her to tell the future… Paul got so exasperated that he turned and said to the demon within her, "I command you in the name of Jesus Christ to come out of her." And instantly it left her. Acts 16:16,18

Trying to find answers or direction outside of God's counsel leads us down a path away from God that will destroy our lives. This is why Isaiah speaks so strongly and calls it disgusting.

Why would we seek anything fake when we have the Holy Spirit, who knows everything, ready to lead us into what Jesus called an "abundant life"?

25 "But I have stirred up a leader who will approach from the north. From the east he will call on my name. I will give him victory over kings and princes. He will trample them as a potter treads on clay.

26 "Who told you from the beginning that this would happen? Who predicted this, making you admit that he was right? No one said a word!

27 I was the first to tell Zion, 'Look! Help is on the way!' I will send Jerusalem a messenger with good news.

28 Not one of your idols told you this. Not one gave any answer when I asked.

29 See, they are all foolish, worthless things. All your idols are as empty as the wind.

Isaiah speaks plainly when it comes to His attack on the idols the Israelites were turning to. These foreign gods, some real, some fake, were imported from the surrounding nations throughout intermarrying and violating a primary directive of God. Once again, we see a God who is jealous to protect us and wants our exclusive devotion, of which He is worthy.

DAY 91
Isaiah 42:1-6

"Look at my servant, whom I strengthen. mHe is my chosen one, who pleases me.

I have put my Spirit upon him. He will bring justice to the nations.

Isaiah now turns his focus to the coming Messiah, Jesus. For the next several chapters, Isaiah paints a prophetic picture of Jesus' nature and character, Divinity clothed in humanity and greatness wrapped in humility.

Over the next several days, we will glimpse Jesus and His Father's love for Him. Remember, this is the same love the Father has for us. When Isaiah writes about God's love and support for His Servant, He sees us through the same lens. This is why Jesus taught us to pray, "Our Father who is in Heaven."

It is not what Jesus did that pleased His Father but who He was, God's Son. You and I spark the same joy in our Heavenly Father. We have been clothed with the same Holy Spirit that empowered Jesus and even raised Him from the dead.

We can either stand outside observing this beautiful prophetic picture through the lens of history and theology or sit at the table as children of God and ask our Father to reveal more of Jesus and His love for us.

He will not shout or raise his voice in public.

3 He will not crush the weakest reed or put out a flickering candle.

This prophetic picture shows Jesus's humility and meekness hundreds of years before He was born into humanity. He is a servant leader who puts others first and is kind and gentle.

Yes, I know this is the same Jesus who rebukes Pharisees and turns over tables, but that is not His nature at its core. His nature is love. He comes alongside the broken and offers them grace. No matter how distant or undeserving I have felt, I know Jesus still loves me and is with me. When I deserve Him the least, He is there to give Himself to me.

When we cry out in pain and even complain that Jesus isn't doing enough to fix the world and particularly my situation, His word assures me that He will not fail to bring justice. It may be that I don't see justice and everything made right within my timeline and according to my plans. In those times of waiting, what does God give me? More of Himself.

> God, the Lord, created the heavens and stretched them out.

> He created the earth and everything in it.

> He gives breath to everyone, life to everyone who walks the earth. mAnd it is he who says, 6 "I, the Lord, have called you to demonstrate my righteousness. I will take you by the hand and guard you, and I will give you to my people, Israel, as a symbol of my covenant with them. And you will be a light to guide the nations.

DAY 92
Isaiah 42:7-12

You will open the eyes of the blind.

You will free the captives from prison, releasing those who sit in dark dungeons.

These verses point to Jesus as God's new covenant and light to the nations. Jesus quoted this text in his first message in His hometown.

The Spirit of the Lord is upon me, for he has anointed me to bring Good News to the poor. He has sent me to proclaim that captives will be released, that the blind will see, that the oppressed will be set free, Luke 4:18

God made a covenant with Abraham and fulfilled both sides by representing Himself and Abraham. He knew man could never be faithful enough to keep a covenant. God repeats this same process when He makes a new covenant with humanity.

Jesus becomes God's sacrificial lamb, sealing the covenant agreement for eternity. We are the benefactors of Jesus' death and shed blood. When we surrender our lives and receive God's gift of salvation, we come under this covenant agreement that cannot be broken.

Nothing can take us away from God or remove us as children born-again into His family.

This is why we honor Jesus as I write these words on Good Friday 2024.

"I am the Lord; that is my name!

I will not give my glory to anyone else, nor share my praise with carved idols.

9 Everything I prophesied has come true, and now I will prophesy again.

I will tell you the future before it happens."

God once again reminds the people that He is jealous of their devotion and worthy of them because of His power and authority.

God is calling His people to think about the times they are and how He had foretold that it would happen. Amos, Hosea, Nahum, and Jeremiah prophesied Israel would be defeated and held captive in Babylon. He has a perfect track record when it comes to fulfilling prophecy. What He speaks always comes to pass.

Now, he looks 800 years into the future and sees deliverance coming for Israel in the form of a Savior Messiah. Notice the phrase "sprouts up." This is the Hebrew word "tsa.mach." It means to spring up like a shoot of grass coming out of the ground. But here in particular, it means "to cause to spring up." I believe God is giving us a prophetic glimpse of Jesus' resurrection—the ultimate victory over the ultimate enemy death.

Peter told the crowd on the Day of Pentecost, "But God released him from the horrors of death and raised him back to life, for death could not keep him in its grip." Acts 2:24

This is not a nice coincidence. It is there for us to review and believe. We see the early prophecies about Israel and Jesus fulfilled. Our only response should be to worship God because He is in control, and all the promises about our future eternal life can be trusted.

Sing a new song to the Lord!

DAY 92

Sing his praises from the ends of the earth!

Sing, all you who sail the seas, all you who live in distant coastlands.

11 Join in the chorus, you desert towns; let the villages of Kedar rejoice!

Let the people of Sela sing for joy; shout praises from the mountaintops!

12 Let the whole world glorify the Lord; let it sing his praise.

The God of all creation certainly deserves our praise. Today especially we honor Jesus' sacrifice and victory over death and grave on our behalf.

We wake up this morning as sons and daughters of God, assured of our eternity and joyful about living in the realm of God's Kingdom. All of this because Jesus loved us so much He would give His life to be brutally tortured and hung on the cross till His blood was shed as payment for our sins.

We are free! Free to live now and into eternity! Free to proclaim God's goodness! Free to live the abundant life Jesus declared! Free to access the power that raised Jesus from the dead by the Holy Spirit within us!

Today is Easter, the day to celebrate and declare HE HAS RISEN INDEED!

DAY 93
Isaiah 42:13-20

The Lord will march forth like a mighty hero; he will come out like a warrior, full of fury.

He will shout his battle cry and crush all his enemies.

14 He will say, "I have long been silent; yes, I have restrained myself.

But now, like a woman in labor, I will cry and groan and pant.

15 I will level the mountains and hills and blight all their greenery.

I will turn the rivers into dry land and will dry up all the pools.

16 I will lead blind Israel down a new path, guiding them along an unfamiliar way.

I will brighten the darkness before them and smooth out the road ahead of them.

Yes, I will indeed do these things; I will not forsake them.

17 But those who trust in idols, who say, 'You are our gods,' will be turned away in shame.

I love that God compensates for all of our weaknesses. If we lack vision and direction, He guides us. If we lack health, He heals us. If we feel unloved or abandoned, He promises to be with us.

There is no situation we can face that God will not see us through. If we trust Him, He will smooth every difficulty in the road ahead.

But this means admitting we are blind to the future and that Jesus knows the best way for us to go. We can walk our path or old paths that have only led to disaster, or we can humble ourselves and allow the Holy Spirit to whisper His guidance.

Prayer: Today, I yield myself to your guidance, Lord Jesus. Holy Spirit, lead me where to go and what to say so I can bring you the honor you deserve.

This passage could be interpreted as a rebuke for spiritual dullness and rebellion to the point where the people are insensitive or dull toward God. Or, it could be God giving credit to His devoted ones who are blind to the things and voices of this world and see what God is doing.

"Listen, you who are deaf! Look and see, you blind!

19 Who is as blind as my own people, my servant?

Who is as deaf as my messenger?

Who is as blind as my chosen people, the servant of the Lord?

20 You see and recognize what is right but refuse to act on it.

You hear with your ears, but you don't really listen."

I believe it is both, we obey with our ears, our eyes, our lips, and our touch. Jesus said, "I tell you the truth, the Son can do nothing by himself. He does only what he sees the Father doing. Whatever the Father does, the Son also does. John 5:19

We should allow no place in our minds for unbelief if we are going to follow God. We read the Scriptures, we sense God responding to us in prayer, and when we hear others' stories of God's faithfulness. All of this should build faith in us as it did in Jesus. He only chose to look where the Father was looking; His greatest focus was on the voice of God. He was blind and deaf to anger, lust, fear, and any noise that interfered with dialed into His Father exclusively.

After he has gathered his own flock, he walks ahead of them, and they follow him because they know his voice. They won't follow a stranger; they will run from him because they don't know his voice." John 10:4-5

DAY 94
Isaiah 42:21-25

Because he is righteous, the Lord has exalted his glorious law.

22 But his own people have been robbed and plundered, enslaved, imprisoned, and trapped.

They are fair game for anyone and have no one to protect them, no one to take them back home.

23 Who will hear these lessons from the past and see the ruin that awaits you in the future?

24 Who allowed Israel to be robbed and hurt?

It was the Lord, against whom we sinned, for the people would not walk in his path, nor would they obey his law.

Isaiah mourns Israel's captivity, but it is due to their rebellion against God. Many complain about feeling trapped in a job, relationship, or difficult situation. The last thing we want to do is blame the victim. But what if the victim is also the perpetrator? What if our rebellion has got us in the place we're in?

When we see friends and family in these places of bondage, one of the most effective things we can do is cry out on their behalf, "Bring them back!"

Bring them back from spiritual blindness. Cause people who love Jesus to cross their path. Continuously put the message of the Gospel and the goodness of God in front of their eyes in miraculous ways. Bring them home to a Father who loves them and wants to heal and deliver them out of bondage.

> May the kindness of God lead them to repentance. Or do you think lightly of the riches of His kindness and restraint and patience, not knowing that the kindness of God leads you to repentance? Romans 2:4

> 25 Therefore, he poured out his fury on them and destroyed them in battle.

> They were enveloped in flames, but they still refused to understand.

> They were consumed by fire, but they did not learn their lesson.

Is God judging the world today? We credit a lot of events with God's judgment that I believe is more the result of a fallen, sinful world.

As Christians, we think a little judgment might be good to awaken people to the truth and God's holiness, to scare some of the Hell out of them.

The reality is that judgment doesn't seem to affect people. Isaiah speaks here about God pouring out His anger, but it doesn't seem to matter. People still went on doing their thing, living their lives.

Jesus tells a parable about a poor man named Lazarus and a rich man. They both die, and the rich man doesn't fare as well as Lazarus, who is on his way to Heaven. The rich man begs Abraham to help him by resurrecting Lazarus and sending him to witness to his family. Look at Jesus' words,

"But Abraham said, 'If they won't listen to Moses and the prophets, they won't be persuaded even if someone rises from the dead.'"
Luke 16:31

It is still the kindness of God that leads people to repentance. People have plenty of pain. What they need is a demonstration of the unconditional love of God. This means presenting God's truth demands wrapped in grace.

DAY 95

Isaiah 43:1-7

But now, O Jacob, listen to the Lord who created you.

O Israel, the one who formed you says,

"Do not be afraid, for I have ransomed you.

I have called you by name; you are mine.

2 When you go through deep waters, I will be with you.

When you go through rivers of difficulty, you will not drown.

When you walk through the fire of oppression,

you will not be burned up; the flames will not consume you.

> 3 For I am the Lord, your God, the Holy One of Israel, your Savior.

One of my favorite passages. God promises to be with us and bring us through storms and fiery circumstances. We must realize that He also allows us to get into these situations as well. Sometimes it is our own doing and sometimes it is the result of an imperfect world whereas Jesus said, "The rain falls on the just and the unjust" (Matt. 5:45).

Regardless of why we are in the storm or fire, God is the way out. Our part is first, not to fear. God is with us so we acknowledge Him and look to Him, rather than the waves or flames.

Finally, we grasp hold of the God who says, "I am your Savior, Yahweh, your mighty God." Your struggle is personal to God. He calls you by name. Your challenge is His challenge, and there is no problem that God cannot overcome.

The people who walked with Jesus were so convinced of this truth James could write,

Dear brothers and sisters, when troubles of any kind come your way, consider it an opportunity for great joy. For you know that when your faith is tested, your endurance has a chance to grow. So let it grow, for when your endurance is fully developed, you will be perfect and complete, needing nothing. James 1:2-4

> I gave Egypt as a ransom for your freedom;

> I gave Ethiopia and Seba in your place.

> 4 Others were given in exchange for you.

> I traded their lives for yours because you are precious to me.

You are honored, and I love you. 5 "Do not be afraid, for I am with you.

I will gather you and your children from east and west.

6 I will say to the north and south,

'Bring my sons and daughters back to Israel

from the distant corners of the earth.

7 Bring all who claim me as their God,

for I have made them for my glory.

It was I who created them.'"

The Father is calling out to His children to come home. I have prayed these verses many times over friends and neighbors. God, bring them from every direction. Draw people to yourself through believers to your church.

God's goal, Jesus' mission, and our commission is to help people discover they are children of God and that Jesus has already paid the price for their sins. They need to surrender control of their life to God and accept His forgiveness to experience His glory and presence.

If you have people you are praying for who are far from God, don't miss the opening promise: God is close to you. When your heart breaks over someone, don't yield to fear. No matter how strong of a grip Satan seems to have on their life or how much they are rebelling. God is bringing them home. Even if they go to the ends of the earth or the depths of pain, God's love and kindness will draw them to Himself.

DAY 96
Isaiah 43:8-13

Bring out the people who have eyes but are blind, who have ears but are deaf.

9 Gather the nations together!

Assemble the peoples of the world!

Which of their idols has ever foretold such things?

Which can predict what will happen tomorrow?

Where are the witnesses of such predictions?

Who can verify that they spoke the truth?

We are called to lead out the blind and deaf. Our job is to love and lead, not condemn and reject. We do not blame people who are physically, emotionally, or spiritually blind or deaf. In the same way, we don't ask physically blind or deaf people what caused them to be in this situation. We want to make them feel accepted.

We realize that if we have abilities that can assist someone else who is struggling, we are obligated to do so. God is calling us to help people move toward Him wherever they are. This is why we are motivated by God's love to see past what the enemy has done to people and have faith in what God can do to transform their lives.

The world condemns people and blames them for their problems. As believers, we want to help everyone experience the same grace we have received from God. We realized that our sins were just as heinous, and we were just as blind and deaf. Jesus accepted us at our worst because He saw ahead and how beautiful we would be to Him once His transforming love filled us.

This is why we are motivated by mercy. We are people of faith who have been loved and have our eyes and ears open. May we use our spiritual sight to see the potential in people and our spiritual hearing to listen to God for particular ways to minister to them.

> 10 "But you are my witnesses, O Israel!" says the Lord.
>
> "You are my servant.
>
> You have been chosen to know me, believe in me, and understand that I alone am God.
>
> There is no other God— there never has been, and there never will be.

Isaiah makes it clear who God is and who we are to be. He is sovereign and reigns overall. He chose us as His people to serve and to tell others of His greatness and goodness. But more than serving Him, God wants us to:

Know Him intimately. When we know someone intimately, we understand the why behind their actions. We understand what motivates them as they open their hearts to us.

Believe Him always. When we know God's character and that He is consistently good and compassionate, faith comes easily.

Comprehend His greatness. We get that our God is omnipotent, omniscient, and omnipresent. He is all-powerful, all-knowing, and always present.

These are the truths on which we build our lives. It is also the message with which we fulfill our commission to tell the world about this God who wants to know us personally and invites us into a relationship that will extend beyond life into eternity.

> 11 I, yes I, am the Lord, and there is no other Savior.
>
> 12 First I predicted your rescue, then I saved you and proclaimed it to the world.
>
> No foreign god has ever done this.
>
> You are witnesses that I am the only God," says the Lord.
>
> 13 "From eternity to eternity I am God.
>
> No one can snatch anyone out of my hand.
>
> No one can undo what I have done."

God is telling His people to lock in their votes for the last time. He is exclusively the Source and Ruler over everything. If we lack confidence in this reality, God offers to reveal more of Himself to us.

As we stand for truth and share our connection with God, He increasingly reveals Himself through us. I have noticed recently that more stories of healing and miracles are taking place as people partner with the Holy Spirit. They describe how God is ministering to others in the church and everyday marketplaces as they follow the Holy Spirit's promptings and trust Him to do His work through them.

We don't have to sit on the sidelines worrying about sin taking us away from God. No one can take us away from Jesus. We humbly ask Him to reveal more of Himself in areas where we are weak in battling temptation.

Our Father wants to help us find freedom to be bold witnesses without condemnation.

DAY 97

Isaiah 43:14-28

This is what the Lord says—your Redeemer, the Holy One of Israel:

"For your sakes I will send an army against Babylon, forcing the Babylonians to flee in those ships they are so proud of.

15 I am the Lord, your Holy One, Israel's Creator and King.

16 I am the Lord, who opened a way through the waters, making a dry path through the sea.

17 I called forth the mighty army of Egypt

with all its chariots and horses.

I drew them beneath the waves, and they drowned,

their lives snuffed out like a smoldering candlewick.

18 "But forget all that—

it is nothing compared to what I am going to do.

19 For I am about to do something new.

See, I have already begun! Do you not see it?

I will make a pathway through the wilderness.

I will create rivers in the dry wasteland.

The calendar today marks another trip around the Sun for me. It is one of those beautiful coincidences where God scheduled, He and I to intersect this morning at these verses in Isaiah.

Every year, as we acknowledge our birth, we also tend to stop and look at our lives. How did I grow in the last year? What is ahead for this 66th year? There is no condemnation for all the goals I didn't hit this past year. For the goals I did accomplish, all the credit goes to Jesus.

As I anticipate a new beginning, I learn from the past but don't dwell there. God is always doing new things. I want to perceive this new path into the wilderness Isaiah describes. I want to focus my time and energy on this new thing. God's vision for me is to continue to grow and mature and impart something to others. I want to drink more from God's flowing stream, which is accessible even in the wilderness.

Today can be your new day, too. Pray to be spiritually sensitive and perceive God's work in you. Take a few moments right now to drink from that flowing stream.

> 20 The wild animals in the fields will thank me, the jackals and owls, too, for giving them water in the desert.
>
> Yes, I will make rivers in the dry wasteland so my chosen people can be refreshed.
>
> 21 I have made Israel for myself, and they will someday honor me before the whole world.

Even if we feel like wild beasts instead of the lambs who devotedly follow Jesus, God still provides refreshing streams of grace for us. God is the only one who can satisfy our thirst for meaning and He goes to outsiders who will turn to Him.

After all, He shaped and formed us for His purpose and we will never be fulfilled in life until we follow God and discover that purpose. You will know when you are moving toward that purpose because you begin praising God more and more.

I believe God's design and direction for us is both macro and micro. Macro describes where we are placed and what our roles are in life. This includes marriage, parenting, career, and anywhere we have a responsibility in leading or influencing others.

The micro level is the everyday listening and obeying God in the small promptings to text, send an email, make a phone call, or just stop and pray for someone. It might be to share a word of prophetic encouragement and communicate God's heart for someone.

Fulfillment comes through following God in the big macro areas and the little micro acts.

> 22 "But, dear family of Jacob, you refuse to ask for my help.
>
> You have grown tired of me, O Israel!

23 You have not brought me sheep or goats for burnt offerings.

You have not honored me with sacrifices, though I have not burdened and wearied you with requests for grain offerings and frankincense.

24 You have not brought me fragrant calamus or pleased me with the fat from sacrifices.

Instead, you have burdened me with your sins and wearied me with your faults.

We get busy, distracted, and have other priorities, so worshiping God becomes another responsibility or burden. This is hard to admit, but we can become too busy and selfish to give God what He is due. Giving and serving can become religious tasks performed from a sense of duty rather than acts of love.

God reminds us that He is the exclusive gateway to eternity through His forgiveness. He is gracious, kind, and loving toward us and always wants what is best for us.

Having our sins forgiven and erased should be enough to redirect our focus from busyness and give God the honor and praise He deserves.

25 "I—yes, I alone—will blot out your sins for my own sake and will never think of them again.

26 Let us review the situation together,

and you can present your case to prove your innocence.

27 From the very beginning, your first ancestor sinned against me; all your leaders broke my laws.

28 That is why I have disgraced your priests;

I have decreed complete destruction for Jacob and shame for Israel.

I like how God gives people the opportunity to make their case. It is, in fact, ridiculous to try to see God in your opinion when he knows everything. Everyone stands before God guilty of sin. We have no case and no grounds on which to argue but must simply appeal to the grace of God given to us through Christ's death. We can only humbly receive God's mercy.

DAY 98
Isaiah 44:1-7

"But now, listen to me, Jacob my servant, Israel my chosen one.

2 The Lord who made you and helps you says:

Do not be afraid, O Jacob, my servant, O dear Israel, my chosen one.

3 For I will pour out water to quench your thirst and to irrigate your parched fields.

And I will pour out my Spirit on your descendants, and my blessing on your children.

4 They will thrive like watered grass, like willows on a riverbank.

5 Some will proudly claim, 'I belong to the Lord.'

> Others will say, 'I am a descendant of Jacob.'
>
> Some will write the Lord's name on their hand and will take the name of Israel as their own."

The first thing that stands out in this passage is the description of God shaping us in His womb. Brian Simmons offers a footnote. "The love God has for us is like a mother's love. The Hebrew concept of compassion carries this thought, for compassion (racham) is the same word as "womb."

The God who transcends time and space can be anything. He is certainly more than the qualities that make up a man and a woman. God fulfills both roles in our lives. We need Him to be our masculine solid leader and our nurturing feminine mother. He is both to us. The Bible uses many metaphors to describe us and our relationship with God: son and daughters, heirs, children, sheep, and even a bride. This is because there are many ways in which God loves us and relates to us.

I love that God tells us not to fear but rather look for the refreshing water God will pour out when we are spiritually empty and dry. I also appreciate that rather than condemnation, we are called "my pleasing one." God is pleased with us, not because of our knowledge or works but simply because we were born-again into His family. We are children loved completely by a good and perfect God.

> 6 This is what the Lord says—Israel's King and Redeemer, the Lord of Heaven's Armies: "I am the First and the Last; there is no other God.
>
> 7 Who is like me?
>
> Let him step forward and prove to you his power.
>
> Let him do as I have done since ancient times when I established a people and explained its future.

I wonder how Isaiah felt hearing these words of God coming to Him. Imagine the authority and conviction as God declares He is the beginning and end and the only true God. He challenges anyone or any god who thinks he can compete with Yahweh. Isaiah had to feel these words down to his bones. Did he sometimes stop and fall on his face in worship, overwhelmed at the privilege of receiving this message?

We have the same opportunity to read these words and experience God's presence as Isaiah did. These "living words," as the writer of Hebrews in the New Testament describes them (Heb. 4:12), are infused with the presence of God. When we read the Bible and pray these words, they declare life and truth. This is the God who says,

"I am watching over my word to perform it." (Jer. 1:12)

God is waiting for us to engage with Him, submit ourselves to this truth, and let it be inculcated into our lives. We are not just reading some ancient text. God speaks to us personally, and we must receive His words as Isaiah did. This is why we always pray as we approach the Word of God. We ask to open our minds and hearts to receive His grace to obey God's words.

DAY 99
Isaiah 44:8-20

Do not tremble; do not be afraid.

Did I not proclaim my purposes for you long ago?

You are my witnesses—is there any other God?

No! There is no other Rock—not one!"

9 How foolish are those who manufacture idols.

These prized objects are really worthless.

The people who worship idols don't know this, so they are all put to shame.

10 Who but a fool would make his own god— an idol that cannot help him one bit?

11 All who worship idols will be disgraced along with all these craftsmen—mere humans— who claim they can make a god.

They may all stand together, but they will stand in terror and shame.

12 The blacksmith stands at his forge to make a sharp tool, pounding and shaping it with all his might.

His work makes him hungry and weak. It makes him thirsty and faint.

13 Then the wood-carver measures a block of wood and draws a pattern on it.

He works with chisel and plane and carves it into a human figure.

He gives it human beauty and puts it in a little shrine.

14 He cuts down cedars; he selects the cypress and the oak he plants the pine in the forest to be nourished by the rain.

15 Then he uses part of the wood to make a fire.

With it he warms himself and bakes his bread.

Then—yes, it's true—he takes the rest of it and makes himself a god to worship!

He makes an idol and bows down in front of it!

16 He burns part of the tree to roast his meat and to keep himself warm.

He says, "Ah, that fire feels good."

17 Then he takes what's left and makes his god: a carved idol!

He falls down in front of it, worshiping and praying to it.

"Rescue me!" he says. "You are my god!"

Who says God doesn't have a sense of humor as He points out the foolishness of man who uses something God created to replace Him in worship? We can do the same. We can put our trust in everything, from our jobs to our investments to other people to our own wisdom and skills to survive this life. But who created us with our capacities or orchestrated events to get us where we are?

Who created the resources that sustain our lives? The only true God who created the trees the ancients carved into idols. Rather than bother with trees we tend to worship ourselves and our own abilities. It's the American way. We celebrate the "self-made" person who did it all on their own. We falsely believe we can make our own life and just turn to God only when we are out of resources, sick, or face eternity. I wonder what stepping into eternity will be like for those who primarily trusted themselves but did at least acknowledge Jesus as their Savior. Will they suddenly see the "abundant life" (John 10:10) Jesus described and realize their philosophy of success and security was misplaced?

> 18 Such stupidity and ignorance!

> Their eyes are closed, and they cannot see.

> Their minds are shut, and they cannot think.

> 19 The person who made the idol never stops to reflect, "Why, it's just a block of wood!

> I burned half of it for heat and used it to bake my bread and roast my meat.

> How can the rest of it be a god?

> Should I bow down to worship a piece of wood?"

> 20 The poor, deluded fool feeds on ashes.

He trusts something that can't help him at all.

Yet he cannot bring himself to ask,

"Is this idol that I'm holding in my hand a lie?"

Isaiah shows us that spiritual blindness and dullness are self-inflicted. It is a choice we make to shut God out. When this happens, we go down a road of rebellion and idolatry because man needs something to worship. If he rejects God, what better way to fill this spiritual void than to create a god in his own image? A god who is accommodating, progressive, and fitted to the times. A god who is light on holiness but heavy on love, perfectly unbalanced to meet the needs of modern man.

This man then finds his people, who help reinforce he is right, and in Isaiah's words, "His deluded heart leads him astray." When confronted with the truth he cannot question this delusion or ask himself if this even makes sense. His food is the ashes of dead religion meant to fool an empty stomach longing for spiritual nutrition and the bread of Heaven.

DAY 100
Isaiah 44:21-28

"Pay attention, O Jacob, for you are my servant, O Israel.

I, the Lord, made you, and I will not forget you.

22 I have swept away your sins like a cloud.

I have scattered your offenses like the morning mist.

Oh, return to me, for I have paid the price to set you free."

23 Sing, O heavens, for the Lord has done this wondrous thing.

Shout for joy, O depths of the earth!

> Break into song, O mountains and forests and every tree!

> For the Lord has redeemed Jacob and is glorified in Israel.

These incredible promises of forgiveness, redemption, and acceptance are made to Israel and us. God's character is unchanging. What He promised in the past holds true for now and eternity.

There are certainly too many periods of time during the day. God is off my radar screen, yet I am always at the center of His attention. He waits to be wanted, not for His sake but for ours.

Nothing stands in the way of our being close to God that He has not removed—no barrier of sin, no requirements of the law, no sacrifice we must make. We simply humble ourselves and come with gratitude.

Isaiah closes with a beautiful picture of all of creation, celebrating that our ransom has been paid, and we, the pinnacle of God's design, are free.

I believe God wants us to out-worship all creation for what He has done for us.

> He (Jesus) replied, "If they kept quiet, the stones along the road would burst into cheers!" Luke 19:40

Today, when you hear a bird sing or the wind passes through the trees, let that be a challenge to worship God.

> 24 This is what the Lord says— your Redeemer and Creator:

> "I am the Lord, who made all things.

> I alone stretched out the heavens.

> Who was with me when I made the earth?

> 25 I expose the false prophets as liars and make fools of fortune-tellers.
>
> I cause the wise to give bad advice thus proving them to be fools.
>
> 26 But I carry out the predictions of my prophets!
>
> By them I say to Jerusalem, 'People will live here again,' and to the towns of Judah, 'You will be rebuilt;
>
> I will restore all your ruins!'

All knowledge and opinions that do not have God as their source are mere foolishness. All truth is God's truth. Every effort to gain insight into the future wastes time and money and results in mere speculation and confusion.

When God prompts us with prophetic insight into the future or wisdom and understanding, He also confirms it. What a contrast between foolish people looking everywhere for knowledge and the omniscient God offering it freely to the humble. This levels the playing field between IQs. It makes the simplest person with faith the smartest person in the room. You may not have the academic credentials to impress others, but if you stay close to God and humbly wait for Him, He will give you the words to speak and confirm them.

> The members of the council were amazed when they saw the boldness of Peter and John, for they could see that they were ordinary men with no special training in the Scriptures. They also recognized them as men who had been with Jesus. Acts 4:13

This is the simple man's superpower, being in the presence of Jesus.

> 27 When I speak to the rivers and say, 'Dry up!' they will be dry.

> 28 When I say of Cyrus, 'He is my shepherd,' he will certainly do as I say.
>
> He will command, 'Rebuild Jerusalem'; he will say, 'Restore the Temple.'"

A little knowledge of ancient history is required to appreciate this passage, which is amazing. Cyrus, king of Persia, reigned from 559 to 529 BC. He conquered Babylon, where the Israelites were held captive. He permitted the Jews to return to Jerusalem and restore the temple (2 Chron. 36:22–23; Ezra 1:1–4).

This is an incredible prophetic declaration because Isaiah prophesies these events and calls Cyrus by name 150 years before these events occur. Josephus, the Jewish historian, wrote that "when Cyrus read this (Isaiah's prophecy), and admired the Divine Power, an earnest desire and ambition seized him to fulfill what was written.

"That part about rivers drying up? That is exactly the strategy Cyrus used to take Babylon. He diverted the rivers and starved the city by cutting off their water supply (See Jer. 50:38; 51:31–36).

What incredible proof that God sees everything and sovereignly oversees our lives. He is always working for our good and leading us down the best road of life. Living under this belief cancels fear or doubt that God is unaware, unable, or unwilling to help us. If God can orchestrate events to affect an entire nation 150 years in advance, you can be assured He has your life under control to the extent you surrender to Him.

DAY 101
Isaiah 45:1-3

This is what the Lord says to Cyrus, his anointed one, whose right hand he will empower.

Before him, mighty kings will be paralyzed with fear.

Their fortress gates will be opened, never to shut again.

2 This is what the Lord says: "I will go before you, Cyrus, and level the mountains.

I will smash down gates of bronze and cut through bars of iron.

3 And I will give you treasures hidden in the darkness— secret riches.

> I will do this so you may know that I am the Lord, the God of Israel, the one who calls you by name.

Cyrus is a pagan king mentioned twenty-two times in the Bible. He is the king who overthrew Babylon and released the Jews to return and rebuild Jerusalem.

Imagine you're Cyrus, and you've conquered this great city-state, and you're riding triumphantly into the city. Suddenly, an older Jewish man comes up to you and says, oh, you're Cyrus, we've been waiting 70 years for you. We knew you were coming 150 years ago. Look right here in our ancient prophetic scroll of Isaiah.

If you are Cyrus, you might also be interested in the rest of this story and be humble enough to realize that there is a sovereign God and that you are part of providence.

This passage has beautiful connections to a later king who would also be called Christ or "anointed one," as Cyrus is described in the first verse.

Both Cyrus (44:28) and Jesus (Heb. 13:20) are called shepherds who will perform all God's pleasure (John 8:29). God takes the right hand of both Cyrus and Christ (Heb. 10:12–13) and subdues nations before them (Ps. 2; Phil. 3:21). Both Cyrus and Christ have open doors before them (Rev. 3:7–8) and are given the treasures of darkness (Matt. 27:45), the hidden riches of secret places (Mark 1:35; Col. 2:3; Rev. 2:17).

Take time to read and study this living Word of God and let its truth shape your life. If God has a destiny marked out for a pagan king, you can be assured He also has one for you.

DAY 102
Isaiah 45:4-11

"And why have I called you for this work?

Why did I call you by name when you did not know me?

It is for the sake of Jacob my servant, Israel my chosen one.

5 I am the Lord; there is no other God.

I have equipped you for battle, though you don't even know me,

6 so all the world from east to west will know there is no other God.

I am the Lord, and there is no other.

7 I create the light and make the darkness.

I send good times and bad times.

I, the Lord, am the one who does these things.

8 "Open up, O heavens, and pour out your righteousness.

Let the earth open wide so salvation and righteousness can sprout up together.

I, the Lord, created them.

9 "What sorrow awaits those who argue with their Creator.

Does a clay pot argue with its maker?

Does the clay dispute with the one who shapes it, saying, 'Stop, you're doing it wrong!'

Does the pot exclaim, 'How clumsy can you be?'

10 How terrible it would be if a newborn baby said to its father,

'Why was I born?' or if it said to its mother,

'Why did you make me this way?'"

11 This is what the Lord says— the Holy One of Israel and your Creator:

"Do you question what I do for my children?

Do you give me orders about the work of my hands?

No matter how unfair life seems, it is never the result of God failing to love or take care of us. We exist because we were the combined elements of life that joined in our mother's womb. Out of millions of possibilities, God chose us to be born. And though we all share unique characteristics, we all have human limitations of strength, health, and understanding.

We were born into a broken world because of sin and live with the consequences every day. At the same time, Heaven has come to earth through Jesus, inaugurating His Kingdom rulership, which will culminate someday in His return.

Until then, we live in anticipation of that Kingdom rule. We believe in the release of God's power and wisdom, which gives us a glimpse of Heaven's order and beauty. When we pray and see miracles, the Kingdom is on display to us and those for whom we intercede.

Rather than questioning God, pray for the Holy Spirit to reveal God's heart to you. If this is the God we are going to trust with our eternity, we should trust Him now for this short life and live as close and connected to God's presence as possible.

DAY 103
Isaiah 45:12-15

I am the one who made the earth and created people to live on it.

With my hands I stretched out the heavens.

All the stars are at my command.

13 I will raise up Cyrus to fulfill my righteous purpose, and I will guide his actions.

He will restore my city and free my captive people— without seeking a reward!

I, the Lord of Heaven's Armies, have spoken!"

Future Conversion of Gentiles

> 14 This is what the Lord says: "You will rule the Egyptians, the Ethiopians, and the Sabeans.
>
> They will come to you with all their merchandise, and it will all be yours.
>
> They will follow you as prisoners in chains.
>
> They will fall to their knees in front of you and say, 'God is with you, and he is the only God.
>
> There is no other.'"

This passage seems like a prophetic declaration of God raising Jesus or us as His children in righteousness. But, the truth is that Isaiah is speaking on behalf of God to a pagan king, Cyrus. This is not a man seeking God or even knowing how God was orchestrating world events through him. Cyrus probably thought it was his effort until he got to Babylon, and Daniel shared the words of Isaiah and Jeremiah. What I take away from this passage is that it reinforces the sovereignty of God. God is in control and uses people to accomplish His purposes.

> The king's heart is like a stream of water directed by the LORD; he guides it wherever he pleases. Proverbs 21:1

Even men as powerful as kings are constantly manipulated today by the gods of this world and God Almighty. We may think the President of the United States is the most powerful person in the world, but God is ultimately in control. We have a part to play in all of this, as our prayers are guided by God to carry out His will. For example, Jeremiah was assigned to pray and speak out, at times to accuse and at other times to encourage.

> Then the Lord reached out and touched my mouth and said, "Look, I have put my words in your mouth! Today I appoint you to stand

up against nations and kingdoms. Some you must uproot and tear down, destroy and overthrow. Others you must build up and plant." Jeremiah 1:9-10

Uprooting in prayer those not planted by God is not a political motivation but is at the guidance of the Holy Spirit to accomplish God's will. Other times, it is to bless and encourage those God has appointed to lead. Because we don't have God's "behind the scenes" knowledge, we trust Him to guide us in praying.

> 15 Truly, O God of Israel, our Savior, you work in mysterious ways.

Does God hide from us?

Sometimes, God feels very close. Whether in times of worship or hearing someone's story of their God encounter. Or maybe it is in those quiet walks where we see something in nature that reveals a new insight into God's character.

There are also times and seasons when God seems quiet and distant. His presence, though always with us, does not seem apparent. Worship does not come as easily, and the words on our Bible page seem less related to our lives. What do we do when God seems to hide Himself? We pursue Him. We keep praying, we keep listening. Not to be overly simple, but I picture a game of tag. Sometimes, God is pursuing me. I feel His presence, I sense His conviction. Other times, I believe God wants me to pursue Him. Worship may not come easily, but we show up anyway. Or maybe we just still ourselves and listen.

> I will offer you a sacrifice of thanksgiving and call on the name of the Lord. Psalms 116:17

The best place to start is with gratitude. Gratitude returns our minds to a place of joy and peace. As we remember how faithful God has been in the past, we are grateful, and we can express this as worship. This is why it is helpful to journal, and in those times when God seems hidden, we review the times He was very close. God never gives up on us.

> You will seek me and find me when you seek me with all your heart. Jeremiah 29:13

DAY 104
Isaiah 45:16-21

All craftsmen who make idols will be humiliated.

They will all be disgraced together.

17 But the Lord will save the people of Israel with eternal salvation.

Throughout everlasting ages, they will never again be humiliated and disgraced.

18 For the Lord is God, and he created the heavens and earth and put everything in place.

He made the world to be lived in, not to be a place of empty chaos.

"I am the Lord," he says, "and there is no other.

19 I publicly proclaim bold promises.

I do not whisper obscurities in some dark corner.

I would not have told the people of Israel to seek me if I could not be found.

I, the Lord, speak only what is true and declare only what is right.

Beneath the dirt and rubble of sin lies a beautiful earth and universe God created. Through the fall of Adam, the deed to what was made was temporarily put in Satan's hands. This is why we see destruction, pollution, and chaos everywhere. Many so-called experts tell us regularly the world will not survive. God's purpose was to shape a world to sustain man. A dwelling that was perfect for Adam and Eve to enjoy. Instead, they chose their way and gave up what was theirs. They had perfection yet were deceived into believing there was more. We do not seek God in vain.

We've lived in darkness and have turned to the light. As we surrender our lives and walk in relationship with Jesus, He reveals Himself to us. The Holy Spirit helps us see beauty in people's lives. He uncovers the hidden beauty of a lost world but will someday be restored when Jesus returns to rule, making all things new.

For now, we press into God's Word and ask for revelation to see what God wants us to see, His truth, and listen as He declares what is right even in a fallen world.

20 "Gather together and come, you fugitives from surrounding nations.

What fools they are who carry around their wooden idol and pray to gods that cannot save!

21 Consult together, argue your case.

Get together and decide what to say.

Who made these things known so long ago?

What idol ever told you they would happen?

Was it not I, the Lord?

For there is no other God but me, a righteous God and Savior.

There is none but me.

One of the strengths of Christianity is that we assemble ourselves. Like refugees in a foreign land, we form bonds in a spiritual family and care for one another. We gain from the revelation we share through our encounters with God. Christians thrive best in community. It is also in community we sort through all the foolishness and lies of a society searching for answers outside of God. It is in community where we are healed and are shaped into the image of God as we encourage and challenge one another.

Jesus calls us to gather in His name. When we do, He is uniquely with us in a special way. I believe a purpose for His presence is to bring insight so we can separate what is true from what is false.

For where two or three gather together as my followers, I am there among them." Matthew 18:20

DAY 105
Isaiah 45:22-25

Let all the world look to me for salvation!

For I am God; there is no other.

23 I have sworn by my own name;

I have spoken the truth, and I will never go back on my word:

Every knee will bend to me, and every tongue will declare allegiance to me."

24 The people will declare, "The Lord is the source of all my righteousness and strength."

And all who were angry with him will come to him and be ashamed.

> 25 In the Lord all the generations of Israel will be justified, and in him they will boast.

God tells us through Isaiah to look at the evidence of all that He promises and all He has done. There is no other god worthy of our complete devotion. He alone is the eternal God and sole means of salvation.

As I sit in God's presence this morning, reading these words of Isaiah in the background, I hear the coronation of King Charles on the television. The pomp and majesty that is placed upon a human king is amazing. Yet, the coronation of a human king is such a limited example of our Heavenly eternal king. The honor and allegiance given to an earthly king pails in comparison to how the angels and saints continually give glory and honor to Jesus on His throne seated next to our Father God.

The Apostle Paul repeats the promise God makes here,

> Therefore, God elevated him to the place of highest honor and gave him the name above all other names, 10 that at the name of Jesus every knee should bow, in heaven and on earth and under the earth, 11 and every tongue declare that Jesus Christ is Lord, to the glory of God the Father. Philippians 2:9-11

Every knee, including those who believed in God and those who did not. Every living being will be overwhelmed with the glory of God. I can't imagine the contrast between those who believed and surrendered their lives to Jesus and those who rejected Him.

DAY 106
Isaiah 46:1-4

Bel and Nebo, the gods of Babylon, bow as they are lowered to the ground.

They are being hauled away on ox carts.

The poor beasts stagger under the weight.

2 Both the idols and their owners are bowed down.

The gods cannot protect the people, and the people cannot protect the gods.

They go off into captivity together.

3 "Listen to me, descendants of Jacob, all you who remain in Israel.

I have cared for you since you were born.

Yes, I carried you before you were born.

4 I will be your God throughout your lifetime— until your hair is white with age.

I made you, and I will care for you.

I will carry you along and save you.

Bel was the chief god of Babylon, and Nebo was the god of wisdom and intellect. Both were revered in the Babylonian culture. Bel means "lord." Isaiah tells the Jewish people that there can only be one lord. He is Yahweh, the Creator and one true God. He doesn't need our support or defense.

We can overlook the many times God carries us, protects us, and supernaturally provides for us. Only eternity will reveal the full extent of God's faithfulness to us. From womb to tomb, God provides unconditional love and care to those who will trust Him. What an incredible promise God makes here. He will carry you. God offers to carry us through every disaster and crisis in our lives. The beauty of being carried is that we can trust God, let Him choose the path, and rest in His arms.

This may be hard for "self-made" people who want to solve their problems and not depend on anyone but themselves. This is not what God wants. He doesn't see trusting Him as a weakness. God is impressed with our humility, faith, and devotion. What would it look like for God to carry you today?

DAY 107
Isaiah 46:5-9

5 "To whom will you compare me?

Who is my equal?

Nothing reaches the majesty and brilliance of God. No created being is as powerful and virtuous as our Heavenly Father. Why would we place our trust in ourselves or any other human? Why do we trust entities like the government and the world economy? Of course, we must interact with people and place a limited amount of trust in man-made systems. When these systems fail us, we're not surprised.

Perfection is in God alone. Power is God's alone. Pure love, grace, and mercy come from God. We are loved and cared for by a benevolent Father who demonstrated His love in the great sacrifice of Jesus for our sins. It is amazing that a perfect God would love and sacrifice Himself for such imperfect people.

So, to answer the obvious question and overstate the obvious, God has no competition. And though it is evident, we must remind ourselves of this truth every day because of the hundreds of little gods who want to steal our allegiance and attention.

To overstate the obvious, God has no competition. And though it is evident, we must remind ourselves of this truth every day because of the hundreds of little gods who want to steal our allegiance and attention.

"So remember this and keep it firmly in mind: The Lord is God both in heaven and on earth, and there is no other. Deuteronomy 4:39

6 Some people pour out their silver and gold and hire a craftsman to make a god from it.

Then they bow down and worship it!

7 They carry it around on their shoulders, and when they set it down, it stays there.

It can't even move!

And when someone prays to it, there is no answer.

It can't rescue anyone from trouble.

8 "Do not forget this! Keep it in mind!

Remember this, you guilty ones.

9 Remember the things I have done in the past.

For I alone am God!

I am God, and there is none like me.

Here again, God directs Isaiah to speak against idolatry. Strong language is required to penetrate a hard heart. The Israelites tended to embrace the pagan cultures around them through intermarriage. Marriage was not the issue; it was the resulting acceptance of the pagan gods of the women they married. To the Israelite men, this did not seem like a big issue until children were born and their mothers began introducing them to these idols and foreign gods.

God is certainly not racist. He desires everyone He created to come into a relationship with him, people from "every tribe, nation, and language," as the Apostle John describes in Revelation. But God is jealous when it comes to idolatry or sharing our affections with a lesser god. He uses the language of marriage and covenant to demonstrate the exclusivity of the relationship with Him.

There is no room to exalt some man-made piece of metal or anything next to God. This is why God is reminding them of all the miracles of deliverance from enemies and famine as they move from Egypt through the wilderness and into the Promised Land. He is the all-powerful God who has carried them.

He is the One who carries us today, just as powerful and jealous.

DAY 108
Isaiah 46:10-13

Only I can tell you the future before it even happens.

Everything I plan will come to pass, for I do whatever I wish.

11 I will call a swift bird of prey from the east— a leader from a distant land to come and do my bidding.

I have said what I would do, and I will do it.

The Hall of Fame baseball player Babe Ruth added to his fame on an afternoon at Wrigley Field in Chicago during the 1932 World Series. As Ruth stepped to bat, he pointed to center field and hit a home run right where he had pointed. "The Babe" had called his shot.

God called His shots repeatedly. He would tell the Israelites exactly what He would do and then carry out exactly what He predicted. Isaiah declares God is faithful in everything He does, whether it is using a pagan gentile king like Cyrus to deliver Israel or keeping one of the promises He has made to us today.

God is faithful to what He says, and we can trust Him. God has plans for each of our lives to bring fulfillment to us and glory to Himself.

12 "Listen to me, you stubborn people who are so far from doing right.

13 For I am ready to set things right, not in the distant future, but right now!

I am ready to save Jerusalem and show my glory to Israel.

The nature of God is always to pursue us in love. Though we reject Him and ignore His grace, God will never stop being who He is. He reveals Himself again and again, hoping we will overcome our stubbornness. You see this quality in Jesus talking about going after the lost sheep who rebels and runs from the safety of his shepherd. Or, when Jesus tells the scribe, "You are not far from the kingdom."

We are either moving toward Jesus or away from Him. What is important is the direction we face and the posture of our hearts. When we turn to God in humility, He is already there to meet us. No matter how rebellious or sinful, like the prodigal, we make a step toward God, and He runs to us. He does not make us grovel or show penance. He welcomes us into His arms.

God is closer than we think and more receptive than we can imagine. We come to Him based on His character, not on our merits.

DAY 109
Isaiah 47:1-10

"Come down, virgin daughter of Babylon, and sit in the dust.

For your days of sitting on a throne have ended.

O daughter of Babylonia, never again will you be the lovely princess, tender and delicate.

2 Take heavy millstones and grind flour.

Remove your veil, and strip off your robe.

Expose yourself to public view.

3 You will be naked and burdened with shame.

I will take vengeance against you without pity."

4 Our Redeemer, whose name is the Lord of Heaven's Armies, is the Holy One of Israel.

God establishes and brings down thrones and leaders. Though God has allowed Babylon to take Israel captive, at a set time, He will have had enough, and He will free Israel and destroy Babylon. Isaiah uses a metaphor of Babylon and Chaldea as queens or female leaders. Throughout the Bible, there is this theme of Babylon as a female deity leading this world's system that tries to establish rulership against God. This culminates in the fall of Babylon in Revelation 18 and the final judgment of those who have opposed God.

> She glorified herself and lived in luxury, so match it now with torment and sorrow. She boasted in her heart, 'I am queen on my throne. I am no helpless widow, and I have no reason to mourn.' Therefore, these plagues will overtake her in a single day— death, mourning, and famine. She will be completely consumed by fire, for the Lord God who judges her is mighty." Revelation 18:7-8

Scripture also metaphorically depicts the church as female and the Bride of Christ. Though we may have rebelled and found ourselves naked and full of shame, we have a Redeemer—a husband in Christ who will rescue His bride.

> Let us be glad and rejoice and let us give honor to him. For the time has come for the wedding feast of the Lamb, and his bride has prepared herself. Revelation 19:7

Our choice is which Kingdom and Ruler will we pledge our allegiance, the Babylonian system or Jesus?

5 "O beautiful Babylon, sit now in darkness and silence.

Never again will you be known as the queen of kingdoms.

6 For I was angry with my chosen people and punished them by letting them fall into your hands.

But you, Babylon, showed them no mercy. You oppressed even the elderly.

7 You said, 'I will reign forever as queen of the world!'

You did not reflect on your actions or think about their consequences.

8 "Listen to this, you pleasure-loving kingdom,

living at ease and feeling secure.

You say, 'I am the only one, and there is no other.

I will never be a widow or lose my children.'

9 Well, both these things will come upon you in a moment: widowhood and the loss of your children.

Yes, these calamities will come upon you, despite all your witchcraft and magic.

10 "You felt secure in your wickedness.

'No one sees me,' you said.

But your 'wisdom' and 'knowledge' have led you astray, and you said, 'I am the only one, and there is no other.'

Just because we do not experience God's judgment does not mean He ignores our sin and rebellion. We often do not think about our actions and the possible consequences. Whether losing our temper with someone in traffic, berating a waitress or clerk because of poor service, or a comment we make on social media. All of these can lead to horrible outcomes we do not anticipate.

Isaiah says this comes from being smug. To be smug, to be prideful and overconfident in ourselves. It is displayed in the foolish person who says they don't need God. They are doing fine on their own. They are the final authority for their life and the source of all truth and wisdom. This conceited and arrogant attitude creates a vacuum of selfishness in which we stop listening to God through our conscience. We neglect the advice of Godly people who love us. In trying to protect ourselves, we isolate ourselves until we are consumed by our darkness.

What is the answer? Humility. Humility opens the door to God, who comes with wisdom and insight. When we invite God in, He guides us into truth and healing. He brings wonderful people along to help free us from loneliness and dark places of isolation.

> Humble yourselves before the Lord, and he will lift you up in honor.
> James 4:10

DAY 110
Isaiah 47:11-15

11 So disaster will overtake you, and you won't be able to charm it away.

Calamity will fall upon you, and you won't be able to buy your way out.

A catastrophe will strike you suddenly, one for which you are not prepared.

12 "Now use your magical charms!

Use the spells you have worked at all these years!

Maybe they will do you some good.

Maybe they can make someone afraid of you.

13 All the advice you receive has made you tired.

Where are all your astrologers, those stargazers who make predictions each month?

Let them stand up and save you from what the future holds.

14 But they are like straw burning in a fire; they cannot save themselves from the flame.

You will get no help from them at all; their hearth is no place to sit for warmth.

15 And all your friends, those with whom you've done business since childhood, will go their own ways, turning a deaf ear to your cries.

Sorcery and witchcraft are not all Ouija Boards and Harry Potter spells. I define witchcraft as any attempt to manipulate spiritual entities, including God Himself. God challenges the people to look to their servers and astrologers for answers. He shows how hopeless it is to trust in any spiritual being outside God Himself.

In some cases, the demonic spirits behind modern witchcraft are real. Your local psychic manipulates you and gets a "cold read;" they then give you general enough information you want to be true, so you unknowingly assist them through body language and responses.

These real or fake reads only have the power over your life you give it. If you believe the predictions they make, you align yourself with Satan to bring it about, and it is you who are being manipulated.

As Christians, we can even try to do this with God, making promises that if He answers our prayers in our way, we will serve Him or honor Him in some way. We will even use threats that if God doesn't come through on our terms, we will turn away from Him. I have seen people fall into this trap. This happens when we do not know God well enough to trust His Divine nature, which is always good and working for our best.

If you are curious about your future, ask the Holy Spirit to show you. Don't expect a clear, mapped-out version of your life for the next 40 years. What you will hear is, "Trust Me today," and that is all we really need.

DAY 111
Isaiah 48:1-6

"Listen to me, O family of Jacob, you who are called by the name of Israel and born into the family of Judah.

Listen, you who take oaths in the name of the Lord and call on the God of Israel.

You don't keep your promises,

2 even though you call yourself the holy city and talk about depending on the God of Israel, whose name is the Lord of Heaven's Armies.

God is always concerned about our inner motives over our outward actions. This especially applies when it comes to our relationship and interaction with God. We can worship by just going through the motions, reading the Bible like a duty, repeatedly praying the exact words, and having no heart. You can tell when your spouse or a close friend says they love you, whether it is sincere. God can read past our surface posture into our hearts. He knows what moves us. Do we fulfill our religious obligation of church attendance, giving, and having suitable bumper stickers only to have a heart far from God?

These people honor me with their lips, but their hearts are far from me. 9 Their worship is a farce, for they teach man-made ideas as commands from God.'" Matthew 15:8-9

Our challenge in today's world is to interpret scripture and worship God on our terms, helping to keep God at a safe distance. If God gets too close, we realize He is consuming and wants control of our lives. He wants us to live by truth, no matter how unpopular or costly. He wants us to be real and have a righteous confession.

Though we may be far from perfect, we are always pressing into God's presence, showing gratitude, worshiping Him, allowing the truth of His Word to come alive and shape us, and living truly dependent upon Yahweh.

> 3 Long ago I told you what was going to happen.

> Then suddenly I took action, and all my predictions came true.

> 4 For I know how stubborn and obstinate you are.

> Your necks are as unbending as iron.

> Your heads are as hard as bronze.

> 5 That is why I told you what would happen; I told you beforehand what I was going to do.

> Then you could never say, 'My idols did it.

> My wooden image and metal god commanded it to happen!'

6 You have heard my predictions and seen them fulfilled, but you refuse to admit it.

Now I will tell you new things, secrets you have not yet heard.

God not only predicts what will happen but fulfills it as well. Because He is not limited by our time and space. Being outside of our boundaries He can never be late or unsure about what is happening. Based on this truth God wants to reveal things to us about what He is doing now and in the future. Rather than waiting for news to happen and then trying to evaluate what happened God focuses on the future. Time spent chasing news might be better spent pursuing revelation from God.

God is inviting us as His children to see and learn new things before they are known to the rest of the world. How crazy and exciting is that? Whether applied to mechanical inventions, science or medicine, or creative ideas for caring for the poor, let's believe God for insight into the secrets of what He is doing now and new things for the future.

To our degree of faith is the level of Revelation God gives about Himself and what He is doing. Pursue Him with all your heart.

DAY 112

Isaiah 48:7-15

7 They are brand new, not things from the past. So you cannot say, 'We knew that all the time!'

8 "Yes, I will tell you of things that are entirely new, things you never heard of before.

For I know so well what traitors you are.

You have been rebels from birth.

9 Yet for my own sake and for the honor of my name,

I will hold back my anger and not wipe you out.

10 I have refined you, but not as silver is refined.

Rather, I have refined you in the furnace of suffering.

11 I will rescue you for my sake— yes, for my own sake!

I will not let my reputation be tarnished, and I will not share my glory with idols!

Too often, we presume upon God's mercy and believe that no matter how much we rebel, He is obligated out of His love to care for us. God's grace is endless, but He also allows us to be purified by the fires of adversity. Isaiah states that God does not purify with the same process as refining silver, which is placed in the heat until all the impurities rise. Our Father is much kinder because He sits in the fire with us. Then, He leads us out and blesses us until we rebel and find ourselves in need of His loving discipline once again. This process happens repeatedly to prepare us for eternity and to bring honor to God.

There will be no rebellion in Heaven or anywhere else in eternity. We must push this from us now. We go through a lifelong process while living in a world, especially a nation that says, "It's all about you; take care of yourself. "

The more we press into a relationship with God, in an ongoing communion of love and obedience, the greater we are blessed, and the more God is honored.

Freedom from Babylon

12 "Listen to me, O family of Jacob, Israel my chosen one!

I alone am God, the First and the Last.

13 It was my hand that laid the foundations of the earth,

my right hand that spread out the heavens above.

When I call out the stars, they all appear in order."

14 Have any of your idols ever told you this?

Come, all of you, and listen: The Lord has chosen Cyrus as his ally.

He will use him to put an end to the empire of Babylon and to destroy the Babylonian armies.

15 "I have said it: I am calling Cyrus!

I will send him on this errand and will help him succeed.

God wants His people to know He is in complete control. Even while the Israelites were captive for seventy years in Babylon, it was not because He had turned away from them or lacked the power to save them. It was their sins that had moved them away from God. Whenever we take steps away from God, we stop listening to His wisdom. We stop following His lead. We make decisions (usually bad) and get ourselves in tough situations.

Our Father watches and waits. He humbly waits for us to acknowledge that He is God and that we are not. If God can love a pagan king like Cyrus, of whom Isaiah is speaking, God will forever love us. He has plans for a pagan king and plans for us as His sons and daughters. He also has a prosperous path for us.

This is difficult to believe because we live in a world without a place for God. We trust science, government, and what marketers tell us. Rather than these modern resources being tools in the hands of God, we have made the tools gods. You can tell when you listen, as people place their trust and invest their emotions in inanimate things.

> They traded the truth about God for a lie. So they worshiped and served the things God created instead of the Creator himself, who is worthy of eternal praise! Amen. Romans 1:25

DAY 113

Isaiah 48:16-22

16 Come closer, and listen to this.

From the beginning I have told you plainly what would happen."

And now the Sovereign Lord and his Spirit have sent me with this message.

17 This is what the Lord says— your Redeemer, the Holy One of Israel:

"I am the Lord your God, who teaches you what is good for you

and leads you along the paths you should follow.

18 Oh, that you had listened to my commands!

> Then you would have had peace flowing like a gentle river
>
> and righteousness rolling over you like waves in the sea.

First, the Holy Spirit is speaking here on behalf of the Trinity. Sent by the Father, the Spirit speaks with all the eternal authority of the Creator. He is giving weight to the truth He is about to speak.

It's mind-blowing to comprehend the eternal God, appealing to us to listen and allow Him to lead. We are a tiny dot on the timeline of human history—one person, alone, insignificant. Yet, if Israel had listened as a people, they would have been the most blessed nation ever. Instead, they followed their way, breaking away from God's leading and His commands. Now, they find themselves in captivity in Babylon.

We have the same promises, and as the book of Hebrews tells us, a "better covenant based on better promises" (Heb. 8:6). We have this history to look back upon God's faithfulness to His promises.

What if we let Him teach us how to succeed by leading us step by step? Sure, it will be awkward initially, but we will stop consistently throughout our day to align ourselves with God's voice and sense His leading. You might have to turn off other noise and distractions.

What sacrifice would be too great compared to having God's presence, like a river of peace and waves of success, wash over you?

> 19 Your descendants would have been like the sands along the seashore— too many to count!
>
> There would have been no need for your destruction, or for cutting off your family name."
>
> 20 Yet even now, be free from your captivity!

Leave Babylon and the Babylonians.

Sing out this message!

Shout it to the ends of the earth!

The Lord has redeemed his servants, the people of Israel.

21 They were not thirsty when he led them through the desert.

He divided the rock, and water gushed out for them to drink.

22 "But there is no peace for the wicked," says the Lord.

We've seen how listening to God and following His leading brings peace and success to our lives. Isaiah continues this thought by declaring that we not only benefit, but our children do as well. We know Israel rejected God's leading and went their way, and now they have been captive for 70 years in Babylon. But God, in a demonstration of His amazing grace, frees the people just as He prophesied He would. He once again rescues rebellious, undeserving people, just like you and me.

There is a beautiful picture here of the foreshadowing of Jesus. He will provide for people who come to Him just as He did for Moses and the Israelites during the Exodus. From ancient times and throughout history, Jesus has been faithful to those devoted to those who are His.

> Jesus stood and shouted to the crowds, "Anyone who is thirsty may come to me! 38 Anyone who believes in me may come and drink! For the Scriptures declare, 'Rivers of living water will flow from his heart.'" John 7:37-38

The river of Jesus' love flowed from His wounds at the Cross, redeeming our lives. Now, as carriers of God's presence, His life, love, and power flow out of us to others.

DAY 114

Isaiah 49:1-4

Listen to me, all you in distant lands!

Pay attention, you who are far away!

The Lord called me before my birth; from within the womb he called me by name.

2 He made my words of judgment as sharp as a sword.

He has hidden me in the shadow of his hand.

I am like a sharp arrow in his quiver.

3 He said to me, "You are my servant, Israel, and you will bring me glory."

What an incredible sense of value and destiny in a preborn life. More than just a clump of cells under the exclusive choice of a mother, we were called before we were born, named by God, and valued by our Creator with purpose and significance.

This passage, of course, points prophetically to Jesus. The Father hid Jesus away in Nazareth for 30 years, preparing Him to be a voice and an arrow in His hand. It takes time to polish an arrow so that it penetrates tough exteriors and gets to the heart. Jesus' words of truth pierced the hearts of people who believed lies about God and themselves.

I pray for mothers to receive revelation into God's incredible design of their conceived child. When tempted to believe the lie that their life and the world would be better if their child's life were ended, they would instead embrace God's truth. This truth is that regardless of the circumstances in which we were conceived or born, God created us with purpose.

> 4 I replied, "But my work seems so useless!
>
> I have spent my strength for nothing and to no purpose.
>
> Yet I leave it all in the Lord's hand; I will trust God for my reward."

We live in constant tension between running our own lives and letting God lead. We forget we exchanged our old life for a new life in Christ—a life lived in surrender to God's will—a life that is better only when God is at the center and directing our steps.

One of the indicators that we have taken back control of our lives is frustration and disappointment. We don't feel like we're hitting our goals or attaining those for which we're reaching. Life generally feels like it is not going our way when we measure it by the world's standards.

When experiencing these emotions, we remind ourselves that we have surrendered all our rights to Jesus. He rules and has control in all areas. All aspects of our lives are placed in His hands.

For example, we can feel frustrated waiting in traffic or at a grocery store. We get angry with people in front of us who are slowing us down from our important tasks. We are not efficient or accomplishing our goals. Of course, we have little control over the situation, so we sit and stew. This is a simple indicator of an unsurrendered part of our lives that must be given to God. We give Him the right to our time and life going our way.

By contrast, if our life is surrendered to God, we wait to pray and worship or reconnect with God during the busyness of our day. We look around at people and ask God if there is anyone we can encourage.

We are not pursuing our reward; we are pursuing God, and our reward is in Him.

DAY 115
Isaiah 49:5-9

5 And now the Lord speaks— the one who formed me in my mother's womb to be his servant,

who commissioned me to bring Israel back to him.

The Lord has honored me, and my God has given me strength.

6 He says, "You will do more than restore the people of Israel to me.

I will make you a light to the Gentiles, and you will bring my salvation to the ends of the earth."

This passage describes three prophetic periods and people. The first is the King of Israel, or maybe Cyrus, who will release the Israelites to return to their homeland.

The second image is that of Christ. He is the One calling Israel back to God and finding His strength in His Father. Jesus is the light to the nations, bringing salvation to every part of the earth.

Finally, we are carriers of God's presence. We bring God's light of revelation to those around us or wherever God directs us. We were shaped in the womb and destined by God to be His followers. We find our strength and direction in Him, and thus, we fulfill our prophetic destiny in obedience to our mission of bringing light to a shadowy world.

7 The Lord, the Redeemer and Holy One of Israel,

says to the one who is despised and rejected by the nations,

to the one who is the servant of rulers:

"Kings will stand at attention when you pass by.

Princes will also bow low because of the Lord, the faithful one,

the Holy One of Israel, who has chosen you."

8 This is what the Lord says: "At just the right time, I will respond to you.

On the day of salvation I will help you.

I will protect you and give you to the people as my covenant with them.

> Through you I will reestablish the land of Israel and assign it to its own people again.
>
> 9 I will say to the prisoners, 'Come out in freedom,' and to those in darkness, 'Come into the light.'
>
> They will be my sheep, grazing in green pastures and on hills that were previously bare.

Our God is a covenant-keeping God. If He makes a promise, we can be assured that He will come through. This is why we seek a closer relationship with Jesus through worship, listening, and meditating on His word. He promises to provide all the stuff we need. As I've heard it said, "We seek the heart of God, not just the hand of God; we seek the giver, not just the gift."

The Father takes care of us as children who trust Him and go about His business. Picture a worker who nervously and continually goes to their boss and asks, "You are going to pay me Friday, right?" The employer would eventually be looking for a new employee because of the lack of trust and probably a lack of anything being accomplished.

God certainly will not fire us. But we miss out on the joy and peace we can experience knowing God is faithful and is free to focus on other's needs rather than just our own. We cannot convincingly declare freedom to others if we are not free. How can we lead others to the light if we are in the dark? We trust God with the temporary stuff of life like sheep who trust their shepherd.

Today, focus solely on God Himself. Even though there is nothing wrong with presenting our needs to God, try not to ask for anything other than to be close to God and to be led by His Spirit. Watch how He takes care of the rest.

DAY 116

Isaiah 49:10-14

They will neither hunger nor thirst.

The searing sun will not reach them anymore.

For the Lord in his mercy will lead them; he will lead them beside cool waters.

11 And I will make my mountains into level paths for them.

The highways will be raised above the valleys.

12 See, my people will return from far away, from lands to the north and west, and from as far south as Egypt."

We've all been hungry, thirsty, hot, and miserable. What God is promising here is not physical comfort but spiritual guidance. Isaiah describes a relationship with God that is so close that we constantly feel joy and peace because we are in God's presence.

As David declared in Psalm 23, "He leads me beside still water." In John's gospel chapter 10, Jesus described Himself as the Great Shepherd who leads His sheep and protects them. In a world filled with chaos, God is telling us we can not only live in peace, but we can also respond to the chaos and bring healing by walking in obedience to God. As our focus becomes more on God than our problems, God takes the responsibility to meet our needs. If we chase anything but God to find fulfillment, it will always lead us away from Him, and any happiness will be fleeting.

All of this comes from the choices we make every day. We choose worship over worry and truth over fear. We press into God until we sense His peace ruling over our selfish thoughts and desires. We push past the temporary into the eternal.

> Since you have been raised to new life with Christ, set your sights on the realities of heaven, where Christ sits in the place of honor at God's right hand. Think about the things of heaven, not the things of earth. For you died to this life, and your real life is hidden with Christ in God. Colossians 3:1-13

> 13 Sing for joy, O heavens!

> Rejoice, O earth!

> Burst into song, O mountains!

> For the Lord has comforted his people and will have compassion on them in their suffering.

> 14 Yet Jerusalem says, "The Lord has deserted us; the Lord has forgotten us."

It is hard for us to comprehend, but there is always a reason for us to be joyful. God will always be faithful to us. He will comfort us in our pain and protect us when we're afraid, and His forgiveness has eliminated guilt and shame from our sins. The world is a witness to the faithfulness of God. Yet, Zion, or the Israelites then, and you and I today, wrestle with doubt. We feel so undeserving or insignificant that we just cannot believe God cares that much about us. This perspective is not only wrong, but also dangerous. If we don't go to God with our pain we will try to alleviate it ourselves or mask it by trying to ignore it. "Just suck it up." This is not God's intention.

The Hebrew word for compassion is racham, which can be translated as "pity, grace, favor, tender affection, or compassion." It can also be translated as "womb." Here, we see the nurturing qualities of a mother in our God, who relates to us as both Father and Mother. He is beyond the limitations of human gender. When children are suffering, they typically run to their Mom for comfort. God invites us to find the same comfort in Him.

DAY 117
Isaiah 49:15-18

15 "Never! Can a mother forget her nursing child?

Can she feel no love for the child she has borne?

But even if that were possible, I would not forget you!

16 See, I have written your name on the palms of my hands.

Always in my mind is a picture of Jerusalem's walls in ruins.

We saw how God loves us as tenderly as a mother does her child. The Bible uses two metaphors to show us the depth of love God has for us: a committed spouse in marriage and as a loving parent. These types of love describe the intimacy and trust God wants between us.

Isaiah recognizes there are exceptions in comparing God to flawed humanity. Parents will be selfish, spouses will be inconsiderate, but God will never stop loving us perfectly and unconditionally. Consider the overwhelming love a couple experiences on their wedding day or the emotions of a mother when her child is first laid in her arms. These examples are given not just for our enjoyment. They are woven into humanity so we can experience a glimpse of God's unfailing love.

God goes as far as tattooing our names on the palm of His hand. He is always thinking about surrounding us with walls of protection and helping us overcome the walls that are obstacles to us.

> 17 Soon your descendants will come back, and all who are trying to destroy you will go away.

> 18 Look around you and see, for all your children will come back to you.

> As surely as I live," says the Lord, "they will be like jewels or bridal ornaments for you to display.

Isaiah prophesies about the Israelites' return to Jerusalem at the end of their captivity in Babylon, which will be over 150 years in the future. The people will return and rebuild the city.

There is also another beautiful message to believers of every generation. The Bible describes crowns we will receive in Heaven bejeweled with the spiritual fruit from our lives. Imagine the person you got to lead to Christ, the prayers you prayed, or the words you shared that brought healing and encouragement. Each of these moments seems to add beauty to our crowns.

What is the significance of a crown in Heaven? Will we parade them around to impress others? Certainly not. There is only one reason we want a beautiful crown with jewels representing our service to Jesus.

> And they lay their crowns before the throne and say, 11"You are worthy, O Lord our God, to receive glory and honor and power. For you created all things, and they exist because you created what you pleased." Rev. 4:10-11

I want a beautiful, bejeweled crown to lay it at Jesus' feet as the best gift I can give for all He has done for me.

DAY 118
Isaiah 49:19-26

19 "Even the most desolate parts of your abandoned land will soon be crowded with your people.

Your enemies who enslaved you will be far away.

20 The generations born in exile will return and say,

'We need more room! It's crowded here!'

21 Then you will think to yourself, 'Who has given me all these descendants?

For most of my children were killed, and the rest were carried away into exile.

I was left here all alone.

Where did all these people come from?

Who bore these children?

Who raised them for me?'"

22 This is what the Sovereign Lord says:

"See, I will give a signal to the godless nations.

They will carry your little sons back to you in their arms;

they will bring your daughters on their shoulders.

23 Kings and queens will serve you and care for all your needs.

They will bow to the earth before you and lick the dust from your feet.

Then you will know that I am the Lord.

Those who trust in me will never be put to shame."

DAY 118

24 Who can snatch the plunder of war from the hands of a warrior?

Who can demand that a tyrant let his captives go?

25 But the Lord says,

"The captives of warriors will be released,

and the plunder of tyrants will be retrieved.

For I will fight those who fight you, and I will save your children.

26 I will feed your enemies with their own flesh.

They will be drunk with rivers of their own blood.

All the world will know that I, the Lord,

am your Savior and your Redeemer, the Mighty One of Israel."

We all face disappointment in life. It's can be as simple as your Amazon package not arriving on time or a big disappointment like losing a job or a spouse who walks out on you. By contrast, God promises to never walk away or let us down.

The only qualification is our heart must be entwined with His. Entwined means to twist or weave two things together so they cannot be separated. Does that describe your connection and relationship with God?

Christ becomes our mighty warrior who will never allow anything to snatch us away from Him if our hearts and our motives are entwined with His. And He promises to save not only us but also our children.

How do we entwine our hearts with God's? We humbly give ourselves to Him. We surrender our plans to God in exchange for His. We live to please Him rather than ourselves. Then our lives can become a beautiful tapestry woven together from the experiences of our lives and the heart of God. Our pains are surrounded by God's healing, weaving a unique story that honors Jesus.

DAY 119
Isaiah 49:19-26

19 "Even the most desolate parts of your abandoned land

will soon be crowded with your people.

Your enemies who enslaved you will be far away.

20 The generations born in exile will return and say,

'We need more room! It's crowded here!'

21 Then you will think to yourself, 'Who has given me all these descendants?

For most of my children were killed, and the rest were carried away into exile.

I was left here all alone.

Where did all these people come from?

Who bore these children?

Who raised them for me?'"

22 This is what the Sovereign Lord says:

"See, I will give a signal to the godless nations.

They will carry your little sons back to you in their arms;

they will bring your daughters on their shoulders.

23 Kings and queens will serve you and care for all your needs.

They will bow to the earth before you and lick the dust from your feet.

Then you will know that I am the Lord.

Those who trust in me will never be put to shame."

24 Who can snatch the plunder of war from the hands of a warrior?

Who can demand that a tyrant let his captives go?

25 But the Lord says,

"The captives of warriors will be released, and the plunder of tyrants will be retrieved.

For I will fight those who fight you, and I will save your children.

26 I will feed your enemies with their own flesh.

They will be drunk with rivers of their own blood.

All the world will know that I, the Lord,

am your Savior and your Redeemer, the Mighty One of Israel."

We all face disappointment in life. It can be as tiny as your Amazon package not arriving on time or a big disappointment like losing a job or a spouse who walks out on you. By contrast, God promises to never walk away or let us down. The only qualification is our heart must be entwined with His. Entwined means to twist or weave two things together so they cannot be separated. Does that describe your connection and relationship with God?

Christ becomes our mighty warrior who will never allow anything to snatch us away from Him if our hearts and our motives are entwined with His. And He promises to save not only us but also our children.

How do we entwine our hearts with God's? We humbly give ourselves to Him. We surrender our plans to God in exchange for His. We live to please Him rather than ourselves. Then our lives can become a beautiful tapestry woven together from the experiences of our lives and the heart of God. Our pains are surrounded by God's healing, weaving a unique story that honors Jesus.

DAY 120
Isaiah 50:1-7

This is what the Lord says: "Was your mother sent away because I divorced her?

Did I sell you as slaves to my creditors?

No, you were sold because of your sins.

And your mother, too, was taken because of your sins.

2 Why was no one there when I came?

Why didn't anyone answer when I called?

Is it because I have no power to rescue?

> No, that is not the reason!
>
> For I can speak to the sea and make it dry up!
>
> I can turn rivers into deserts covered with dying fish.
>
> 3 I dress the skies in darkness, covering them with clothes of mourning."

It was easy for the Israelites, who faced oppression from the nations around, to feel like it was God's fault. Why isn't God coming through? Why isn't He answering my prayers?

We must remember that God is always good and will never abandon His children. God is pointing out the truth. It was the people of God rebelling and choosing to enjoy the pleasures of sin that caused them to abandon God. In a marvelous display of His grace, the Father reaches out to His children in their rebellion, offering to deliver them. His unlimited power is available, and He is ready to respond if His people stop running from Him.

I can easily pursue my schedule and even ask God to bless my plans. My challenge is to stop, be still, and listen because I value God's leading. I'm trying more and more not to miss those opportunities to meet God and respond with a yes to whatever He desires, knowing it is always better.

> 4 The Sovereign Lord has given me his words of wisdom,
>
> so that I know how to comfort the weary.
>
> Morning by morning he wakens me and opens my understanding to his will.

5 The Sovereign Lord has spoken to me, and I have listened.

I have not rebelled or turned away.

6 I offered my back to those who beat me and my cheeks to those who pulled out my beard.

I did not hide my face from mockery and spitting.

7 Because the Sovereign Lord helps me,

I will not be disgraced.

Therefore, I have set my face like a stone, determined to do his will.

And I know that I will not be put to shame.

From this point forward in Isaiah's writing, he highlights the Servant of the Lord. Did Isaiah comprehend what he was writing, what would take place over seven hundred years into the future when God would come to earth in the flesh? Regardless, the rest of the Book is a prophetic picture of Jesus. We see His power, rulership, humility, and sacrifice. Everything Isaiah describes Jesus will fulfill in His time on earth.

The Gospel writers confirm these words of Isaiah when they describe how Jesus suffered at the hands of the Jewish leaders and the Romans just before His crucifixion. It all starts with a Servant that is submitted and willing. The opening phrase about opening His ear is not about listening; it is about the ear being pierced as a sign of ownership and the commitment of the Servant to the Owner. Jesus did not resist, and He did not rebel. Jesus was willing to be the sacrifice for our sins as well as to offer Himself to be rejected, abused, and beaten as part of the process.

Notice the strength Jesus carried in the knowledge He is empowered by His Father and the Holy Spirit dwelling in Him. This gave Him the motivation to endure everything He faced with holy determination. I must remember the same Holy Spirit that dwelt in Jesus dwells in me. I am also empowered and sense His presence and leading. There is no reason for me to be ashamed, but with holy determination, like Jesus, to be a servant of God.

DAY 121
Isaiah 50:8-11

8 He who gives me justice is near.

Who will dare to bring charges against me now?

Where are my accusers? Let them appear!

9 See, the Sovereign Lord is on my side!

Who will declare me guilty?

All my enemies will be destroyed like old clothes that have been eaten by moths!

Isaiah makes an amazing statement in verse 8: "The One who makes me righteous is close to me." If we can grasp this truth, it can become the bedrock of our lives. When we feel God has left us, or we have left God, or the enemy condemns our failures, we hold to this truth.

It is not me who makes me righteous. God has made me a new creation, and I want to be holy like Jesus. Yes, I get tempted and distracted by a sinful, fallen world and can lose sight of who I am. In those moments, I remind myself how close God is and that if I lean into Him, He will guard and guide me in righteousness. What was once at the center of my life, me has been replaced by Jesus. The more I center my life around this truth, the less influence the enemy and old desires have on my life. Perfection will not come until Heaven, but our life in Jesus far exceeds those old rags of condemnation that identified us in our past.

>10 Who among you fears the Lord and obeys his servant?
>
>If you are walking in darkness, without a ray of light,
>
>trust in the Lord and rely on your God.
>
>11 But watch out, you who live in your own light and warm yourselves by your own fires.
>
>This is the reward you will receive from me: You will soon fall down in great torment.

Isaiah finishes this chapter with a very direct challenge. His challenge is in the form of a question: do you love God? If not, you walk in darkness and have God's wisdom and direction. Many live this way, giving lip service to God when it is convenient, but they do not rely on God at heart. If this is the case, where do they place their trust? They presumptuously live by their own experience and wisdom. Their light is their cleverness in navigating life, and they are always motivated by what will make them happy and comfortable. This sounds cynical, but it is true of so many who profess to be fully devoted followers of Christ and who live so compartmentalized that the spiritual part is kept separate from everything else.

Our God is not just a little candle to inspire us like mood lighting. He is a fire that envelops us until we are consumed. He takes our old lives in exchange for eternal life with Him, but that begins here and now, not some future time when we die. We serve a loving, holy, and jealous God. He is jealous of anything that would harm us by leading us away from Him.

Unfortunately, the greatest enemy we face each day is our thinking. We need a bigger picture of God, a fresh revelation of the depth of His love, and a new understanding of what it means to live in a covenant relationship.

DAY 122
Isaiah 51:1-3

1 "Listen to me, all who hope for deliverance— all who seek the Lord!

Consider the rock from which you were cut, the quarry from which you were mined.

2 Yes, think about Abraham, your ancestor, and Sarah, who gave birth to your nation.

Abraham was only one man when I called him.

But when I blessed him, he became a great nation."

Before Abraham, God had not made a personal covenant with any man. Though God walked with Adam and Enoch and spared Noah from the flood, it was not until Abraham that God entered into a binding relationship with a man. Isaiah reminds the Israelites and us as heirs of that Abrahamic covenant that our righteousness, or right to stand before God, is secure.

Throughout the Bible, we see the story of covenant. God makes an agreement with man and then fulfills both sides of the agreement. Even when we are unfaithful, God remains committed to His covenant and will never go back on His promises. We can reject His love, refuse His leading, and completely miss out on God's best by choosing our own way. Instead, we choose to rely on God and trust He will always keep His promise to guide us into what is best: living in peace and with hope about the future.

And now that you belong to Christ, you are the true children of Abraham. You are his heirs, and God's promise to Abraham belongs to you. Galatians 3:29 NLT

> 3 The Lord will comfort Israel again and have pity on her ruins.

> Her desert will blossom like Eden, her barren wilderness like the garden of the Lord.

> Joy and gladness will be found there.

> Songs of thanksgiving will fill the air.

Isaiah is building on God's covenant, keeping promises we looked at yesterday. The people are going to enter captivity in Babylon for 70 years. They are going to feel abandoned by God. Isaiah is encouraging them that God will remain faithful and eventually restore them.

I love the language Isaiah uses as he speaks for God. The phrase "comfort all her broken places" stands out to me. God's restoration isn't just about restoring them to a land and a nation; He also cares about all the broken places inside them.

In the times we feel broken and disappointed, Jesus comforts us. He sits with us in our pain and gives us hope for our future.

We are promised restoration and a transformation from what feels like a dry wilderness into a lush garden of Eden. This garden is a place of joy and laughter, with songs overflowing from our grateful hearts. In this life, we may not see a restoration of Eden in our world, but we can have God's garden within us—a place where, like with Adam, God provides for us, shows us His created beauty, and walks with us. This is a taste of eternity we can experience now.

DAY 123
Isaiah 51:4-7

"Listen to me, my people.

Hear me, Israel, for my law will be proclaimed, and my justice will become a light to the nations.

5 My mercy and justice are coming soon.

My salvation is on the way.

My strong arm will bring justice to the nations.

All distant lands willGod has sent out His Word across the world. His message came through prophets like Isaiah here in the Old Testament. The purpose of God's Word is to draw us to the Father and lead us into truth. It is not just to gain knowledge about God.

Send out your light and your truth; let them guide me. Let them lead me to your holy mountain, to the place where you live. Psalm 43:3

Ultimately, God sent His Son Jesus, who is God's righteousness, salvation, and mighty arm. Through Jesus, God's righteousness and salvation are made available to us. Through Jesus' death, God's mighty arm is displayed to defeat the enemy who blinds people and holds them back. Jesus also came to reveal the Father's heart of God. He showed us we could have the same connection with our Heavenly Father He displayed here on earth.

> The Word gave life to everything that was created, and his life brought light to everyone. The light shines in the darkness, and the darkness can never extinguish it. John 1:4-5

> 6 Look up to the skies above, and gaze down on the earth below.

> For the skies will disappear like smoke, and the earth will wear out like a piece of clothing.

> The people of the earth will die like flies, but my salvation lasts forever.

> My righteous rule will never end!

> 7 "Listen to me, you who know right from wrong, you who cherish my law in your hearts.

> Do not be afraid of people's scorn, nor fear their insults.

Perspective becomes clearer, and the higher and further you get from your immediate situation. Have you ever noticed how a highway construction project seems complex and indefinable, but if you can see it from above at a good distance, you see how it comes together?

Our lives are this way. We live in a complex world where we gather information from news outlets, internet opinions, extremist claims, and rumors. We lose perspective on what is true.

We need a higher view. As children of God, we are offered another perspective. We can see our lives and the world from a Heavenly view being seated next to Father on His throne. From there, we see that this earth is wearing out. And, though we should honor God's creation, our life mission is not to serve the planet.

Instead, God calls us to focus on our eternal salvation. Our desire should be God's eternal truths rather than the latest news and theories. If we want a Godly perspective, focus on the Word of God. Even if those around you say you are too Heavenly-minded or you're ignoring problems in the world, keep your focus upward.

> Set your mind and keep focused habitually on the things above [the heavenly things], not on things that are on the earth [which have only temporal value]. Colossians 3:2 Ampl.

DAY 124
Isaiah 51:8-12

For the moth will devour them as it devours clothing.

The worm will eat at them as it eats wool.

But my righteousness will last forever.

My salvation will continue from generation to generation."

9 Wake up, wake up, O Lord! Clothe yourself with strength!

Flex your mighty right arm!

Rouse yourself as in the days of old when you slew Egypt, the dragon of the Nile.

Isaiah is not saying God is asleep and unaware of His people's needs.

> He will never slumber nor sleep; he is the Guardian-God for his people, Israel. Yahweh himself will watch over you; he's always at your side to shelter you safely in his presence. Psalms 121:4-5

Isaiah is praying on behalf of the people that God would display His power again and that they would be awakened. One way we awaken to God is to remember His faithfulness and past deeds.

The Sea monster God defeated is a reference to Egypt who He struck with plagues until Pharoah relented and released the Israelites and then destroyed the Egyptian army in the Red Sea when they pursued the Israelites. The dragon from long ago takes us back to the Garden when God confronted and judged the serpent—two pivotal miracles by God to save His people. In the same way, we have been delivered from the enemy's power when Jesus won our victory on the Cross.

Jesus forgives and sets us free from our past, just as God defeated the Egyptians who chased after the Israelites. The Egyptians being swallowed up in the Red Sea is a picture of water baptism where we leave our old past in the waters.

> 10 Are you not the same today, the one who dried up the sea, making a path of escape through the depths so that your people could cross over?
>
> 11 Those who have been ransomed by the Lord will return.
>
> They will enter Jerusalem singing, crowned with everlasting joy.
>
> Sorrow and mourning will disappear, and they will be filled with joy and gladness.
>
> 12 "I, yes I, am the one who comforts you.

> So why are you afraid of mere humans, who wither like the grass
> and disappear?

Isaiah continues this heart cry of the Israelites for God to repeat the miracle of deliverance He performed in freeing them from Egypt so many centuries earlier. This time, Babylon would have freedom from bondage. Isaiah reveals a great principle of prayer. He prays for deliverance and then pictures what that deliverance will look like. This builds joy and gratitude and increases faith. He sees the people marching out, celebrating in worship. All of their despair and depression will be gone. This is faith seeing a future result of prayer being answered.

A word of caution: picturing a specific outcome can also be presumptuous. We can fix our thoughts on an exact outcome, and if God does not respond in this way, we can feel disappointed. However, I do not think Isaiah is concerned about how God will deliver specifically. He is just grateful for freedom; however God wants to bring it about.

God is honored by this kind of faith because He responds to prayer by assuring Isaiah and the people of His protection. This is another great principle of prayer: trust God to take care of you until you experience the freedom you've prayed for. Have a reverence for God that is greater than any fear of man.

DAY 125
Isaiah 51:13-18

13 Yet you have forgotten the Lord, your Creator, the one who stretched out the sky like a canopy and laid the foundations of the earth.

Will you remain in constant dread of human oppressors?

Will you continue to fear the anger of your enemies?

Where is their fury and anger now?

It is gone!

14 Soon all you captives will be released!

Imprisonment, starvation, and death will not be your fate!

15 For I am the Lord your God, who stirs up the sea, causing its waves to roar.

My name is the Lord of Heaven's Armies.

Sometimes, God's goodness seems unnatural in our "real world" of brokenness. We can forget how gracious and powerful God is to His children and fall into the trap of living as though God doesn't care or is unaware of our suffering. Then, we feel we are left to our own devices to survive. This puts us in a vulnerable space of doubt and fear without feeling security.

The truth is that God promises our deliverance and provision if we remember who He truly is and trust Him. What He promised to do for Israel and accomplished becomes a solid foundation on which we place our faith. He is the faithful God who never neglects us but is always there as our refuge.

16 And I have put my words in your mouth and hidden you safely in my hand.

I stretched out the sky like a canopy and laid the foundations of the earth.

I am the one who says to Israel, 'You are my people!'"

17 Wake up, wake up, O Jerusalem!

You have drunk the cup of the Lord's fury.

You have drunk the cup of terror, tipping out its last drops.

18 Not one of your children is left alive to take your hand and guide you.

In verse 9, the people cried out to God to awaken or respond to their time or crisis. God is telling them it is they who need to wake up. Through the prophets of His covenant, God has promised them to keep love and protection. He carried them through the wilderness and led them to conquer the Promised Land. They are the people of God.

But the Israelites and we as His children wander. We get distracted from walking with God, or frustrated because we get what we want in our time frame, or someone says something that wounds us. We rebel or escape into some momentary pleasure and forget about this Divine connection. As this rebellion continues, it spreads within families, churches, and society. People suffer in these periods where the presence of God seems absent. This is why tens of thousands of people rushed to a small college in Kentucky last year because it was said God is visiting Asbury Seminary.

The people of God are renewed in their hunger for a deep relationship with God and to encounter His presence and power. We have felt what it is like to be dry, and now we urgently desire our God. We need to be restored to Him and lead others to know Him.

> This is all the more urgent, for you know how late it is; time is running out. Wake up, for our salvation is nearer now than when we first believed. The night is almost gone; the day of salvation will soon be here. So remove your dark deeds like dirty clothes, and put on the shining armor of right living. Romans 13:11-12

DAY 126
Isaiah 51:19-23

19 These two calamities have fallen on you: desolation and destruction, famine and war.

And who is left to sympathize with you?

Who is left to comfort you?

20 For your children have fainted and lie in the streets,

helpless as antelopes caught in a net.

The Lord has poured out his fury; God has rebuked them.

The four calamities are grouped into disaster and devastation. These may come from health issues, relational breaks, or job loss, famine and war or other global factors. Either circumstance can radically change our lives, and we feel trapped and not in control. God allows these situations to come into our lives to capture our attention, especially when we stray from our relationship with God. I believe we become more vulnerable to disasters in our personal lives. Add to this natural disasters and wars from living in a broken, sinful world, and you see the constant battles we face within and without.

The Israelites are suffering because of their rebellion. They are drinking the cup of God's wrath, which we looked at yesterday in verses 17-18.

The Good News for us today is that Jesus took this cup for us. He took the judgment we deserved upon Himself.

> **He walked away, about a stone's throw, and knelt down and prayed, "Father, if you are willing, please take this cup of suffering away from me. Yet I want your will to be done, not mine." Luke 22:41-42**

21 But now listen to this, you afflicted ones who sit in a drunken stupor, though not from drinking wine.

22 This is what the Sovereign Lord, your God and Defender, says: "See, I have taken the terrible cup from your hands.

You will drink no more of my fury.

23 Instead, I will hand that cup to your tormentors, those who said, 'We will trample you into the dust and walk on your backs.'"

Here, we see it repeated: the promise of God reconciling all things and bringing to justice those who have harmed His people.

DAY 127

Isaiah 52:1-6

Wake up, wake up, O Zion!

Clothe yourself with strength.

Put on your beautiful clothes, O holy city of Jerusalem,

for unclean and godless people will enter your gates no longer.

2 Rise from the dust, O Jerusalem. Sit in a place of honor.

Remove the chains of slavery from your neck,

O captive daughter of Zion.

3 For this is what the Lord says:

"When I sold you into exile, I received no payment.

Now I can redeem you without having to pay for you."

4 This is what the Sovereign Lord says: "Long ago my people chose to live in Egypt. Now they are oppressed by Assyria.

In chapter 51, God calls the people to wake up and continues this plea. He sees His people in their majestic strength; they see themselves crawling in the dust. In Genesis, God cursed the serpent to crawl in the dust, and it is his delight to have us there.

The unclean entering our gates can be applied to the gateway of our mind. What thoughts we entertain and dwell upon either raise us to glorious worship and communion with Jesus or drag us down into the dust with the Enemy.

Isaiah reminds us that it is up to us. We are the gatekeepers who choose what enters our gates—everything from the people we connect with to what we put into our bodies and the entertainment we consume. We have the authority to step out of the prison of spiritual bondage. We do not have to be victims. God has empowered us to be victors. We need to wake up and open our eyes.

5 What is this?" asks the Lord. "Why are my people enslaved again? Those who rule them shout in exultation. My name is blasphemed all day long.

6 But I will reveal my name to my people, and they will come to know its power. Then at last they will recognize that I am the one who speaks to them."

I often remind people praying for God's intervention that they have a "righteous cause." When they pray with pure motives and their request is Biblical and aligned with God's nature, they can pray confidently because what they are contending for is right.

God desires justice. We see it throughout the Bible, in the Old and New Testaments. He delivers His people who have been unjustly accused or attacked. He also delivers for His name's sake. We are His children, and like any good Father, we can have confidence that God is working out everything to grow us in faith and shape us in character.

I like how God our Father finishes with this promise, "Behold, I am here!" God promises He is with us continually, but we can also behold Him. Behold is used 1,298 times in the Bible and means to "perceive through our sight." More than a glance, behold conveys looking with intention, gazing with undistracted focus. This is where faith is forged.

DAY 128
Isaiah 52:7-10

7 How beautiful on the mountains are the feet of the messenger who brings good news,

the good news of peace and salvation, the news that the God of Israel reigns!

Isaiah sees several hundred years into the future when God would come to earth and proclaim a new Kingdom. This would have been a familiar sight in ancient times as Kings dispatched runners throughout the Kingdom to announce a royal victory or birth. Jesus came as the King, bringing the message Himself.

What incredible news Jesus brought to the world. The offer of salvation

Notice there is only one messenger mentioned here but when we read Paul's quotation of this verse in Romans 10:15 he sees multiple messengers. We are the current-day messengers sent to declare good news to captives under the control of the Kingdom of this world. What marvelous news we must share with others to set them free.

8 The watchmen shout and sing with joy, for before their very eyes they see the Lord returning to Jerusalem.

9 Let the ruins of Jerusalem break into joyful song, for the Lord has comforted his people.

He has redeemed Jerusalem.

10 The Lord has demonstrated his holy power before the eyes of all the nations.

All the ends of the earth will see the victory of our God.

Watchmen were appointed to stand guard from a high place to see and warn of an approaching army. They also were the first to see their conquering army coming home.

Here, the watchmen are not viewing this vaguely in the distance. They are seeing close up and clearly what God is going to do. Isaiah is shouting out to the Israelites as a watchman what God has shown him prophetically. Freedom is not only coming for Israel but is coming in the future for all of mankind through Jesus. This is how God wants to reveal Himself to us, close up and personally.

Jesus here is described as the Redeemer or Kinsman-Redeemer, as in the book of Ruth. Naomi and her daughter-in-law Ruth found a "Kinsman-Redeemer" in Boaz whose responsibility was to "act on behalf of a relative who was in trouble, danger, or need." This is just another picture of what Jesus came to do for us. Isaiah draws a picture of a mighty hero with strong arms to fight for us and who simultaneously brings comfort and care for His children. Jesus is our Mighty Warrior and our Kinsman-Redeemer.

DAY 129

Isaiah 52:11-15

11 Get out! Get out and leave your captivity, where everything you touch is unclean.

Get out of there and purify yourselves, you who carry home the sacred objects of the Lord.

12 You will not leave in a hurry, running for your lives.

For the Lord will go ahead of you; yes, the God of Israel will protect you from behind.

Babylon was probably the most modern and impressive city of its day. It was also one of the most materialistic and hedonistic cities. During their seventy years of captivity, it would have been easy for the Israelites to grow attached to the modern comforts rather than their agrarian roots back in Jerusalem. This place would have been even more tempting to their children.

But God is not centered in this place like He is in Jerusalem. This is where God is and where His people should be. God tells them to leave the place of bondage no matter how comfortable and not to touch anything or take any of the culture with them.

DAY 129

Today, we are the vessels who carry God's presence. We have been freed from Satan's bondage, and God is calling us away from our past and the values of this world. We cannot be filled with God and Satan at the same time. God wants us free; if we trust Him, He will lead us out. Step by step, He will guide us away from panic and feeling rushed by the pace of life.

God goes before us and guards us from behind so we do not have to live in any fear. We do not have to constantly look over our shoulders, wondering when our past will catch up with us. That past is gone, carried to the Cross and sacrificed through Jesus' death. We are free to be wholly consumed with God.

The Lord's Suffering Servant

> 13 See, my servant will prosper; he will be highly exalted.

> 14 But many were amazed when they saw him.

> His face was so disfigured he seemed hardly human, and from his appearance, one would scarcely know he was a man.

> 15 And he will startle many nations.

> Kings will stand speechless in his presence.

> For they will see what they had not been told; they will understand what they had not heard about.

Isaiah begins his revelation of God's Servant, Jesus. He provides amazing clarity to Jesus' mission and sacrifice for us. In his New Testament epistle, Peter contemplates the prophetic insights the Holy Spirit revealed to prophets like Isaiah.

> "They wondered what time or situation the Spirit of Christ within them was talking about when he told them in advance about Christ's suffering and his great glory afterward." 1 Peter 1:11

In chapter 53, Isaiah describes Jesus's obedience and willingness to offer Himself to take the punishment we deserve. Though sinless, Jesus took the weight of mankind's sin and suffered for us. The scene Isaiah saw must have been gruesome. To see someone beaten and disfigured to such an extent they no longer look human.

I must admit I find this scene hard to contemplate. For example, I have only seen the movie "The Passion of the Christ" once. I want to think it is because I don't want to see Jesus' suffer like He did at the hands of the Jewish leaders and Roman soldiers. But at a deeper level, I don't want to feel the weight of Jesus doing this for me, an obligation I can never repay. What would be my obligation to Him if Jesus did all this for me? Grace says nothing is required but to accept this overwhelming gift with no strings attached.

I am reminded that Jesus suffered and sacrificed so we could become His sons and daughters. His substitution for us was so that we could reign with Him.

Like these kings and leaders, as I contemplate what Jesus has done, I am forever grateful and want to give Him my whole worship and devotion for which He is worthy.

DAY 130
Isaiah 53:1-5

Who has believed our message?

To whom has the Lord revealed his powerful arm?

2 My servant grew up in the Lord's presence like a tender green shoot, like a root in dry ground.

There was nothing beautiful or majestic about his appearance, nothing to attract us to him.

3 He was despised and rejected— a man of sorrows, acquainted with deepest grief.

We turned our backs on him and looked the other way.

He was despised, and we did not care.

Now, we get to one of the most powerful sections of the Old Testament. Isaiah shares his vision of Jesus. Almost the entire chapter will be quoted in the New Testament as Jesus fulfills everything spoken of here by the prophet some 700 years before His birth.

Isaiah first wonders which generation will get to experience what he is seeing. He sees Jesus being born in a vulnerable human body. He's coming when Israel is dry regarding spiritual passion for God. I believe the conditions in which Jesus came this first time will be similar to those in which He will return. There was nothing special about Jesus' appearance. His looks or physic drew no one. They were drawn by the presence of God in Him—the love He displayed.

Yet, for the love He showed, Jesus was despised and rejected. He felt the pain of rejection and grief from loss and betrayal. Jesus experienced all the human emotions we face. Eventually, when the crowd turned away, even Jesus' closest friends denied Him and ran. Imagine God in the flesh loving His people and then being completely abandoned by them. This had to be one of the hardest things for Him to endure.

Because Jesus lived a life facing all the human tragedies we encounter, He can relate to us, and we can relate to Him. All of His suffering was for us. This is why we can only respond with humble gratitude and worship at His feet.

> 4 Yet it was our weaknesses he carried; it was our sorrows that weighed him down.

> And we thought his troubles were a punishment from God, a punishment for his own sins!

> 5 But he was pierced for our rebellion, crushed for our sins.

I could break down the theological implications of what Isaiah prophesies and what Jesus accomplished for us on the cross. But today, I want to sit in awe that the God of creation looked past my weaknesses and rebellion and did this all for me. The omnipotent God of Heaven took my sins and sicknesses. He took my punishment. He bore my cross and took the nails and spear that should have pierced me, for I was the one who was guilty, not Him.

How did you respond to that level of giving and sacrifice by someone on your behalf? How do you possibly say thanks in such a way that it acknowledges the significance of Jesus' sacrifice and His forgiveness? I think I will say it again and again and again and never stop for eternity, expressing gratitude to the only One who could free me in this way and give me a new life. He is worthy of nothing less.

DAY 131

Isaiah 53:6-9

6 All of us, like sheep, have strayed away. We have left God's paths to follow our own.

Yet the Lord laid on him the sins of us all.

7 He was oppressed and treated harshly, yet he never said a word.

He was led like a lamb to the slaughter.

And as a sheep is silent before the shearers, he did not open his mouth.

What a contrast between these two verses. We are the rebellious ones, choosing to reject God's way over our own. Jesus is the humble lamb, the most compliant creature possible, and the greatest and most powerful entity ever.

The pride and arrogance is astounding when we consider the infinite God invites us into a personal relationship. He is willing to guide us into a fulfilled life. Still we think we know what is best for us.

Jesus bore all the sins of all people in the past and future on the cross. The Good News for man is we are forgiven. We just need to accept this gift of freedom and a new life in exchange for surrendering our old life. It is not enough to pray and be forgiven, only to go back to our life of wandering, here meaning "self-deception." Though we will still struggle with sin, our heart's intent must be to walk with Jesus.

We must take on the same quality as Jesus, who "humbly submitted" to God. Even though He knew what He faced, Jesus didn't defend Himself. He didn't need to as He was resolved to follow the will of God regardless of the pain and sacrifice. Silent submission to God is always the best way forward. Entrusting ourselves to the God of all wisdom and goodness is always the best path.

> 8 Unjustly condemned, he was led away.
>
> No one cared that he died without descendants,
>
> that his life was cut short in midstream.
>
> But he was struck down 8for the rebellion of my people.
>
> 9 He had done no wrong and had never deceived anyone.
>
> But he was buried like a criminal; he was put in a rich man's grave.

We must remember that these words were written about Jesus not after His death but 700 years prior. The amazing details and perspective are revelations from the God who is planning and orchestrating these events.

This is such an encouragement to me. Nothing in my life takes God by surprise. God is aware of every choice I make, and because He sees my life from beginning to end, He knows the outcome. Yes, I have free will, but God has foreknowledge. This means I don't have to sweat or fret over decisions. I trust God and follow what I sense is right, and God takes care of the rest.

Isaiah somehow saw how Jesus was betrayed, falsely accused, and murdered, and though he was considered a criminal, he was placed in a rich man's tomb. What must have seemed like chaos, what Isaiah was shown was all a part of God's plan to redeem mankind.

This reminds us that we don't need to stress and worry about tomorrow. God is in control. Just as He revealed these events in Jesus' life to Isaiah, He can do the same for us. We may not get all the details of our lives mapped out before us, but if we trust God, He will give us glimpses of our future and more specific directions each day.

DAY 132

Isaiah 53:10-12

10 But it was the Lord's good plan to crush him and cause him grief.

Yet when his life is made an offering for sin,

he will have many descendants.

He will enjoy a long life, and the Lord's good plan will prosper in his hands.

God is not sadistic. He did not take joy in watching His Son suffer through the injustice, the beatings, and then death on the Cross. What pleased Our Father was the selflessness of Jesus to give Himself so we could be redeemed. Jesus "prolonged His days" in the sense that He now indwells every believer, and His reach on the earth is greater because He is not limited to one body and one place. The sacrifice of Jesus was in God's plans before the world was ever created. There was no other way to free us.

…the Lamb who was slaughtered before the world was made. Rev. 13:8

Jesus willingly faced the horror of taking on all of our sins and enduring the Cross because He saw how our lives could be transformed. The sacrifice was worth the shame.

> We do this by keeping our eyes on Jesus, the champion who initiates and perfects our faith. Because of the joy awaiting him, he endured the cross, disregarding its shame. Now, he is seated in the place of honor beside God's throne. Hebrews 12:2

We are challenged in the same way to see past the sacrifice of not giving in to temptation or taking the risk of praying for someone when we feel prompted. These are small discomforts compared to Jesus' sacrifice for us. It helps to see the other side of victory over a temptation or how God can use our simple prayer to do miracles. Focus on pleasing God and the long-term joy rather than the short-term pain.

> 11 When he sees all that is accomplished by his anguish, he will be satisfied.
>
> And because of his experience, my righteous servant will make it possible
>
> for many to be counted righteous, for he will bear all their sins.
>
> 12 I will give him the honors of a victorious soldier,
>
> because he exposed himself to death.
>
> He was counted among the rebels.

He bore the sins of many and interceded for rebels.

Jesus understands the anguish of our souls. The ongoing pains and frustrations we face. He reminds us there is light coming. There will be peace and satisfaction as God's presence surrounds us and leads us out. Our responsibility is to be steadfast and continue to trust God. This qualifies us to be counted with the "mighty ones" who share the joys of an eternity with God. The Apostle Paul uses the metaphor of a race.

> Hold firmly to the word of life; then, on the day of Christ's return, I will be proud that I did not run the race in vain and that my work was not useless. Philippians 2:16

> I have fought the good fight, I have finished the race, and I have remained faithful. 2 Timothy 4:7

Jesus loves and intercedes for rebels. He values us and sees beyond what sin has done to us. He sees the potential of a "mighty one" in us, someone who will finish the race, not in their strength but by wholly trusting in God.

DAY 133
Isaiah 54:1-5

"Sing, O childless woman,you who have never given birth!

Break into loud and joyful song, O Jerusalem, you who have never been in labor.

For the desolate woman now has more children than the woman who lives with her husband," says the Lord.

2 "Enlarge your house; build an addition.

Spread out your home, and spare no expense!

3 For you will soon be bursting at the seams.

Your descendants will occupy other nations and resettle the ruined cities.

Barrenness was seen as a curse from God. A woman especially felt that God had abandoned her from her primary purpose today and in her culture. Yet, God speaks a word and says rejoice, celebrate, sing!

This is where real faith steps up. We rejoice and worship God before the evidence of a miracle. Note that this is God speaking; it is not just someone working up faith and then manipulating God to do what they want. This is humbly submitting to God's will while at the same time presenting our desires in prayer. Then, when God speaks a word to us, it is time to party like it has already happened. Our prayers turn from petitions to thanksgiving and worship.

When God makes a promise, we respond. We don't hold back on being prudent. God says, go ahead and get a giant tent, not just for one child but many. Make the house stronger to hold more capacity. I've watched people who wanted something so wrong they went ahead and made their arrangements, but they hadn't heard from God, so they looked foolish and presumptuous.

The best posture is to stay in God's presence and surrender our will to His. Most of the time, it is letting go of being fixed on a particular outcome and simply trusting Jesus, who always does what is best for us.

> 4 "Fear not; you will no longer live in shame.
>
> Don't be afraid; there is no more disgrace for you.
>
> You will no longer remember the shame of your youth and the sorrows of widowhood.
>
> 5 For your Creator will be your husband; the Lord of Heaven's Armies is his name!
>
> He is your Redeemer, the Holy One of Israel, the God of all the earth.

In verse 4, Isaiah mentions six characteristics or weaknesses of man. Fear, shame, embarrassment, feeling disgraced, youthful inadequacy, and the emptiness and loneliness of widowhood. Widowhood here relates to being alone spiritually and not having any real relationship with God.

In verse 5, we are given seven names or qualities of God. Each name declares an aspect of our relationship with God and how He cares for us. God is our Maker, husband, Yahweh, Commander of Armies, Kinsman-Redeemer, Holy One, and Mighty God. God is greater than our struggles. I like that it lists six of man's weaknesses but seven of God's strengths. His power and His love are always greater than our weaknesses.

This encouragement was given to people coming out of captivity who would feel inadequate among the nations surrounding them. We read about this in Ezra and Nehemiah.

This also applies to us as we have come out of spiritual captivity and into a new life with Christ. We still feel the draw at times from our past, or we can become distracted by temptation and feel inadequate spiritually. God is always there to fight for us to overcome our fears and our shame and be as committed to us as a faithful husband is to his wife.

DAY 134

Isaiah 54:6-10

6 For the Lord has called you back from your grief—

as though you were a young wife abandoned by her husband," says your God.

7 "For a brief moment I abandoned you, but with great compassion I will take you back.

8 In a burst of anger I turned my face away for a little while.

But with everlasting love I will have compassion on you," says the Lord, your Redeemer.

Here the love of the Father is displayed prophetically to Israel and to us as His children today. When we feel depressed and deserted God invites us to come to Him as the one who will not reject us. In fact, God is always there drawing us to Himself.

The text indicates that God had not abandoned His people; it only felt like it to them. I believe there are times we turn away from God, and it seems He has turned away from us as well. God never breaks or ignores His covenant with us (Deut.

31:6). Under the New Covenant, Jesus repeats this promise to never forsake us (Heb. 13:5).

For God to be silent or seem to hide Himself so that we pursue Him is part of our maturity. I remember my son always wanting to walk alone when we were in a store. One day I let him wander away, and I hid behind a rack where I could see him, but he could not see me. Suddenly, he looked around, couldn't see me, and panicked in fear. I came around the corner, and he ran and clung to me. He realized He needed me close. We never outgrow this childlike dependence on Jesus, our Kinsman-Redeemer, who protects and cares for us.

> 9 "Just as I swore in the time of Noah that I would never again let a flood cover the earth,
>
> so now I swear that I will never again be angry and punish you.
>
> 10 For the mountains may move and the hills disappear,
>
> but even then my faithful love for you will remain.
>
> My covenant of blessing will never be broken," says the Lord, who has mercy on you.

I find it amazing that God would make a vow to us. He is God. He can do whatever He chooses to do at any time. He is the Creator and Ruler of all and doesn't answer to anyone. Yet, because of His tender heart towards us, He makes promises to which He binds Himself.

Water comes and goes. It is fluid and eventually turns to gas and evaporates. Mountains and hills, on the other hand, do not move easily. They are steadfast and solid, just like God and His love for us. Isaiah is peering forward to a New Covenant relationship God will have with His people. He will never abandon or leave us, even when we turn from Him. His commitment to us is so much greater than our commitment to Him.

Jesus probably had this promise from His Father in mind when he said we should build our lives upon the rock (Lk. 6, Matt. 7). We find security and live in peace when we hold fast to God's promise.

We have peace with God because of Jesus' sacrifice for our sins on the Cross. He has given us a covenant He will never break, always showing love and compassion to us. Our only response can be humility, gratitude, and worship.

DAY 135
Isaiah 54:11-17

11 "O storm-battered city, troubled and desolate!

I will rebuild you with precious jewels and make your foundations from lapis lazuli.

12 I will make your towers of sparkling rubies, your gates of shining gems, and your walls of precious stones.

13 I will teach all your children, and they will enjoy great peace.

Isaiah prophesies to the Israelites, who will be held captive by Babylon but released after seventy years. When they return to Jerusalem, they will find a city in ruins. They will have to rebuild the walls for protection, farms for food, and, most importantly, restore the Temple so they can connect with God. Yahweh knew this would feel overwhelming, so He assured them He would lead and provide for them. God's first promise is to rebuild the people. His promise is not just to a city or a kingdom but to people individually. This is what God does for us. He frees us from captivity and then rebuilds our lives around His presence and His peace within us.

The precious jewels represent the works of grace and spiritual gifts from the Holy Spirit dwelling in us. We reflect God's character just as precious stones reflect the light that shines through them. Even though we may feel poor, God wants us to know how rich we are with His presence.

The last portion reminds us of our purpose in helping others discover God's love so He can rebuild their lives. They become spiritual sons and daughters who bring fulfillment to us as we watch God transform their lives.

14 You will be secure under a government that is just and fair.

Your enemies will stay far away.

You will live in peace, and terror will not come near.

15 If any nation comes to fight you, it is not because I sent them.

Whoever attacks you will go down in defeat.

16 "I have created the blacksmith who fans the coals beneath the forge and makes the weapons of destruction.

And I have created the armies that destroy.

17 But in that coming day no weapon turned against you will succeed.

You will silence every voice raised up to accuse you.

> These benefits are enjoyed by the servants of the Lord;
>
> their vindication will come from me. I, the Lord, have spoken!

Everything changes When we grasp that God has imparted His righteousness to us. Righteousness is the ability to stand before God unashamed because we have been given His perfection. This doesn't mean we don't sin and still mess up. It means, at our core, what we are being transformed into, and reflecting more each day, the image of God.

This means we do not have to fear any person or spiritual entity, and we do not have to live under oppression. This is such an important realization when renewing our minds. God declares He is in control and has anyone or anything that would harm us on a leash. No strategy of man or the Devil can succeed unless God allows it for testing and to equip us. Whatever accusations or condemnation come at us, we stand in the truth that though we make mistakes, we indeed are children of God and part of His royal family.

In verse 17, Isaiah changes from talking about the Son to sons. Here, through the end of the book, Isaiah shifts from referring to the Servant of the Lord, Jesus, to His followers. The picture is that Jesus has done His work of redemption on the Cross, and the rest of Isaiah highlights what that means to us and how we should live in light of what Jesus has accomplished through His death and resurrection. We'll explore some great promises in the days ahead. These promises are not to the self-righteous but to the humble servants of God.

DAY 136
Isaiah 56:1-5

This is what the Lord says: "Be just and fair to all.

Do what is right and good, for I am coming soon to rescue you

and to display my righteousness among you.

2 Blessed are all those who are careful to do this.

Blessed are those who honor my Sabbath days of rest and keep themselves from doing wrong.

After announcing the blessings in the last few chapters, Isaiah presents two qualifications for walking in those blessings. In justice, we care for others, and in keeping the Sabbath, we care for ourselves.

In caring about justice, we benefit from God delivering us and unveiling more of Himself. God takes care of those who care for others.

In honoring God with the Sabbath, we choose to put Him before anything and value rest. God takes care of those who take responsibility for resting and enjoying Him.

If we love others and highlight a day each week to renew ourselves with rest, worship, and experiencing God through His Word, we will also distance ourselves from sin.

We constantly return to what God values rather than adopting the values of this world that say to put yourself first.

> 3 "Don't let foreigners who commit themselves to the Lord say,
>
> 'The Lord will never let me be part of his people.'
>
> And don't let the eunuchs say, 'I'm a dried-up tree with no children and no future.'
>
> 4 For this is what the Lord says: I will bless those eunuchs who keep my Sabbath days holy
>
> and who choose to do what pleases me and commit their lives to me.
>
> 5 I will give them—within the walls of my house— a memorial and a name far greater than sons and daughters could give.
>
> For the name I give them is an everlasting one. It will never disappear!

What an incredible promise to those who feel alone and like outsiders. God embraces two groups the Jewish people typically reject: foreigners or Gentiles and those incapable of having children. Since children were considered a blessing from God, to be barren meant you must be under God's curse. These were the people the church of the day rejected. The people representing God were not welcoming the people God was accepting. They had a higher standard than the God they served.

Jesus reinforced this value of openness when He spoke to the woman at the well, the woman caught in prostitution, or the many Gentiles He healed. He wanted outcasts to know they were included in His family. He modeled something from which the church has moved away. God says He will never forget the outsiders, and we must keep them at the forefront of our mission.

An outcast must come humbly, embrace God's truth, and grow in maturity. As we say in the Vineyard, "come as you are, but don't stay that way".

DAY 137

Isaiah 56:6-12

6 "I will also bless the foreigners who commit themselves to the Lord,

who serve him and love his name, who worship him and do not desecrate the Sabbath day of rest,

and who hold fast to my covenant.

7 I will bring them to my holy mountain of Jerusalem and will fill them with joy in my house of prayer.

I will accept their burnt offerings and sacrifices,

because my Temple will be called a house of prayer for all nations.

DAY 137

> 8 For the Sovereign Lord, who brings back the outcasts of Israel, says: I will bring others, too,

> besides my people Israel."

When we read these words, our thoughts immediately go to the New Testament story of Jesus going through the Temple and turning over the tables of the merchants and money changers. These people were excluding the women and Gentiles from worship by taking over their place in the courtyard. They set up bizarres to make money off worshippers coming to Jerusalem for the annual feasts. Jesus quotes Isaiah,

> "My house will be called a house of prayer for all the nations'. But you have made it a den of robbers" (Mark 11:17).

God is always open to any honest seeker who comes to Him, and He is against anyone who stands in their way. God welcomes everyone and invites them in. He offers joy in His presence, acceptance, and a place in His family. Our Father has open arms no matter where we've come from or what we've come through.

There are some rules to follow in God's family. We are called to love and serve God and honor the Sabbath as a time to experience His presence. These seem to be essentials to God; they should also be to us.

> 9 Come, wild animals of the field!

> Come, wild animals of the forest!

> Come and devour my people!

> 10 For the leaders of my people—

the Lord's watchmen, his shepherds— are blind and ignorant.

They are like silent watchdogs that give no warning when danger comes.

They love to lie around, sleeping and dreaming.

11 Like greedy dogs, they are never satisfied.

They are ignorant shepherds,

all following their own path

and intent on personal gain.

12 "Come," they say, "let's get some wine and have a party.

Let's all get drunk.

Then tomorrow we'll do it again and have an even bigger party!"

These sobering words are for leaders who ignore their responsibility. They are not watching for God or spiritual attacks coming to the people. They have no voice, no current word from God, from not being in His presence. They rely on their knowledge, what others have received, or television or social media opinions. To be sleeping when we should be awake and watching is due to selfishness and spiritual burn-out.

I know many good pastors who came out of the last few years tired and less motivated to pray, listen, and lead. Many are afraid to speak about what is happening today for fear of offending someone on either side of the political spectrum. What they do instead is keep everything light and happy. Let's have a party, make church fun, and focus on the Good News and how to be blessed. This appeals to the consumer hearts of people who follow their leaders in shallow commitment.

But what happens to these people who follow God solely for their benefit? Isaiah says they become easy targets of the enemy and are devoured. God has called all of us to lead and speak out when we see someone stumbling toward destruction. If we listen to God and take the risk of caring, we can see lives redeemed and transformed.

Pray for God to awaken, refresh, and equip His leaders to shepherd their people.

DAY 138
Isaiah 57:1-5

Good people pass away; the godly often die before their time.

But no one seems to care or wonder why.

No one seems to understand that God is protecting them from the evil to come.

2 For those who follow godly paths will rest in peace when they die.

Once again, we are challenged to view life and death from God's perspective. Our view is so finite. All we can think of is our loss and the lost potential in the life of the person who has passed away.

Isaiah says God, in His love, protects people from some evil they will face later in life. Here, we embrace God's wisdom and love to stop the loop of sorrow. If we genuinely embrace death as a promotion and reward, we would probably celebrate someone's passing more than we do. The person we love and who followed God has finished their race or completed their time on earth and entered into an eternal rest and reward. They've won!

This perspective may not make sense on this side of Heaven. There have been many untimely deaths I have to put in a mental folder to be addressed in eternity. But I have this feeling, though, that the moment I see Jesus' face to face in eternity,

I will forget all about that folder. All my questions will be gone, and it will all make sense.

Idolatrous Worship Condemned

> 3 "But you—come here, you witches' children,
>
> you offspring of adulterers and prostitutes!
>
> 4 Whom do you mock, making faces and sticking out your tongues?
>
> You children of sinners and liars!
>
> 5 You worship your idols with great passion beneath the oaks and under every green tree.
>
> You sacrifice your children down in the valleys, among the jagged rocks in the cliffs.

Isaiah describes the many forms of idolatry and the type of worship each God required. As the Israelites moved into the Promised Land, they were to remove every idol and every form of false worship. God strongly warned them not to intermarry with the local tribes. This is not because God is against mixing ethnicities; it is so the Israelites would not be tempted to embrace the gods of the people they married. This, again and again, was Israel's downfall.

Our God, the One True God, is jealous of an exclusive relationship with us. When we dabble with horoscopes, psychics, and other means of tapping into the supernatural realm, we connect with real spiritual beings. That is hard for us to embrace in our modern world, but these entities still exist and seek to draw us away from God.

The people described here are children of people who dabbled in false religions and then allowed themselves to be drawn away from God. Isaiah uses the strongest language to expose what they excuse as "Both big deals." To God, spiritual adultery is just as actual as physical adultery is to a marriage. Every generation draws their family closer to God or toward pagan gods and practices. It might be dressed up in a modern form, but it is the same god wanting to steal us and our children and grandchildren away from following Jesus.

I love that God is jealous of me, and I want to be exclusively for Him and, boy, allow any other gods to get in the way of my worship.

DAY 139
Isaiah 57:6-10

6 Your gods are the smooth stones in the valleys.

You worship them with liquid offerings and grain offerings.

They, not I, are your inheritance.

Do you think all this makes me happy?

We get or become what we worship. If we worship God, we reflect His character qualities and image. If we worship the gods of this world, we will sacrifice our lives to them and, in exchange, get nothing of eternal value. This certainly is pleasing to us or God.

7 You have committed adultery on every high mountain.

There you have worshiped idols and have been unfaithful to me.

8 You have put pagan symbols on your doorposts and behind your doors.

You have left me and climbed into bed with these detestable gods.

You have committed yourselves to them.

You love to look at their naked bodies.

9 You have gone to Molech with olive oil and many perfumes,

sending your agents far and wide, even to the world of the dead.

10 You grew weary in your search, but you never gave up.

Desire gave you renewed strength, and you did not grow weary.

All of the Israelites' pursuits led them away from God. They thought they could find meaning and fulfillment in other ways, but every new hopeful search left them empty and with nothing. I am amazed at how many people I see today who are on the same pursuits. The goal is to be financially independent, free of the exclusiveness of marriage, the rules of society, or moral attributes of the past.

Learn a lesson from these people in Isaiah's audience. Pursuing the next thing to make us happy seldom fulfills more than a moment, and then we must be on to the next thing.

DAY 140
Isaiah 57:11-15

11 "Are you afraid of these idols?

Do they terrify you?

Is that why you have lied to me and forgotten me and my words?

Is it because of my long silence that you no longer fear me?

12 Now I will expose your so-called good deeds.

None of them will help you.

13 Let's see if your idols can save you when you cry to them for help.

> Why, a puff of wind can knock them down!

> If you just breathe on them, they fall over!

> But whoever trusts in me will inherit the land and possess my holy mountain."

I don't know where I first heard it, but I have repeated the statement many times: "Big God, little problems. Little God, big problems." In other words, the bigger our fears become by focusing on our problems, the less we look to God, and the smaller He becomes in our thoughts.

This is what seems to have happened with the Israelites. They intermarried with the local tribes and took on their gods. Then, they started to live to appease these gods rather than to please the one true God. As a result, God goes silent and allows them to stumble without Him.

It is easy for us to fall into the same pattern in modern times. We quit going to church, stop worshiping, and stopped giving and serving. In our minds, we know we have our savings, abilities, and resourcefulness to care for ourselves. Do we need to bother God? But, all of these things in which we invest our lives are unstable. God is the solid rock on which we build our lives. He is our provider. He is the one in whom we stand in awe and humbly worship.

God Forgives the Repentant

> 14 God says, "Rebuild the road!

> Clear away the rocks and stones so my people can return from captivity."

> 15 The high and lofty one who lives in eternity, the Holy One, says this:

> "I live in the high and holy place
>
> with those whose spirits are contrite and humble.
>
> I restore the crushed spirit of the humble and revive the courage of those with repentant hearts.

More important than the captivity from which the Israelites were being freed was their destination. Returning to Jerusalem meant returning to God's presence. Jerusalem held the Temple, and the Temple was where God met His people.

The rocks in the road represent whatever keeps us from God. Distractions can be work, entertainment, pleasure, anything that consumes more time than necessary, the times we could meet with God. If our life is about us and our schedule and desires, then we are at the center rather than Jesus.

God frees us so we can live in close communion with Him and obey Him. This is why the invitation to deeper intimacy with God is only for those who are contrite and humble. The Israelites found themselves in captivity because they had rejected God. We humble ourselves and ask God to help order our lives so that we can make time to be with Him.

Father, help us clear the stones of distraction that get in the way of our access to You. Help us to humbly follow as the Holy Spirit leads away from captivity and into Your presence.

DAY 141

Isaiah 57:16-21

16 For I will not fight against you forever;

I will not always be angry.

If I were, all people would pass away— all the souls I have made.

17 I was angry, so I punished these greedy people.

I withdrew from them, but they kept going on their own stubborn way.

18 I have seen what they do, but I will heal them anyway!

I will lead them.

I will comfort those who mourn,

How does God show His displeasure with His people? Here, under the old covenant, He withdraws His presence. God hopes that they will sense how empty and vulnerable they are in His being distant and run to God. But humans are slow to learn and stubborn rebels by nature. It is God who is merciful, heals, and leads them anyway. They are His children, and He will not let them go.

Now fast-forward to today. We have a new covenant, and God's presence is within us. God promises never to leave or forsake us. Can we still feel distant from God, though He is constantly with us? Of course, we can turn from God and ignore Him in our thoughts and decisions. We choose our way without consulting the God we call the Lord and the Great Shepherd who is supposed to lead us.

Life is tough. It is especially tough for those who know God but ignore Him. The tension in trying to please God and fulfill our own needs becomes frustrating and futile.

What is the answer? Humble submission and trust in our loving Savior who heals leads and comforts us. The last verse of the old hymn, **Blessed Assurance** captures this idea well.

Perfect submission, all is at rest,
I in my Savior am happy and blest;
Watching and waiting, looking above,
Filled with His goodness, lost in His love
This is my story, this is my song
Praising my Savior all the day long.

19 bringing words of praise to their lips.

May they have abundant peace, both near and far," says the Lord, who heals them.

20 "But those who still reject me are like the restless sea,

which is never still but continually churns up mud and dirt.

21 There is no peace for the wicked," says my God.

As we draw close to God in worship, He fills us with peace. He heals our wounds and restores our faith. It doesn't matter whether we feel close to God or far away; the moment we turn to Him, He meets us right there and begins the healing process. Whether it is our bodies, minds, or emotions, God desires to make us whole.

By contrast, those who continue to rebel and seek their way will live lives of constant turmoil. All their efforts to succeed and find happiness will only become a mess. Frustration and disappointment rule the lives of those who reject God.

Ultimately, there is no rest in this life and for eternity for those who are too strong, proud, and self-confident to need a God to care for them.

> So let us do our best to enter that rest. But if we disobey God, as the people of Israel did, we will fall. Heb. 4:11

DAY 142
Isaiah 58:1-5

"Shout with the voice of a trumpet blast.

Shout aloud! Don't be timid.

Tell my people Israel of their sins!

2   Yet they act so pious!

They come to the Temple every day and seem delighted to learn all about me.

They act like a righteous nation that would never abandon the laws of its God.

They ask me to take action on their behalf, pretending they want to be near me.

This 58th chapter of Isaiah focuses on fasting. Fasting is simply denying ourselves something so we can draw closer to God. It can be a powerful spiritual discipline that helps us gain control over our physical appetites and leads to greater devotion to God. Fasting is about humility and giving ourselves to God, not trying to impress Him with our religious efforts.

These are all lessons the Israelites have forgotten. They fast as the Jews did one day per week, but it has become a religious obligation. God calls this rebellion and sin. It is taking our relationship with God and turning it into a practice with no meaning. The people only pretended to be passionate about God. In the same way, many attend church today out of tradition or habit rather than a deep desire to worship God.

God is always after truth more than appearances. A married couple can fall into a routine and neglect each other. Everything may look fine on the outside, but inside, the relationship is empty and hollow.

The good news is that God only requires us to be honest and lay down all pretenses. We just come humbly and admit our distractions and need for His love. This posture of the heart pleases God and restores our relationship with Him.

The people are offended that God is not impressed with their religious display. He should appreciate that they went an entire morning and afternoon without food, a whole 12 hours from sunup to sundown according to the Law! Shouldn't that depth of devotion be honored? So what if Moses and Jesus fasted 960 hours or 40 days?

Right here is the issue. The people were focused on themselves. Maybe they thought God would be impressed and bless them. They not only missed God's intention, but they hurt others. They displayed no love for God or people. No matter how they outwardly displayed their devotion, God saw the real problem. It was not their bellies that were empty, but their hearts.

Can we fall into the same trap of feeling like we're pretty good on our own? This trap makes us feel like God should be pleased that we go to church, give some, don't do what we would consider heinous crimes, and always have justification for when we sin. But this type of empty religious activity is deceptive and worthless. Humility pleases God, and that is what fasting is about.

DAY 143

Isaiah 58:6-10

6 "No, this is the kind of fasting I want:

Free those who are wrongly imprisoned;

lighten the burden of those who work for you.

Let the oppressed go free, and remove the chains that bind people.

7 Share your food with the hungry, and give shelter to the homeless.

Give clothes to those who need them, and do not hide from relatives who need your help.

8 "Then your salvation will come like the dawn, and your wounds will quickly heal.

Your godliness will lead you forward, and the glory of the Lord will
protect you from behind.

As Isaiah shares the kind of fast God approves, we notice, and probably surprising to many, that the fast is not just about God or me. This fast, "God's Chosen Fast," as Arthur Wallace calls it in his great book, involves others in selfless acts of compassion. Don't get me wrong, fasting honors God and has a tremendous spiritual impact on our lives, but there is also an element of humble service that pushes our needs out and places our attention on the suffering of others.

Suffering from a lack of food is our choice. The poor and oppressed have no choice; this is their life. By identifying with their hunger, we may be moved to help free them somehow.

Strangers and family are included in Isaiah's challenge to lay down our lives or our resources to care for others.

As we sacrificially humble ourselves and put God and others before us, the timeless principal kicks in wherein God refreshes us and provides for us. We get free from our darkness as we help others get free from theirs.

9 Then when you call, the Lord will answer.

'Yes, I am here,' he will quickly reply.

"Remove the heavy yoke of oppression.

Stop pointing your finger and spreading vicious rumors!

10 Feed the hungry, and help those in trouble.

Then your light will shine out from the darkness,

and the darkness around you will be as bright as noon.

Isaiah continues his exhortation concerning fasting as a means of motivating one to identify with the suffering and the poor. God promises to take care of us as we care for others.

The Christian life is never to be lived in isolation. It is about a spiritual family and a larger community where we are to engage. As much as we like our independence, we are our brother's keeper.

This message is repeated for clarity. As we meet the needs of others, God takes care of us. This is very different from what society decrees: we care for ourselves first and let others run their lives. This idea is flipped when we are followers of Christ.

It seems from the text that there is a direct cause-and-effect relationship between God responding to our needs and our meeting the needs of others. We look to see how we can bless somebody else if we have an urgent need. This is another example of how God's Kingdom values are the opposite of this worlds.

DAY 144
Isaiah 58:11-14

11 The Lord will guide you continually,

giving you water when you are dry and restoring your strength.

You will be like a well-watered garden, like an ever-flowing spring.

12 Some of you will rebuild the deserted ruins of your cities.

Then you will be known as a rebuilder of walls and a restorer of homes.

One of the great benefits of fasting is drawing close to God and the increased clarity that comes with hearing His voice. Isaiah presents a picture of God leading us and filling us with His peace that overflows to others. In fasting God brings us into closer alignment with His vision for people and communities. He wants to use us to heal brokenness and restore people to Himself.

If our thoughts are consumed with anxiety and fear and concerns for our own lives we will not be in the place where we can think about helping others. As followers of Christ, we seek Him and His mission and trust that all of our needs are in His hands. This is the life of faith. It is the life to which we return when we fast and renew our devotion to Jesus and His purpose for us.

When we read these verses, they can seem like a fantasy that is not grounded in the reality of everyday life. But this is God's kingdom reality. It is a taste of what eternity will be. It is the way we experience the future now.

> 13 "Keep the Sabbath day holy.
>
> Don't pursue your own interests on that day,
>
> but enjoy the Sabbath and speak of it with delight as the Lord's holy day.
>
> Honor the Sabbath in everything you do on that day, and don't follow your own desires or talk idly.
>
> 14 Then the Lord will be your delight.
>
> I will give you great honor and satisfy you with the inheritance I promised to your ancestor Jacob.
>
> I, the Lord, have spoken!"

In addition to placing a high value on fasting, Isaiah highlights another often-neglected spiritual discipline, honoring a Sabbath. Whereas fasting is a discipline of our appetites, the Sabbath is controlling our time and focusing our attention on God. Both of these disciplines bring us closer to God by centering on Him rather than ourselves. Whenever we put God before our plans we are making a statement of faith. We are declaring my strength and wisdom come from God. He is my source for all things.

If these disciplines are believed to be just religious duty and obligation, they'll be seen as a means to appease God rather than a means of knowing Him better and receiving the joy and peace that comes from being in His presence.

Fasting and Sabbath keeping are a great measure of my devotion and trust in God compared to pursuing my own life. I want to live in that "joyous bliss." I want to prosper in all ways. I want to experience God triumphantly carrying me through difficult times.

The choice is ours. We can humbly surrender control over a small portion of our time and appetites and offer them to God as a gift. In exchange, we receive all the promises Isaiah mentions. This is something we will only learn by doing from a heart of worship and a hunger to know God.

DAY 145
Isaiah 59:1-5

Listen! The Lord's arm is not too weak to save you,

nor is his ear too deaf to hear you call.

2 It's your sins that have cut you off from God.

Because of your sins, he has turned away and will not listen anymore.

3 Your hands are the hands of murderers, and your fingers are filthy with sin.

Your lips are full of lies, and your mouth spews corruption.

4 No one cares about being fair and honest.

> The people's lawsuits are based on lies.
>
> They conceive evil deeds and then give birth to sin.
>
> 5 They hatch deadly snakes and weave spiders' webs.
>
> Whoever eats their eggs will die; whoever cracks them will hatch a viper.

Whenever we feel distant from God, it is never His fault. It is always our rebellion or neglect to prioritize our relationship with God. It begins with small distractions that keep us from worship. We get busy with life and soon give up reading the Bible. Church becomes optional because of our busyness and obligations. Whether justified or not, all the things and time consumers build a wall between us and God.

This formerly resulted in a harsh Old Covenant reality. By not keeping the Law, feasts, and temple worship, the people found God ignoring them. In desperate times, they would suddenly get religious and start praying, but to no avail.

Today, under the New Covenant, we have unlimited access to God based not on what we do but on what Christ has done. God will never turn His back on us. Our challenge is to not allow the distractions of life to put us in the same place as Isaiah's audience. Even though we have a better covenant, we can still turn from God. We can drift so far that we do not hear the voice of God leading us away from danger and into places of blessing.

Remember, if God feels distant, it is never Him who has moved. All we have to do is move toward Him in humility. This can be done simply with gratitude and worship. We remind ourselves the God of all creation loves us and wants to refresh us and equip us to live a fulfilling life that honors Him.

DAY 146
Isaiah 59:6-12

6 Their webs can't be made into clothing, and nothing they do is productive.

All their activity is filled with sin, and violence is their trademark.

7 Their feet run to do evil, and they rush to commit murder.

They think only about sinning.

Misery and destruction always follow them.

8 They don't know where to find peace or what it means to be just and good.

They have mapped out crooked roads, and no one who follows them knows a moment's peace.

> 9 So there is no justice among us, and we know nothing about right living.

> We look for light but find only darkness.

> We look for bright skies but walk in gloom.

The truth is not always easy to confront. The sin that seems like no big deal to us grieves God. When we try to hide or justify sinful behavior, wrong attitudes, or maybe unforgiveness, we leave a path of destruction that hurts others and misrepresents God. How do we get here? The writer of Hebrews says we "drift away" from the truth (Heb. 2:1). Sometimes, it is not intentionally turning from God; it is a step away from the distractions that maybe are not even that bad, but they cause us to drift away slowly.

This distance we create shuts down any insight or leading from God. Instead, we are left alone to figure out life without God's wisdom and love guiding us. Prayers are prayed, but God doesn't seem to hear or respond.

What do we do when we find ourselves in this place? We approach God in humility. We confess our distractions and turn from the things we have tried to escape or fill our lives with. God is always quick to forgive and receive us. He brings us out of the darkness so we can see Him more clearly.

> 10 We grope like the blind along a wall, feeling our way like people without eyes.

> Even at brightest noontime, we stumble as though it were dark.

> Among the living, we are like the dead.

> 11 We growl like hungry bears; we moan like mournful doves.

We look for justice, but it never comes.

We look for rescue, but it is far away from us.

12 For our sins are piled up before God and testify against us.

Yes, we know what sinners we are.

Drawing close to God is always the result of honestly acknowledging our stepping away from Him in the first place. We feel our world is not right. We feel alone and empty inside, and something sparks within. The Holy Spirit nudges us and reminds us of God's grace, that we are forgiven, and that we are able to approach Him. His unconditional love is stored up and waiting for us.

We awaken to the fact we have been walking in darkness and cannot make it on our own. We repent or become aware that our direction is wrong and adjust our course toward God rather than away from Him. When we turn toward God, He runs to meet us where we are, just like the Father in Jesus' story of the prodigal (Luke 15). It took the young man in Jesus' parable to come to the end of himself. He had to look at his sins and failures and realize they were his and his fault alone.

It is good to remember that our sins have been forgiven under the New Covenant through Jesus bearing them on the cross. We may know our "rebellious deeds," but God does not hold them against us. They are not "stacked high" and condemn us as Isaiah describes here under the Old Covenant.

We have no reason to stay distant from God for fear of rejection or punishment. We are only punishing ourselves and missing out on a fulfilling life because we have chosen to keep our distance from the one source that can improve our lives. Thank God for His grace that draws us into His arms.

DAY 147

Isaiah 59:13-17

13 We know we have rebelled and have denied the Lord.

We have turned our backs on our God.

We know how unfair and oppressive we have been,

carefully planning our deceitful lies.

14 Our courts oppose the righteous,

and justice is nowhere to be found.

Truth stumbles in the streets, and honesty has been outlawed.

> 15 Yes, truth is gone, and anyone who renounces evil is attacked.

> The Lord looked and was displeased to find there was no justice.

Isaiah confesses the people's sins. Their rebellion has brought them to this place. The Israelites have turned away from God and their identity as His people. They begin to believe lies and then repeat them as truth. They are deceived and eventually carried away captive to Babylon.

We also see a prophetic picture of modern times here. In many places, the church has adapted its beliefs to fit the culture rather than the timeless orthodoxy it has held since the New Testament writings. Therefore, rather than being a voice to stop injustice and immorality, the truth of God has been silenced. Even those who walk according to God's Word become victims of ridicule and are called hate mongers. Babylon is the prophetic metaphor representing the kingdoms men build.

Unfortunately, this is the pattern of human history and societies. Prosperity leads to pride and arrogance. We don't need God. Man's wisdom and science have the answers. The good of others and society is replaced with a focus on individual freedoms regardless of morality.

This is a pattern in every great empire, including the Greeks, Romans, Spain, Holland, England, and America today. There are economic factors that historian's debate, but there has always been the underlying factor of faith in God. When people are desperate, they help each other and work together for justice. Their faith in God sustains them, and each one helps the other. The more affluent and independent they become, the more selfish they become. Where we once exported the Gospel, now we export the immorality we have embraced, and our influence is waning as nations reject our new truth.

Can we become the first empire to learn from our past, humble ourselves, and seek God? Can the church lead with humility and justice and restore its voice of influence?

History shows that He responds when God's children cry out to Him. When we become radically committed to living for God and loving others, the church is revived, and society is awakened to righteousness. This must be our prayer.

> 16 He was amazed to see that no one intervened to help the oppressed.

So he himself stepped in to save them with his strong arm, and his justice sustained him.

17 He put on righteousness as his body armor and placed the helmet of salvation on his head.

He clothed himself with a robe of vengeance and wrapped himself in a cloak of divine passion.

God works through people, everyday people who are willing to take on a cause and rather than just complain they are moved to action. Isaiah shares that God is willing to work through anyone, especially when His choices are few. Availability has always been more important than capability to God, because He does the equipping and empowering.

The champion described here can also be translated as "intercessor," and "rescue" means to intercede or pray on behalf of others.

When we think of a champion, we think of human ability, charisma, and strength. God seeks someone compassionate and available and will allow Him to lead them in where to intercede or direct His power.

James tells us, The earnest prayer of a righteous person has great power and produces wonderful results (James 5:16). This is the way of God's Kingdom. Everyone is qualified to be a champion and rescue others through our prayers.

Ultimately, man couldn't save himself, so Isaiah predicts again, hundreds of years in advance, the coming of Jesus. Jesus came as our Champion to destroy the works of the enemy (1 Jn. 3:8). He came to set captives free (Luke 4:18). As Jesus has ascended to His place at the right hand of the Father, we are empowered as intercessors to put on our holy armor (Eph. 6:10-18) and change the world through prayer.

DAY 148
Isaiah 59:18-21

18 He will repay his enemies for their evil deeds.

His fury will fall on his foes.

He will pay them back even to the ends of the earth.

19 In the west, people will respect the name of the Lord;

in the east, they will glorify him.

For he will come like a raging flood tide driven by the breath of the Lord.

Someday, accounts will be settled, and God will reconcile all things. Justice will come to those who have been oppressed. Even a lifetime of suffering will seem but a moment compared to eternity. God will bring judgment to those who reject Him. He will give them what they desire: separation and isolation from His presence. Only those who exalt Yahweh and pursue Him will spend eternity fulfilling that desire. To those who love Him, God will come to their aid like a flood, washing away their enemies.

Jesus became that flood that broke into this world to bring God's Kingdom rule to all who will receive it. He came in the name of His Father, Yahweh, driven by the breath or spirit, representing the Holy Spirit. The Holy Trinity of God came to rescue us and invite us into their perfect union.

When we walk in this union with Jesus, the same Holy Spirit that directed and empowered Jesus dwells in us. We are to be conduits of that power to a broken world. Jesus promised that rivers of living water would spring up and overflow from our lives to reveal God's love (John 7:38).

Prayer: Father, fill and saturate us with your presence so that we overflow and your love spills out to everyone around us today.

> 20 "The Redeemer will come to Jerusalem to buy back those in Israel
>
> who have turned from their sins," says the Lord.
>
> 21 "And this is my covenant with them," says the Lord. "My Spirit will not leave them, and neither will these words I have given you. They will be on your lips and on the lips of your children and your children's children forever. I, the Lord, have spoken!

Isaiah once again points to the future when Jesus, our Redeemer, will come to free the people who desire Him. In the book of Ruth, we see Boaz as the Kinsman-Redeemer who rescues Ruth. This theme throughout the Old Testament is the anticipation of God coming to rescue His people.

Jesus inaugurates a New Covenant through His death. He saves us and dwells within us with the Holy Spirit. Under the Old Covenant, the Holy Spirit would come upon people, give them words to speak or empower them for a moment, but He could not dwell in them because of their sinful nature. Now that Jesus has redeemed us through His sacrifice for our sins on the cross, we have the Holy Spirit dwelling in us continually (1 John 2:27).

God promises His word will always be available to us for generations. We teach our descendants to be sensitive to the voice of the Holy Spirit and not rebel against God.

What if we valued God's leading so that we wouldn't move or make decisions without hearing from Him? Or, if we wouldn't speak unless we sensed He was giving us the words to say?

Let's take every opportunity to be empowered by the indwelling presence of God and speak His words.

DAY 149
Isaiah 60:1-4

"Arise, Jerusalem! Let your light shine for all to see.

For the glory of the Lord rises to shine on you.

2 Darkness as black as night covers all the nations of the earth,

but the glory of the Lord rises and appears over you.

3 All nations will come to your light;

mighty kings will come to see your radiance.

Isaiah launches into the final movement of this beautiful prophetic symphony. He describes the glory of God that radiates to us and through us. God's glory is His presence on display. We experience God's glory when we worship to the point of being in awe at the sense of His presence with us, or when the peace of God overwhelms us and our focus is solely on Him rather than the noise and distractions of this world.

Isaiah describes this glory, or manifest presence of God, 23 times in the last six chapters of his book. Even though darkness surrounds us, God's Shekinah, or glory, penetrates wherever we are with light. We then reflect His light.

Our Moon has no light source of its own but can only reflect the light of the Sun. In the same way, we absorb and reflect God's glory. Jesus came to reveal God's glory. He calls us to display what it means to walk in the light of God's presence. People are drawn to the light when they see God's glory reflected in us.

> "You are the light of the world—like a city on a hilltop that cannot be hidden. Matthew 5:14 NLT

> 4 "Look and see, for everyone is coming home!

> Your sons are coming from distant lands;

> your little daughters will be carried home.

We live in a time when we are flooded with negative news and opinions. Even if we try to ignore what is being reported in the media, we still have social media and conversations with people that focus on all the imminent bad happenings and disasters. If the environment or some plague doesn't kill us, then AI robots probably will.

Isaiah calls us to lift our eyes higher. See the world from where Christ has seated us with Him at the right hand of God. See what God is doing. This raises our faith to pray more significant prayers that have an eternal effect on people's lives. We're to call sons and daughters, biological and spiritual, who are far from God to come home to Him. Rather than worry about their political views or how many tattoos they have, our focus is joined with Jesus on their hearts. We pray the Holy Spirit will draw them so they become the next generation of the church.

John Wimber always challenged us in the Vineyard to see where God is at work and join Him there. God is working in every generation. We can either criticize them or see them with eyes of love and compassion, see opportunities to pray and connect and invite them into our homes and hearts. This is what enabled the Jesus Movement in the 1970s to reach thousands of young adults.

Let's partner with God in loving this generation and bringing it into a relationship with Jesus.

DAY 150
Isaiah 60:5-9

5 Your eyes will shine, and your heart will thrill with joy,

for merchants from around the world will come to you.

They will bring you the wealth of many lands.

6 Vast caravans of camels will converge on you,

the camels of Midian and Ephah.

The people of Sheba will bring gold and frankincense

and will come worshiping the Lord.

7 The flocks of Kedar will be given to you,

and the rams of Nebaioth will be brought for my altars.

I will accept their offerings, and I will make my Temple glorious.

There is debate regarding whom Isaiah is describing and in what period this portion of the prophecy applies. The good news is that Isaiah reveals more of our God's amazingly generous nature. Whatever timeframe this applies reveals blessings and resources being poured out to His people. Because God is unchanging, we can draw from Isaiah the truth that all we need of His love and favor is available because of God's generosity.

God would never spoil or corrupt us as His children. I do believe He looks for those who will hold His gifts loosely and see them as a tool to extend His love. Someone said, "There are plenty of resources in the world for everyone's needs but not for everyone's greed."

How we handle money says so much about our trust in God. This is why Jesus often used money and stewardship as a measure of devotion. When we think the resources in our hands are ours rather than God's, we think of ourselves first. We will hoard, protect, and value things more than people.

In this passage, God appeals to us to grasp how generous He is toward His people. If we live open-handed like God, then He can entrust us with more resources to pass through us to bless others. We, in turn, gain the true joy of seeing lives changed through generosity.

8 "And what do I see flying like clouds to Israel, like doves to their nests?

9 They are ships from the ends of the earth,

from lands that trust in me, led by the great ships of Tarshish.

They are bringing the people of Israel home from far away,

carrying their silver and gold.

They will honor the Lord your God,

the Holy One of Israel, for he has filled you with splendor.

It's difficult for us to comprehend God's love for us. We live in a world of limited resources, so we are taught to be frugal and not waste anything. Extravagance is seen as more of a sin than a virtue. Even love tends to be conditional and measured out. After all, we don't want to spoil someone we love.

God operates on a completely different set of values. He lavished love on His people. His grace is endless, and His love is boundless. Jesus proved this by going as far as one can go to express love by giving His life for us so we could draw even closer to God as sons and daughters.

We are God's temple or dwelling place. Look in these verses how God speaks of adding "more glory to His glorious temple." This speaks of God revealing more of Himself to us, filling our lives with His joy, peace, and power. The God of endless resources is a God of love looking for temples He can fill.

We must not put stops on God or filter His love. As we embrace more of God, others are drawn to His presence, which overflows from our lives. This is how the Kingdom of God grows.

Let's open our lives to all God wants to impart to us.

DAY 151
Isaiah 60:10-14

10 "Foreigners will come to rebuild your towns,

and their kings will serve you.

For though I have destroyed you in my anger,

I will now have mercy on you through my grace.

11 Your gates will stay open day and night

to receive the wealth of many lands.

The kings of the world will be led as captives in a victory procession.

12 For the nations that refuse to serve you will be destroyed.

The power of covenant is on display in these verses. Because God is a covenant keeper, His grace and kindness will always exceed punishment for our failures. The favor of God is mentioned as a work of God to cause others to bless us at His direction. We may not have done anything to deserve it, but God compels someone to prefer us. This may apply to a career position, special access others do not have, or a place of influence that seems beyond what we could ever reach on our own.

God takes delight in opening doors, making His children look better than they are, and allowing them to receive more than they deserve; that is favor from being in covenant with God.

If our minds begin to race toward wealth, power, and popularity, we have missed the point, and God will withdraw His favor to keep us from corrupting ourselves.

It is usually the humblest people who walk in Divine favor and barely notice God's blessings until later. They live simply to love God and obey Him. They trust He will be faithful to do the supernatural work and take care of them along the way.

13 "The glory of Lebanon will be yours—

the forests of cypress, fir, and pine—to beautify my sanctuary.

My Temple will be glorious!

14 The descendants of your tormentors

will come and bow before you.

Those who despised you will kiss your feet.

> They will call you the City of the Lord,
>
> and Zion of the Holy One of Israel.

Some Bible scholars see this section of Isaiah's writing as representing the throne Jesus will establish in Jerusalem for 1,000 years. Others see it as Jesus' permanent throne when He returns. These issues can be debated, but what is most critical is the fact that Jesus will return and reign forever, and every enemy will be defeated, and every knee will humbly bow and acknowledge Jesus truly is the Son of God and Lord Supreme.

The good news for us today is that God is doing this work spiritually in us. He is shaping us into His image. He is beautifying our lives and giving us favor. He is even capable of making peace between us and our enemies.

The more we look like Jesus, the more people are drawn to Christ in us. People see a change in us when we allow God to mold us into His image. Let Jesus remodel your life, and the world will be blessed by Christ in you.

DAY 152

Isaiah 60:15-18

15 "Though you were once despised and hated,

with no one traveling through you,

I will make you beautiful forever, a joy to all generations.

16 Powerful kings and mighty nations

will satisfy your every need,

as though you were a child nursing at the breast of a queen.

You will know at last that I, the Lord,

am your Savior and your Redeemer, the Mighty One of Israel.

Doesn't everyone want a hero like this? To think the God of all creation takes a rejected and undesirable person, like you and I, and makes us majestic.

Isaiah, of course, is painting this prophetic picture of the future city of Jerusalem and the nation of Israel. He also describes the work of Jesus, who was rejected and despised for our sake when He took our sins on the Cross. This also means Isaiah points to citizens of God's Kingdom like you and me today. We become a source of joy as we carry God's love and display His power to the nations.

Everything in scripture points forward to eternity. What we live in now is a taste of that eternal Kingdom. We experience a more profound sense of God's presence in worship and see His power at work in answers to prayer. All of these ancient prophetic words and current experiences we have allowed us a taste of eternity. They are an invitation to know our Father, Yahweh, our Savior, our hero, and Redeemer, more intimately. To have this opportunity to know God in such a personal way begs the question, how or why would we ever feel insignificant?

17 I will exchange your bronze for gold,

your iron for silver, your wood for bronze, and your stones for iron.

I will make peace your leader and righteousness your ruler.

18 Violence will disappear from your land;

the desolation and destruction of war will end.

Salvation will surround you like city walls,

and praise will be on the lips of all who enter there.

God's blessing is always far greater than what we can accomplish through our efforts. Our work to gain wealth and peace always falls short. The world's system is heavy, full of stress, and fragile, but living in God's Kingdom and under His rule brings contentment and joy.

> The blessing of the LORD makes a person rich, and he adds no sorrow with it. Proverbs 10:22

By contrast, the person who lives independently from God and trusts in himself discovers that his hard work does not have the same benefits. In fact, he experiences the opposite.

> You have planted much but harvest little. You eat but are not satisfied. You drink but are still thirsty. You put on clothes but cannot keep warm. Your wages disappear as though you were putting them in pockets filled with holes! Haggai 1:6

Isaiah says our security, our protection, is in walls as strong as our salvation. If we live by faith in Christ, nothing can penetrate those walls. The only access for going in and out are gates of praise. What we allow in our lives is filtered through our worship and devotion to Jesus. God secures our walls, and we guard our gates.

DAY 153
Isaiah 60:19-22

19 "No longer will you need the sun to shine by day,

nor the moon to give its light by night,

for the Lord your God will be your everlasting light,

and your God will be your glory.

20 Your sun will never set; your moon will not go down.

For the Lord will be your everlasting light.

Your days of mourning will come to an end.

21 All your people will be righteous.

They will possess their land forever,

for I will plant them there with my own hands

in order to bring myself glory.

22 The smallest family will become a thousand people,

and the tiniest group will become a mighty nation.

At the right time, I, the Lord, will make it happen."

The beauty of the New Heavens and the New Earth is revealed to Isaiah. To be present with God is to experience His light, His glory. Dwelling in perfection and being perfectly loved. No more sadness, pain, or fear for eternity.

How difficult and distant this seems to us when we struggle through life. This is our hope. We can experience it now to the degree we draw close to God. He is with us in our sadness and pain, offering comfort and healing.

We grow in faith from the tender sapling into a mighty Oak. Notice that God does this work by His hand; he will accomplish His will in our lives. Our part is to embrace God's plans and cooperate with how He is working in us.

DAY 154
Isaiah 61:1-3

The Spirit of the Sovereign Lord is upon me,

for the Lord has anointed me to bring good news to the poor.

He has sent me to comfort the brokenhearted

and to proclaim that captives will be released

and prisoners will be freed.

This is a familiar passage because Jesus quotes these words from Isaiah during His first public message in Nazareth (Luke 4:16–21). It begins with the Holy Spirit being present, surrounding, and deeply integrated into the life of this coming Messiah. This is unique because the Holy Spirit would "come upon" people to prophesy or release miracles under the Old Covenant. Under the New Covenant, the Holy Spirit continually dwells in us.

> But you have received the Holy Spirit, and he lives within you… 1 Jn. 2:27a

Jesus will walk in this Messianic role and announce that day in the synagogue that it is a time of Jubilee (Lev. 25). This means all indentured slaves are to be freed and debts canceled. The Jews saw this as an economic restoration. Jesus saw it as a spiritual restoration of relationship with the Father. This is why it is such good news.

The poor represent anyone who realizes they are empty spiritually and hungering to fill their life with God.

> "God blesses those who are poor and realize their need for him, for the Kingdom of Heaven is theirs. Matt. 5:3

Jesus came to bring light into a world of spiritual darkness. He is still doing that today through the same Holy Spirit leading and shining through us. If we have been freed, our task is to be lights that lead others out of darkness into the light of Christ's grace and freedom.

> 2 He has sent me to tell those who mourn
>
> that the time of the Lord's favor has come,
>
> and with it, the day of God's anger against their enemies.
>
> 3 To all who mourn in Israel,
>
> he will give a crown of beauty for ashes,
>
> a joyous blessing instead of mourning,

festive praise instead of despair.

> In their righteousness, they will be like great oaks
>
> that the Lord has planted for his own glory.

How beautifully accurate Isaiah describes Jesus' ministry. No one in all history has fulfilled anything like Isaiah describes. Jesus comes and simultaneously brings a message of grace and hope while destroying the enemy's work. He demonstrates the power and wisdom of God by tenderly touching the poor and breaking authority while confronting the religious.

Isaiah predicts this new season or era will be called the "last days." This period is when the Kingdom of God breaks in and reverses the effect of a fallen world and sin. It is the era of the Church where the intimate connection between God and His sons and daughters is restored. This is the period in which we get to live.

Don't miss the effect Jesus has on people. He doesn't just patch them up; He renews and fills them. They move from one extreme, such as sorrow represented by ashes, to becoming a beautiful bouquet, from heaviness and tears to joy. Such wonderful contrasts.

This also has a powerful effect as people Jesus touches become Mighty Oaks of Righteousness. They have experienced something so deep it has transformed their faith into something solid and unshakeable.

The more we encounter God, the deeper our roots go into Him, and the stronger we become. God has planted us to be a living display of His presence and glory. Guided by the Holy Spirit, we bring the same transforming power to others.

DAY 155
Isaiah 61:4-7

4 They will rebuild the ancient ruins, repairing cities destroyed long ago.

They will revive them, though they have been deserted for many generations.

5 Foreigners will be your servants.

They will feed your flocks and plow your fields and tend your vineyards.

Isaiah saw the destruction of Jerusalem, the captivity in Babylon, the release and return under King Cyrus, and the restoration of Jerusalem and the Temple. He also got a glimpse of the Messiah who would come and liberate the people and rebuild Israel into a mighty nation. This last part was probably the most difficult for Isaiah to grasp. The Jews had long believed since the time of Solomon that God would raise up a Messianic figure like David. Though it was prophesied, they could not imagine God Himself coming to earth in the form of a child. They also could not grasp the idea of a spiritual Kingdom versus a physical one.

What Jesus came to rebuild were lives, who would spiritually revitalize neighborhoods, cities, and nations. We have watched this happen throughout history as spiritual awakening and revivals have changed cities and nations. We've recently revisited one of these awakenings in the Jesus Movement, which is documented in the movie "Jesus Revolution. "

These times of encountering God begin in individuals or small groups, where God draws so close that His presence is undeniable. Recently, word got out, and 100,000 people descended on Wilmore, KY, because God is coming close to hungry students at Asbury Seminary.

Isaiah sees the Kingdom thriving to the point where God's blessing is so great He provides resources and workers to carry out the daily tasks so the people of God can minister to Him. This is what happened in the Jesus Movement. Many mainline churches are experiencing a decline in attendance, and resources have opened their doors to thousands of young people who need a place to gather and worship.

I believe we desperately need another encounter in which God's desire meets people's hunger and the church is revived.

> 6 You will be called priests of the Lord, ministers of our God.

> You will feed on the treasures of the nations and boast in their riches.

> 7 Instead of shame and dishonor, you will enjoy a double share of honor.

> You will possess a double portion of prosperity in your land, and everlasting joy will be yours.

Isaiah continues his description of God's blessings, which He will pour out on His children. Even though they have rebelled against God and gone their own way, He is willing to restore them. He also makes them priests. Remember, in the Old Testament, only descendants of the tribe of Levi could be priests. This points to the New Testament, where we all become a kingdom of priests (Rev. 1:6, 5:10).

Why is this important? First, only Priests could enter the Holy Place within the Temple, so they had access to the very presence of God. Secondly, they had two responsibilities: to go to God on behalf of the people, hear from God, and take a word back to them. This is fulfilled today in our ministry of prayer and prophecy.

We pray for those in need as the Holy Spirit guides us in what to pray. Then we hear a word from God and take this to the people to encourage (1 Cor. 14:1-2).

In addition, we hear in Isaiah the promise Jesus will add to this blessing: If we seek Him and His Kingdom and put serving Him before everything else, He will meet our needs and fill us with double the joy and contentment of any momentary pleasure in this world (Matt. 6:33).

Why would we doubt or not take advantage of this incredible opportunity to know God and receive all this from His hand now and for all eternity?

DAY 156

Isaiah 61:8-11

8 "For I, the Lord, love justice.

I hate robbery and wrongdoing.

I will faithfully reward my people for their suffering

and make an everlasting covenant with them.

9 Their descendants will be recognized and honored among the nations.

Everyone will realize that they are a people the Lord has blessed."

10 I am overwhelmed with joy in the Lord my God!

For he has dressed me with the clothing of salvation

and draped me in a robe of righteousness.

I am like a bridegroom dressed for his wedding or a bride with her jewels.

11 The Sovereign Lord will show his justice to the nations of the world.

Everyone will praise him!

His righteousness will be like a garden in early spring,

with plants springing up everywhere.

In addition to giving His life for our sins on the Cross, Jesus takes us as His bride. Laying down His life for us is such an incredible act of mercy and grace. We who are undeserving of God's grace receive it just because we are loved unconditionally. To be loved so deeply that we are made a perfect bride, beautifully pure and righteous, is overwhelming.

These prophetic pictures are almost too much to take in. Maybe this is why stories like Cinderella resonate with us. The idea of someone broken down by life, who is not a royal or someone of high birth, would be chosen to be the bride of the God of the universe. Our only response is unrestrained worship from the joy spilling out because it is impossible to contain. This is the root of our worship. The knowledge of what Christ has done radiates through our minds. We meditate on how unbelievable this all seems, yet it's true.

Can you imagine the world's impact if Christians really believed this truth? It is worth taking time to stop and meditate on who we are in Christ and letting this generate a fresh expression of worship to Yahweh.

DAY 157
Isaiah 62:1-5

Because I love Zion, I will not keep still.

Because my heart yearns for Jerusalem,

I cannot remain silent. I will not stop praying for her

until her righteousness shines like the dawn,

and her salvation blazes like a burning torch.

2 The nations will see your righteousness.

World leaders will be blinded by your glory.

Isaiah responds to all of the incredible ways God has described His love and intervention for His covenant children, Israel. But Isaiah also sees Israel's current condition. They are rebellious against God and, as a result, are broken and lost. Isaiah has perceived what they can be and what God will do if they only take a step toward Him. All Isaiah can do at this point is intercede in prayer. He must stand between the Israelites and their destruction.

Sometimes, we see in others what they cannot see in themselves. A rebellious or wounded heart that is more dangerous than they realize. Maybe they are ignoring the potential we see in them. Intercession is intervening when we may not be able to confront someone. It is a way of gaining insight into what is happening in them. The Holy Spirit will show us issues at the root of their problems.

There is a way to pray for someone even though our prayers may not seem effective. Do what Isaiah does. He keeps the outcome before him. He keeps before him a picture where he sees Israel completely transformed into God's image and walking with Him in a close relationship. That is how to intercede and stay in faith until what we pray for becomes a reality.

> And you will be given a new name by the Lord's own mouth.
>
> 3 The Lord will hold you in his hand for all to see—
>
> a splendid crown in the hand of God.
>
> 4 Never again will you be called "The Forsaken City" or "The Desolate Land."
>
> Your new name will be "The City of God's Delight" and "The Bride of God,"
>
> for the Lord delights in you and will claim you as his bride.
>
> 5 Your children will commit themselves to you, O Jerusalem,

> just as a young man commits himself to his bride.

> Then God will rejoice over you as a bridegroom rejoices over his bride.

This picture of being the bride of God certainly foreshadows Jesus' statements about Himself being the bridegroom (Matt. 9:15). Paul describes the church as the bride of Christ in Eph. 5:25-32. The culmination of this era and the entrance into the New Heavens and Earth is celebrated as a wedding feast (Rev. 19:7; 21:1-2).

This language can be a little challenging for men to grasp. We don't look at marriage and love the same way a woman can imagine her wedding day. Men have difficulty focusing on intimacy without it, leading to physical connection. A woman can embrace emotional intimacy much more deeply. Of course, our marriage will be richer than any physical or emotional connection. It will be a spiritual union that is so amazing that it will blow our romanticized pictures away.

What I take from this passage and the references in the New Testament is there is so much more of God's love for us to experience. I know God is taking delight in me and can't wait to show me what He has prepared for all of us as we come together in perfect union.

Our current task is to tell others of this wonderful God who is crazy in love with us and preparing for an eternity of perfection and beauty. He wants everyone there. That is the Good News of the Gospel.

DAY 158
Isaiah 62:6-9

6 O Jerusalem, I have posted watchmen on your walls;

they will pray day and night, continually.

Take no rest, all you who pray to the Lord.

7 Give the Lord no rest until he completes his work,

until he makes Jerusalem the pride of the earth.

Prayer reminds God of His promises. It is not that He forgets, but we do. We get caught up in our fears and pain. We get distracted by a world that does not live in union with God. We must remind ourselves of His love and power to intervene in our lives.

Jesus always admired, or as the Gospels state, "He marveled" at people's faith (Matthew 8:5-13; Mark 6:1-6). Jesus never rebuked anyone for having too much faith. Hebrews tells us, "Without faith, it is impossible to please God (Hebrews 11:6)."

The Father loves it when we pray big prayers, hold tight to His promises, and continually look to God rather than worry over our circumstances. As we remind God, we are reinforcing God's truth while simultaneously submitting to His will.

The best approach for me is to pause and ask God what He desires to do. Then, I ask the Holy Spirit to lead me through God's Word to reveal the faith foundation for my prayers. I pray with more faith or confidence when my request is based on a promise He has directed me to.

> 8 The Lord has sworn to Jerusalem by his own strength:
>
> "I will never again hand you over to your enemies.
>
> Never again will foreign warriors come
>
> and take away your grain and new wine.
>
> 9 You raised the grain, and you will eat it,
>
> praising the Lord.
>
> Within the courtyards of the Temple,
>
> you yourselves will drink the wine you have pressed."

When God makes a promise, He backs it up with His word and His power. He stops the enemy from stealing what He has provided for us. This is why the festivals were so important to the Israelites. They would gather their harvest and offer the first portion or first fruits to God. They would give these offerings with praise and thanksgiving, acknowledging that it was because of God's blessing that they prospered.

As with any promise of blessing from God, our responsibility is to worship Him with the first portion of His provision for us. This is why we honor God from our income today and return the first portion to Him.

Giving our offerings to God keeps us from becoming selfish and somehow thinking we created these resources exclusively ours. This only invites the enemy in to steal from us. This is why so many people who claim to follow Jesus find themselves broke and struggling.

Put God first, and He will see to your harvest, and you will be able to enjoy it in peace and feast on new grain and new wine. The new grain also represents insights and truth revealed from God's Word. The new wine represents the Holy Spirit. As we put Jesus first, we experience God's revelation and are empowered.

DAY 159
Isaiah 62:10-12

10 Go out through the gates!

Prepare the highway for my people to return!

Smooth out the road; pull out the boulders;

raise a flag for all the nations to see.

11 The Lord has sent this message to every land:

"Tell the people of Israel, 'Look, your Savior is coming.

See, he brings his reward with him as he comes.'"

12 They will be called "The Holy People"

and "The People Redeemed by the Lord."

And Jerusalem will be known as "The Desirable Place"

and "The City No Longer Forsaken."

Isaiah's prophecy covers the period from 150 years before Israel's captivity to the coming of Jesus to the very end of this age, culminating in the return of Christ.

When Jesus returns, one of His first symbolic acts will be to enter Jerusalem through the Eastern Gate. This Gate was walled in by Muslims years ago as if some stones could stop the one who created the stones. In passing through this Gate, Jesus fulfills His promise to reign from Jerusalem and make "all things new" (Rev. 21:5).

You hear the cry of God's heart coming through these words to the church today. Preparing a smooth path for the nations to come to God is our first and foremost mission. Our message is to point to Jesus as the one who is our Deliverer. He is returning with rewards but also judgment.

We are God's Holy people, redeemed, and the ones whom God loves. This is our life now and for eternity. Our assurance of God's love motivates us to tell others they can experience this love, too.

DAY 160
Isaiah 63:1-6

Who is this who comes from Edom,

from the city of Bozrah, with his clothing stained red?

Who is this in royal robes, marching in his great strength?

"It is I, the Lord, announcing your salvation!

It is I, the Lord, who has the power to save!"

Isaiah begins this chapter with a question. God answers the question as to who He is and what He is doing. Bozrah is believed by some scholars to be the capital city of Edom, a people who always contended with Israel. Others see Edom as a symbol of all the nations that rebelled against Israel and God. It typifies spiritual warfare between good and evil and the battle we face to follow God or go our own way.

It is important to note that God overcomes this enemy. Whether in breaking down every opposing Kingdom when He returns (Rev. 11:15), or His ultimate destruction of Satan (Rev. 20:10), all of the enemies of God and His people will be defeated.

Today, God wants to enforce Jesus' victory on the Cross. He is ready to defeat those spiritual enemies that seek to distract and turn us away from God. He is our champion, with power and might greater than any temptation if we only trust Him.

> 2 Why are your clothes so red, as if you have been treading out grapes?
>
> 3 "I have been treading the winepress alone; no one was there to help me.
>
> In my anger I have trampled my enemies as if they were grapes.
>
> In my fury I have trampled my foes.
>
> Their blood has stained my clothes.
>
> 4 For the time has come for me to avenge my people, to ransom them from their oppressors.
>
> 5 I was amazed to see that no one intervened to help the oppressed.
>
> So I myself stepped in to save them with my strong arm, and my wrath sustained me.

6 I crushed the nations in my anger and made them stagger and fall to the ground,

spilling their blood upon the earth."

This isn't one of those passages you read to your children before bed at night. It describes a gruesome scene of vengeance. But what is being communicated? Is this God pouring out His wrath on people? I believe God communicates through Isaiah's words what Jesus accomplished for us in His sacrificial death. He took on Himself our sins and, therefore, God's punishment for sin. This is why He calls it "my redeeming work". Jesus did this on His own with no support as His disciples fled at His arrest and crucifixion. The people who walked by Him hanging there on the cross hurled insults and rejected Him. Yet, all His suffering was for them.

There is also a picture of Jesus defeating nations and kingdoms. Jesus redeemed us and came to destroy the enemy's works (1 Jn. 3:8). He did it all. He set us free from sin and the control of Satan (Eph. 2:1-5).

So, rather than retribution, this is a picture of redeeming love.

DAY 161
Isaiah 63:7-10

7 I will tell of the Lord's unfailing love.

I will praise the Lord for all he has done.

I will rejoice in his great goodness to Israel,

which he has granted according to his mercy and love.

8 He said, "They are my very own people.

Surely they will not betray me again."

And he became their Savior.

9 In all their suffering he also suffered,

and he personally rescued them.

In his love and mercy he redeemed them.

He lifted them up and carried them through all the years.

10 But they rebelled against him and grieved his Holy Spirit.

So he became their enemy and fought against them.

Once again, Isaiah contrasts God's faithfulness with Israel's rebellion. This truth applies to every generation and people throughout time. God's "endless love" is described and celebrated. The Hebrew word is "hesed". This word is so full of meaning it is hard to capture the depth of love it represents. Hesed has been translated as loving-kindness, steadfast, unconditional, endless, and covenantal love. The New Testament equivalent is "agape." This is the God kind of love that never abandons or turns away from us. It is endless and abundant, undeserved and lavished upon us.

When we are hurt, God is there. He comforts and saves us by carrying us through every difficult circumstance. The Angel of His Presence is Jesus. God Himself shows up when we face a crisis. He may show up in the form of a friend, a pastor, or anyone through whom He can display His compassion.

Amid this outpouring of God's love, His people can still rebel. They can turn their backs on God, choose their way, and blame God for their problems. This "grieving of the Holy Spirit" refuses God's love, and in their minds, they make God the enemy as they idolize themselves. This is what happened to Ananias and Sapphira in Acts 5. The more we rebel against God, the more distant we become and the more deformed the image of God becomes of us (Heb. 6:4-6).

What a contrast in choices. We can humbly receive God's "hesed" and live an "abundant life" (John 10:10), or we can reject God's love, choosing a path that only leads to destruction.

DAY 162

Isaiah 63:11-16

11 Then they remembered those days of old

when Moses led his people out of Egypt.

They cried out, "Where is the one who brought Israel through the sea,

with Moses as their shepherd?

Where is the one who sent his Holy Spirit

to be among his people?

12 Where is the one whose power was displayed

when Moses lifted up his hand—

the one who divided the sea before them,

making himself famous forever?

13 Where is the one who led them through the bottom of the sea?

They were like fine stallions

racing through the desert, never stumbling.

14 As with cattle going down into a peaceful valley,

the Spirit of the Lord gave them rest.

You led your people, Lord,

and gained a magnificent reputation."

Our God is consistent in character and timeless in power. What He did in the past, He can and will do again. It took the Jewish people going back to read the miracles God did on behalf of their Israelite ancestors in the past to stir faith in them now.

I picture the people being gathered and the priests reading from Moses' account of the Exodus, how God passed over the homes where He saw the blood applied to the door frames, how he delivered the people and blew a path through the Red Sea that swallowed their enemies, how God led them with the cloud and pillar of fire. He provided manna and water from the rock and protected them through their wilderness journey.

As the people revisit these stories, their faith grows, and they begin to ask one another, why can't God do this today? Why can't He deliver us?

This renewed faith forms their prayer of petition. God, deliver us as you did the Israelites in the past. We are your people, and we trust you, Holy Spirit, to lead us to a place of peace and rest. He leads us out of struggling to trust in His leading.

Prayer for Mercy and Pardon

15 Lord, look down from heaven;

look from your holy, glorious home, and see us.

Where is the passion and the might

you used to show on our behalf?

Where are your mercy and compassion now?

16 Surely you are still our Father!

Even if Abraham and Jacob would disown us,

> Lord, you would still be our Father.

> You are our Redeemer from ages past.

One of the great truths Jesus came to reveal was the Father heart of God. The Jewish religious leaders criticized him for calling God His Father. Yet, 750 years before Jesus is incarnated in human flesh, Isaiah cries out to God, calling Him Father. It is this Father's heart that Isaiah appeals to in prayer. This is not some stoic God unmoved by our requests. Isaiah had the revelation that God could be approached as a loving, compassionate father who would never ignore or turn from His children.

This is the same Father Jesus displays in His parable of the prodigal son. Luke 15 records Jesus' story of a rebellious son who comes to the end of Himself and humbly returns to his father. The father doesn't scold or shame him. Instead, the father embraces his son, restores his dignity, and then affirms him before everyone. We can approach this God with boldness (Heb. 4:16).

DAY 163
Isaiah 63:17-19

17 Lord, why have you allowed us to turn from your path?

Why have you given us stubborn hearts so we no longer fear you?

Return and help us, for we are your servants,

the tribes that are your special possession.

18 How briefly your holy people possessed your holy place,

and now our enemies have destroyed it.

19 Sometimes it seems as though we never belonged to you,

as though we had never been known as your people.

God's grace tolerates our rebellion and continues to love us. Isaiah is appealing to God to keep His people close to Him. This seems like an unusual request. Can you imagine a spouse saying, please keep me close to you because you know I want to pursue other lovers?

Yet, this was Israel's history and dilemma. They would devote themselves to God in a crisis and ignore Him when things were going okay. This is also the common pattern of man throughout history. There even seems to be a complaint in Isaiah's words that God is not doing enough. I have often confessed my weakness and asked God to surround me and fill me with His Spirit because I can get distracted from God's best for my life. I can get caught up in what I want or think I need and pursue those things instead of God. I believe Isaiah looks honestly at how easily the human heart can turn from God. He understands the stakes, and that there is too much to gamble away.

Prayers admitting our dependence on God are not weakness but wisdom.

DAY 164
Isaiah 64:1-5

Oh, that you would burst from the heavens and come down!

How the mountains would quake in your presence!

2 As fire causes wood to burn and water to boil,

your coming would make the nations tremble.

Then your enemies would learn the reason for your fame!

3 When you came down long ago,

you did awesome deeds beyond our highest expectations.

And oh, how the mountains quaked!

Isaiah has been allowed to see and communicate an entire timeline of human history, from the Exodus to Israel's return from captivity to Jesus's life and return reign.

Like Isaiah, we often wish God would come down and reveal Himself in a display of power that would humble people and leaders. This would certainly rock our world and cause a lot of sudden interest in religion. This, however, is not how God works in this season. We do have the promise of Jesus' return, and every person will witness Him in all His glory and fall to their knees in awe.

Until Jesus returns to reveal Himself globally, He is revealing Himself to us. He is setting our hearts ablaze. He is shaking us and wanting us to tremble in His presence.

Many times, I have prayed, Lord rend the Heavens, tear through any veil over my heart and flood my life with Your thoughts and dreams. I want to engage you fully and continually. I want to hear your voice, see where you are working, and join you there.

I wonder what would happen today if people claiming to be Christ's followers prayed this prayer and hungered for God's presence.

> 4 For since the world began,
>
> no ear has heard and no eye has seen a God like you,
>
> who works for those who wait for him!
>
> 5 You welcome those who gladly do good, who follow godly ways.
>
> But you have been very angry with us, for we are not godly.

DAY 164

> We are constant sinners; how can people like us be saved?

Isaiah is reminding the Israelites to consider everything God has done for them. From delivering them from Egypt to a parting of the Red Sea to miraculous provision and constant protection, God has been faithful. He did things way beyond their comprehension with perfect timing.

You also see our responsibility to live holy lives. When we cultivate good character and choose what is right over what is convenient, God meets us and does His supernatural work. Whenever we take a step toward God, He is always there to meet us.

Do we cherish God's ways? Do we long for Him? We are saved because of what Jesus did for us, but real life begins with our desire for His presence and choosing to walk His path.

DAY 165
Isaiah 64:6-7

6 We are all infected and impure with sin.

When we display our righteous deeds,

they are nothing but filthy rags.

Like autumn leaves, we wither and fall,

and our sins sweep us away like the wind.

7 Yet no one calls on your name

or pleads with you for mercy.

> Therefore, you have turned away from us
>
> and turned us over to our sins.

We live in a fallen world where man's selfishness has been corrupted. David said For I was born a sinner— yes, from the moment my mother conceived me (Psalm 51:5). If you ever wonder if this is true, spend a few hours with a toddler. You will see how selfish humans can be. A child will only think of themselves and choose to lie to cover their guilt. No one had to teach them it is hard-wired into them. This is how we come from the factory.

We love the story in Gen. 1:26-28 describing how man was made in God's image, which is certainly true for Adam and Eve. But not for us. If you read a few chapters later, after the fall, Genesis 5 tells us, When Adam had lived 130 years, he fathered a son in his likeness, after his image, and named him Seth (Genesis 5:3). No longer the image of God. Still, now humanity was to be made in the image of a fallen man.

This is why we need to be born again. We needed Jesus, who would sacrifice His life to pay the penalty for our sins, make a new creation, and become spiritually alive (see Eph. 2:1-6).

God is not impressed by our religious activities or self-righteousness. Isaiah calls us, "fallen leaves". Jesus warned His disciples to stay connected to Him as branches must be sustained through attachment to the vine (John 15).

God draws near to the humble, those who know they need a Savior and who live moment by moment nourished by a life-giving attachment to God.

DAY 166
Isaiah 64:8-12

And yet, O Lord, you are our Father.

We are the clay, and you are the potter.

We all are formed by your hand.

9 Don't be so angry with us, Lord.

Please don't remember our sins forever.

Look at us, we pray, and see that we are all your people.

10 Your holy cities are destroyed.

DAY 166

> Zion is a wilderness; yes, Jerusalem is a desolate ruin.
>
> 11 The holy and beautiful Temple
>
> where our ancestors praised you
>
> has been burned down, and all the things of beauty are destroyed.
>
> 12 After all this, Lord, must you still refuse to help us?
>
> Will you continue to be silent and punish us?

This timeless wrestling with surrender to God is displayed here in the Israelites. They realize they are clay in God's hands, and He can shape them any way He wishes. The question they face is, can they willingly submit to God and trust His work in them?

We want God's blessing, yet we struggle with obedience and devotion. It seems the people here have come to the end of themselves. Their cities and lives are in ruins. They are without resources and desperately crying out to God in repentance. They have abused their creative potential, for which God formed them. Yet, they are searching for undeserved mercy, a New Covenant concept Jesus will establish.

No longer does God's judgment hang over those who have been forgiven and received new life in Christ. But we can still wreck our lives and ignore or mismanage the gifts God has given us. He is the Master Potter who crafts beautiful lives when we place ourselves on the wheel and allow God to shape us into the unique image of Himself.

DAY 167

Isaiah 55:1-5

The Lord says,

"I was ready to respond, but no one asked for help.

I was ready to be found, but no one was looking for me.

I said, 'Here I am, here I am!'

to a nation that did not call on my name.

2 All day long I opened my arms to a rebellious people.

But they follow their own evil paths and their own crooked schemes.

The Apostle Paul quotes this first verse verbatim in Romans 10. He sees God extending the mission of the church to Gentiles as the fulfillment of this prophetic declaration by Isaiah. Repeating a phrase more than once was the ancient way to add emphasis, like an exclamation mark. When God says, "Here I am" twice, He is stressing how desirous He is to receive people outside of Judaism.

The Israelites fell into the trap of taking God's presence and leading for granted. Yet, God still graciously reached out to His people. So we see God extending His love to everyone, including those who are unaware they are sinners and even to those who willfully sin. He is always standing with open arms to receive anyone who humbly turns and surrenders to Him.

What a beautiful view of God's grace hundreds of years prior to Jesus coming in flesh to display God's outstretched arms.

> 3 All day long they insult me to my face by worshiping idols in their sacred gardens.

> They burn incense on pagan altars.

> 4 At night they go out among the graves, worshiping the dead.

> They eat the flesh of pigs and make stews with other forbidden foods.

> 5 Yet they say to each other,

> 'Don't come too close or you will defile me!

> I am holier than you!'

> These people are a stench in my nostrils,
>
> an acrid smell that never goes away.

Hypocrisy is such a deceptive sin. We think of ourselves as healthy with good motives. As the saying goes, "We judge others by their actions and ourselves by our motives." The people God is addressing are those who are self-confident and have developed a religious view that justifies their views and confirms God into their image. They are untouchable in regards to anyone addressing weaknesses in their lives. Their blindness keeps them isolated from others for fear of being exposed as sinful.

God demands holiness, but He also has made us holy in Christ. Through His unconditional love, He has made us completely righteous. Our response is gratitude, honoring what Jesus has done. We can now live in relationship with others in the body of Christ and invite them to help us overcome the temptation to return to our old way of living.

DAY 168

Isaiah 55:6-10

6 "Look, my decree is written out in front of me:

I will not stand silent;

I will repay them in full!

Yes, I will repay them—

7 both for their own sins

and for those of their ancestors," says the Lord.

"For they also burned incense on the mountains

and insulted me on the hills.

I will pay them back in full!

Self-righteousness always presents man as more spiritual and less guilty of sins. Charles Spurgeon once preached on this passage and said, "If a man should willfully break the windows of your shop, I warrant you, you would not take it as an excuse if he pleaded, 'I did not break them all; I only smashed one sheet of plate glass.' Pleas that would not be mentioned in a human court are thought good enough to offer to God. O, the folly of our race!"

As we saw in the previous verses, God takes sin seriously. Under the Old Covenant, sins can be covered with an annual series of sacrifices. The constant threat of judgment was to be a deterrent to sinning. It did not bring the people closer to God. Jesus comes announcing a New Covenant. A covenant in which sin more than just being covered over, it would be washed away. The person who committed the sins was formerly spiritually dead and becomes spiritually alive as a new creation without sin (Rom. 6; Eph. 2). We now are drawn to God because of His grace and acceptance rather than being repelled by sin. Our sins of the past are no longer held against us.

This is the Good News Jesus came to reveal. Through His sacrifice, we are now sons and daughters of God and co-heirs with Christ (Rom. 8:17). This is our motivation of love to please God and live holy lives.

I think of all the small clusters of New Wine that are being established everywhere: home groups and prayer gatherings before work or school, teams that go out and care for the poor, or teams that travel to another nation to bring God's Good News. There is a blessing in joining these small groups of like-minded seekers of God who bless one another. God doesn't criticize these groups but applauds what they do to gather around Him and His mission.

Isaiah pictures the people of God settling in the mountains. Mountains or high places were always used by pagan religions as places of worship for idols. He sees these idols displaced by worshippers of the One True God.

God will bless His worshippers on the mountain and give them the valleys for their livestock and farms. In other words, God will care for those who seek Him and have no place in their lives for idols of any kind.

DAY 169
Isaiah 55:11-14

11 "But because the rest of you have forsaken the Lord

and have forgotten his Temple,

and because you have prepared feasts to honor the god of Fate

and have offered mixed wine to the god of Destiny,

12 now I will 'destine' you for the sword.

All of you will bow down before the executioner.

For when I called, you did not answer.

When I spoke, you did not listen.

You deliberately sinned—before my very eyes—

and chose to do what you know I despise."

Isaiah addresses the people who will be taken captive to Babylon when Jerusalem is conquered. Many of the people will be taken over 1,000 miles away to the nation of Babylon, where they will be reeducated and brainwashed in the Babylonian culture. This means worshiping the Babylonian gods like Gad and Meni described here. Imagine you have grown up around other farmers in the small community that is left of Jerusalem. Then you are taken to the biggest city in the world. You might be tempted to dive into the more modern culture and leave your culture and faith behind. An old expression during WW1 was, "Once they've seen Paris, you'll never get them back on the farm". This was the concern for the people of Israel.

We all face this kind of temptation in our day. It might be gambling or pornography or being consumed with shopping for things to impress others. All of these distractions are the draws of the gods who are drawing us away from God to bow down to them.

God says these things lead to our destruction. Even now, God calls us to Himself. He calls us to be different from this world's culture and seek Him rather than the latest trending thing and lure us away from Him.

Choose the eternal over the temporary. Choose an intimate relationship with God that will fill your life with joy, peace, and meaning.

13 Therefore, this is what the Sovereign Lord says:

"My servants will eat,

but you will starve.

My servants will drink,

but you will be thirsty.

My servants will rejoice,

but you will be sad and ashamed.

14 My servants will sing for joy,

but you will cry in sorrow and despair.

One of the most difficult characteristics of God that people struggle to comprehend is that He is holy and Lord over all creation. God sets the rules according to His desire and wisdom. While we celebrate God's grace and mercy, we tend to play down His holiness. It doesn't fit in a world where the personal pursuit of pleasure is the central focus of man.

This struggle comes from the misunderstanding that we attempt to be holy through our efforts rather than trusting God to make us holy. We are holy because God sets us apart as we lean into Him.

In these verses, Isaiah contrasts those who serve or place their trust in God versus those who rebel and go their way or pursue other gods. Just as a marriage is exclusive to one man and one woman, our relationship with Jesus has no place for any other gods. The person who wants God's grace must also embrace the exclusivity of a life set apart for God. We make poor gods, but when we submit to Jesus, He heals our broken hearts and fills us with gladness.

DAY 170
Isaiah 65:15-18

Your name will be a curse word among my people,

    for the Sovereign Lord will destroy you

    and will call his true servants by another name.

    16 All who invoke a blessing or take an oath

    will do so by the God of truth.

    For I will put aside my anger and forget the evil of earlier days.

The contrast between the righteous and the unrighteous goes beyond death. The legacy and memory of a Godly person will hold honor, but those who rejected God will be cursed and become a cautionary tale at best. It is a beautiful thought that our lives have the potential to speak to others beyond the grave and influence them to follow God.

God is called faithful. He is faithful in blessing His children and the source of all good things.

> Whatever is good and perfect is a gift coming down to us from God our Father, who created all the lights in the heavens. He never changes or casts a shifting shadow. James 1:17

God can be counted on to be good, faithful, and true because that is His nature. He will never go against the essence of who He is. You see this in His willingness to forgive and not hold anything from our past against us.

> 17 "Look! I am creating new heavens and a new earth,
>
> and no one will even think about the old ones anymore.
>
> 18 Be glad; rejoice forever in my creation! And look! I will create Jerusalem as a place of happiness.
>
> Her people will be a source of joy.

As Isaiah closes the last chapters of his book, he focuses on eternity. You see many of the same themes shared by the Apostle John in his Revelation.

God is not given to exaggeration. Therefore, when He says He is creating such a wonderful place for us, we will never think of earth as it is now. I hear people talking about taking their memories with them into eternity. How wonderful must the new heavens and earth be that we will have no interest in reminiscing about this portion of our lives? This is a difficult concept to grasp because this is the only world and life we know. I have a pretty good imagination, so to be beyond my comprehension for eternity blows my mind.

In the meantime, God invites us to be filled with joy. He offers us a taste of eternity in His presence now.

> You will show me the way of life, granting me the joy of your presence and the pleasures of living with you forever. Psalm 16:11

DAY 171

Isaiah 65:19-20

19 I will rejoice over Jerusalem and delight in my people.

And the sound of weeping and crying

will be heard in it no more.

20 "No longer will babies die when only a few days old.

No longer will adults die before they have lived a full life.

No longer will people be considered old at one hundred!

Only the cursed will die that young!

Isaiah seems to shift timeframes and discuss a time when the earth is restored, health is increased, and people will not be in distress. This could refer to the

Millennium view of a 1,000-year-old Christ, as some believe. It is a time when Satan is locked up, and Jesus rules on the earth and sets things in order.

In the Amillennial view, this could be a future restoration of the earth that could come through people turning to God for revival. We have seen cities and nations respond to the Gospel in such a way that crime was all but eliminated, thus relieving stress. Who knows? With continued progress in medicine, we are finding cures for many forms of infant death. Our medical advances now make it more common for people to live to one hundred and beyond.

How and when God brings this about is something we cannot know, but we can certainly pray for. We now have the privilege of walking in the blessings of God's Kingdom in obedience to Jesus' command to pray, "Thy Kingdom come, Thy will be done on the earth as it is in Heaven". We don't have to wait for revival, or a Millenium, or eternity, we can believe and see the Kingdom of God come into our lives and touch the world through us today.

DAY 172

Isaiah 65:21-25

21 In those days people will live in the houses they build

and eat the fruit of their own vineyards.

22 Unlike the past, invaders will not take their houses

and confiscate their vineyards.

For my people will live as long as trees,

and my chosen ones will have time to enjoy their hard-won gains.

23 They will not work in vain,

and their children will not be doomed to misfortune.

When reading prophetic scripture, we can complicate and miss the message by getting caught up in figuring out what future dates these promises apply. The good news is that we can look forward to Isaiah's description of our lifestyle under the reign of Christ when He returns.

As children of the Kingdom, we get a taste of this life now—an abundant life, as Jesus referred to it. These are promises we can pray and ask God for in this time before His return. We may not live in perfect peace and harmony, but God can certainly give us favor with others so that even our enemies see us at peace (Proverbs 16:7).

Ask God to highlight a promise such as these in scripture. It may be something He wants you to pray and believe for. Jesus never criticized anyone for too much faith. Why not believe Him for protecting our home, work, health, children, and grandchildren? God does not make these promises just for the future; they are to be believed now.

> For they are people blessed by the Lord,

> and their children, too, will be blessed.

> 24 I will answer them before they even call to me.

> While they are still talking about their needs,

> I will go ahead and answer their prayers!

> 25 The wolf and the lamb will feed together.

The lion will eat hay like a cow.

But the snakes will eat dust.

In those days no one will be hurt or destroyed on my holy mountain.

I, the Lord, have spoken!"

Isaiah goes back to the words God spoke almost exactly in Isaiah 11:6. After describing the Messiah (Jesus), he goes on to describe the world in which Christ will rule. There will be peace in every realm of the earth, peace between man and even animals. We will be so close to God that before we speak, He knows us so well that He will respond to us.

Notice the renewed earth will be similar to what God created in Eden. Genesis mentions animals as herbivores, so there was no death.

And I have given every green plant as food for all the wild animals, the birds in the sky, and the small animals that scurry along the ground—everything that has life." And that is what happened. Genesis 1:30

I guess you cannot improve on perfection. This renewed earth time will have one factor different from Eden: only sons and daughters who have given their lives to God will be there. Serpents will exist but not be influenced by Satan to tempt man. Ironically, the serpent will still crawl and eat what is in the dust, thus fulfilling God's promise in Genesis 3.

Living every day with this knowledge of eternity led the early church to proclaim "Maranatha!" meaning, "Our Lord is coming" (1 Cor. 16:22).

DAY 173

Isaiah 66:1-4

This is what the Lord says:

"Heaven is my throne,

and the earth is my footstool.

Could you build me a temple as good as that?

Could you build me such a resting place?

2 My hands have made both heaven and earth;

they and everything in them are mine.

I, the Lord, have spoken!

God is the omnipresent Creator of all existence. Every tiny molecule to billions of stars and galaxies is under his rule and domain. But there is a place where He has restricted Himself: the human heart. God will not force His way into our hearts. We must invite Him. When we invite God in, He comes to rule here as well. The beauty of humbling ourselves and inviting God to dwell in us is that we now dwell with Him. We become one, united together. We are made new and become children of God and Temples of His presence.

Before we become too arrogant because we can reject God and keep Him out of our lives, we must realize the consequences of our choices. There is no greater contrast in the world than a person who has embraced God and stands in awe of Him versus the one who sits on the throne of their little kingdom, thinking they are special. All they build in their kingdom will end in destruction and dust.

There is no wiser choice in this life than to be united with our Heavenly Father and to live the abundant life Jesus promised that extends into eternity.

"I will bless those who have humble and contrite hearts,

who tremble at my word.

3 But those who choose their own ways—

delighting in their detestable sins—

will not have their offerings accepted.

When such people sacrifice a bull,

it is no more acceptable than a human sacrifice.

When they sacrifice a lamb,

it's as though they had sacrificed a dog!

When they bring an offering of grain,

they might as well offer the blood of a pig.

When they burn frankincense,

it's as if they had blessed an idol.

4 I will send them great trouble—

all the things they feared.

For when I called, they did not answer.

When I spoke, they did not listen.

> They deliberately sinned before my very eyes
>
> and chose to do what they know I despise."

God does not play games and will not be deceived. What we may take lightly, God takes very sincerely. He knows how we can be manipulated and how it is in our humanity to think we are more holy than we are.

Thankfully, today, as believers, we live under a New Covenant in which Jesus made the once-and-for-all sacrifice. I believe God still cares about our motivation and heart posture when we come to Him.

If worship becomes more entertainment, and Bible study becomes a token act rather than seeking transformation, we are no different from the people who approached with their sacrifices out of duty rather than devotion.

We live humbly in God's presence, grateful for His grace. We seek revelation and life-changing truth. We desire to be shaped into His image and live to honor the God who saved us. This is the way to live free and fearless as followers of Jesus.

DAY 174
Isaiah 66:5-9

5 Hear this message from the Lord, all you who tremble at his words:

"Your own people hate you and throw you out for being loyal to my name.

'Let the Lord be honored!' they scoff.

'Be joyful in him!'

But they will be put to shame.

These words are to the religious people of the day who judged others based on outward expressions of others they deemed either righteous or unrighteous. They thought they were representing God, but in fact they were usurping God's role as Judge. Religious people who feel it is their responsibility to share their disagreements or disappointments with Christian leaders on social media use this same justification.

When the disciples mentioned to Jesus, that others were preaching in his name, they wanted Jesus to condemn them. Jesus instead said no. He knew criticism of a Christian leader could also sow seeds of distrust of other leaders. Going after the weeds was to risk pulling out wheat grains (see Matt. 13:24-43). We pray for leaders and trust God to lead His church. It doesn't mean we sit under someone we do not trust. We find a place and Christian leaders we can trust. This also means not criticizing or attacking another brother or sister in Christ.

This judgment is God's exclusive domain, and it is best left to Him. Jesus prays for us continually (Heb. 4:14-16). It would be wise to follow His example, pray for leaders in the church, and then let God build His church.

> 6 What is all the commotion in the city?
>
> What is that terrible noise from the Temple?
>
> It is the voice of the Lord
>
> taking vengeance against his enemies.
>
> 7 "Before the birth pains even begin,
>
> Jerusalem gives birth to a son.
>
> 8 Who has ever seen anything as strange as this?
>
> Who ever heard of such a thing?
>
> Has a nation ever been born in a single day?

Has a country ever come forth in a mere moment?

But by the time Jerusalem's birth pains begin,

her children will be born.

9 Would I ever bring this nation to the point of birth

and then not deliver it?" asks the Lord.

"No! I would never keep this nation from being born,"

says your God.

God can do in a moment what man can not accomplish in a lifetime. Here is the rebirth of Jerusalem after the seventy-year captivity in Babylon. One day, God moves on the heart of the Persian King Cyrus to release the Israelites and allow them to go back and rebuild the temple. Many accounts in the Bible indicate God delivering His people, providing resources, or turning a battle. God can do miracles beyond our capacity to grasp. This picture or metaphor used here is a quick and painless childbirth. Wouldn't every pregnant woman want to believe in this experience?

What Isaiah is saying is that God is not limited by natural laws or our timeframe. He is outside our time so that He can insert Himself into our world and our lives at any point. His supernatural power and authority allow God to intervene and change any circumstance. We do no need to go through painful processes unless God wants us to grow through the pain or the waiting. He promises that in the end, He will not ignore or leave us but will accomplish what He began. This is what the Apostle Paul believed when he wrote,

"And I am certain that God, who began the good work within you, will continue his work until it is finally finished on the day when Christ Jesus returns" Phil. 1:6.

DAY 175
Isaiah 66:10-13

10 "Rejoice with Jerusalem!

Be glad with her, all you who love her

and all you who mourn for her.

11 Drink deeply of her glory

even as an infant drinks at its mother's comforting breasts."

12 This is what the Lord says:

"I will give Jerusalem a river of peace and prosperity.

> The wealth of the nations will flow to her.
>
> Her children will be nursed at her breasts,
>
> carried in her arms, and held on her lap.
>
> 13 I will comfort you there in Jerusalem
>
> as a mother comforts her child."

Isaiah's message is targeted at all Jews everywhere. This would include the ten nations that split away and became the Northern Kingdom of Israel. Assyria conquered this nation, and the people scattered. We refer to them as the Ten Lost Tribes of Israel. Isaiah directly addresses the people of Jerusalem, which is the remnant of only two tribes, Judah and Benjamin, just before they were conquered by Babylon.

When Isaiah speaks of God's promise to restore Jerusalem, it should be good news to all Jews everywhere. This includes those who have been dispersed throughout the world and are now known as the diaspora. The lesson for us today applies to our relationship with other Christians and other churches. We are to rejoice when a brother or sister prospers. This doesn't mean there is less for us; it is a sign of God's abundance and love. We should be happy because it displays the nature of God to bless His children.

The story Jesus tells of the Prodigal Son includes a cautionary portion about the elder brother, who could not rejoice in His father's grace and the extraordinary love He displayed to the undeserving brother.

Don't miss out on what God wants to do for you by being selfish or jealous. When we can genuinely rejoice with others who prosper in some way, we open ourselves to be blessed through them.

DAY 176

Isaiah 66:14-17

When you see these things, your heart will rejoice.

You will flourish like the grass!

Everyone will see the Lord's hand of blessing on his servants—

and his anger against his enemies.

15 See, the Lord is coming with fire,

and his swift chariots roar like a whirlwind.

He will bring punishment with the fury of his anger

and the flaming fire of his hot rebuke.

16 The Lord will punish the world by fire

and by his sword.

He will judge the earth,

and many will be killed by him.

17 "Those who 'consecrate' and 'purify' themselves in a sacred garden with its idol in the center—feasting on pork and rats and other detestable meats—will come to a terrible end," says the Lord.

It is amazing how God shows love and kindness to humanity, yet they reject Him again and again. Here, Isaiah is being shown the future and the end of man's time on earth. Future man is in the same place as the earliest humans regarding rebellion against God.

The LORD observed the extent of human wickedness on the earth, and he saw that everything they thought or imagined was consistently and totally evil. Gen. 6:5

This is the period of corruption on the earth just before the great flood in which only Noah and his family were spared. Jesus said men's hearts would be in the same condition at the time of His return.

For as were the days of Noah, so will be the coming of the Son of Man. Matt. 24:37

Every generation of humanity and every individual must choose whom we will worship, but in the words of Bob Dylan, "you're going to serve somebody".

DAY 177
Isaiah 66:18-21

"I can see what they are doing, and I know what they are thinking. So I will gather all nations and peoples together, and they will see my glory. 19 I will perform a sign among them. And I will send those who survive to be messengers to the nations—to Tarshish, to the Libyans and Lydians (who are famous as archers), to Tubal and Gre and to all the lands beyond the sea that have not heard of my fame or seen my glory. There they will declare my glory to the nations. 20 They will bring the remnant of your people back from every nation. They will bring them to my holy mountain in Jerusalem as an offering to the Lord. They will ride on horses, in chariots and wagons, and on mules and camels," says the Lord. 21 "And I will appoint some of them to be my priests and Levites. I, the Lord, have spoken!

Isaiah paints a beautiful picture of the church being outwardly focused on the ends of the earth as Jesus mandated His disciples. God is still sending people to far-away places to share God's love and preach the Gospel message. Jim and Vicki Egli, Dan and Brenda Salas, Jack and Sherry Harris, Ryan and Andrea Crozier, are people we support through our church to pursue God's calling, as described here hundreds of years before Jesus would challenge His disciples. Notice the focus is on Gentiles, which includes anyone who is outside of Judaism. The Gospel is for all people.

When we introduce someone to Jesus, we are fulfilling our mission. It becomes an act of love and a wonderful offering to God.

Eventually, Jesus will return to this earth He created and purified it so that people from "every tribe, nation, and tongue" (Rev. 7:9) will come together to worship our King and gaze upon His radiance. This will be a party that will last for eternity.

DAY 178
Isaiah 66:22-24

22 "As surely as my new heavens and earth will remain,

so will you always be my people,

with a name that will never disappear,"

says the Lord.

23 "All humanity will come to worship me

from week to week

and from month to month.

> 24 And as they go out, they will see
>
> the dead bodies of those who have rebelled against me.
>
> For the worms that devour them will never die,
>
> and the fire that burns them will never go out.
>
> All who pass by
>
> will view them with utter horror."

As Isaiah closes out his book, he stays true to his theme of communicating God's words clearly and forthrightly. The great contrast between those who are devoted to God and those who reject Him is the message emphasized once again. The choice is clear, so man is without excuse. To accept God's rulership in our lives is to be invited as sons and daughters to live in a new heaven and earth. To ignore God's offer of eternal salvation means separation from everything good.

Isaiah is a microcosm of the entire Bible and conveys the central message of God creating man in His image for a relationship with Himself. Man rebels again and again, and God, through His enduring love, provides a means of salvation. This back-and-forth pursuit and rejection will one day end for each one of us, and we will live for eternity with the outcome we chose.

I pray that you see the amazing unconditional love of God and give your life completely to Him. The only requirement is that you come humbly and acknowledge He is the One True God who is worthy of our complete devotion.

Thank you for joining me on this journey. I am praying about which book of the Bible to travel next. Hopefully, we'll connect on that trip as well.

GLOSSARY OF KEY WORDS

Ahaz – The king of Judah whom Isaiah gave the prophetic sign of a virgin conceiving a son (Immanuel) as a promise of God's presence and deliverance.

Anointing – In the context of Isaiah 10:27, it represents the presence and power of God poured upon a person, designated exclusively for Him. This power is described as significant enough to break all oppression and bondage.

Assyria – A powerful nation that God used as "the rod of my anger" to scatter the northern kingdom of Israel and execute judgment. Its king, Sennacherib, was later punished by God for his arrogance.

Babylon – The nation God allowed to overrun Judah and take the Israelites captive. The text also describes its future judgment and downfall, which is prophesied by Isaiah.

Covenant – A sacred agreement. The source notes that God's "unfailing love" for His people is like a covenant He will never break, and that Jesus mediates a "better covenant" based on better promises.

Cyrus – A Persian king referred to as God's "anointed one" in Isaiah 45. God used him to subdue nations and deliver Israel from captivity in Babylon.

Diaspora – The scattering of the Jewish people, which began with the Assyrian conquest of the ten northern tribes of Israel.

Egypt – A nation the Israelites were warned against trusting for help, as they are "mere humans, not God." Trusting in Egypt's military might instead of the Holy One of Israel is presented as an act of rebellion.

Grace – God's unmerited favor. The source repeatedly highlights that even in the Old Testament and amidst judgment, God's grace, mercy, and unfailing love are always present and offered to His people.

Hesed (or chesed) – God's unconditional love. Word is translated many different ways to try to encompass the greatness of God's never ending love.

Hezekiah – A king of Judah who, after being told by Isaiah he would die, prayed to God and was granted fifteen more years of life. He later made the mistake of proudly showing all his treasures to envoys from Babylon.

Holiness – God's absolute purity and perfection. In Isaiah's vision in chapter 6, the seraphim cry "Holy, holy, holy is the LORD," and the sight causes Isaiah to become acutely aware of his own sinfulness.

Idolatry – The worship of idols or false gods. The source condemns it as foolishness, describing craftsmen who create gods from wood or metal that cannot save them, contrasting this with the one true, living God.

Immanuel – A name meaning "God with us." It was given as a sign to King Ahaz and is interpreted as a prophecy pointing to Jesus, who came to earth to reveal the nature and character of God the Father.

Isaiah – A Hebrew prophet whose prophetic messages are a central focus of the study. His ministry occurred during the reigns of kings Uzziah, Jotham, Ahaz, and Hezekiah of Judah. His vision and calling are described in chapter 6.

Israel – Originally the twelve tribes descended from Jacob. At the time of Isaiah, it refers to the northern kingdom of ten tribes, which was conquered by Assyria. The name is also used to refer to God's covenant people as a whole.

Jerusalem – The capital city of Judah, also referred to as **Zion**. It is central to many of Isaiah's prophecies, described as both a place of judgment for its sin and the future center of God's glorious reign.

Judah – The southern kingdom of Israel after the nation split. It consisted of the tribes of Judah and Benjamin, with Jerusalem as its capital. It was eventually conquered by Babylon.

Justice – A core attribute of God. The source explains that God will establish His eternal kingdom with fairness and justice, and He calls on His people to "learn to do good; seek justice, correct oppression."

Messiah – The "anointed one" prophesied to be the savior and king. The text extensively identifies this figure with Jesus, detailing prophecies about His birth, titles (Isaiah 9:6), suffering (Isaiah 53), and righteous reign (Isaiah 11).

Prophetic Act – An action a prophet is instructed by God to perform as a living symbol of a message. Isaiah naming his son Maher-Shalal-Hash-Baz is an example of a prophetic act.

Remnant – A theme in Isaiah's prophecies that even after judgment and exile, a small group of faithful people will survive and return to God. This remnant will be the seed for the future restoration of Israel.

GLOSSARY OF KEY WORDS

Righteousness – A state of being right with God. The study explains that the Messiah will rule with righteousness, and believers are vindicated through the righteousness God imparts to them.

Sennacherib – The king of Assyria who besieged Jerusalem but was defeated by God's intervention after King Hezekiah prayed. He is an example of a human ruler used as God's instrument who then became arrogant.

Servant of the LORD – A key figure in Isaiah's prophecies, most extensively described in chapters 42, 49, 50, and 53. The source identifies this suffering but ultimately triumphant servant as the Messiah, Jesus Christ.

Uzziah – A king of Judah whose death in 740 B.C. marks the year that Isaiah had his foundational vision of the LORD in the temple (Isaiah 6).

Zion – Another name for Jerusalem, often used poetically to refer to the city as the dwelling place of God and the heart of His people.

THE ISAIAH PAULINE CONNECTION

It is easy when you read Isaiah and the Apostle Paul's writings, the connection between the two. Paul uses Isaiah's text as the foundation for his understanding of the gospel.

Isaiah Text	Paul's Citation	Other NT Citations
1:9	Rom 9:29	—
8:14	Rom 9:33	1 Pet 2:8
10:22-23	Rom 9:27-28	—
11:10	Rom 15:12	—
22:13	1 Cor 15:32	—
15:8	1 Cor 15:54	—
27:9	Rom 11:27	—
28:11-12	1 Cor 14:21	—
28:16	Rom 9:33	1 Pet 2:6 & Rom 10:11
29:10	Rom 11:8	—
29:14	1 Cor 1:19	—
29:16	Rom 9:20	—
40:13	Rom 11:34 & 1 Cor 2:16	
45:23	Rom 14:11	—

- 49:8   2 Cor 6:2   —
- 52:5   Rom 2:24   —
- 52:7   Rom 10:15   —
- 52:11   2 Cor 6:17   —
- 52:15   Rom 15:21   —
- 53:1   Rom 10:16   John 12:38
- 54:1   Gal 4:27   —
- 55:10   2 Cor 9:10   —
- 59:7-8   Rom 3:15-17   —
- 59:20-21   Rom 11:26-27   —

I have not covered John's use of Isaiah, but we see in Revelation the culmination of many of Isaiah's prophecies concerning the last days. This is a future study.

MORE MIND AND HEART SERIES WORKS

The Bible clearly addresses our minds and emotions. Isaiah, as well as other Old Testament writers, understood and distinguished between heart and mind and wisdom and knowledge. They saw wisdom as revelation from God and knowledge we pursue through study.

In this series Tony Portell addresses in each book study aspects of understanding how discipleship must involve our intellect and our relational connection with God. God is a relational being. We see Jesus expressing all types of emotions, such as joy, anger, sadness, frustration, and so on. We have not focused on this aspect of spiritual growth. To be mature in our spiritual life, we must seek maturity in our emotions. This means healing from past trauma, poor attachment as a child and wounds we pick up along the path of life.

For more information on the connection between mental and spiritual health, check out Tony's bestseller, **No Longer Stuck**. You can also get the Course and Workbook and the Leader's Guide for small group study.

As of December 2025, I am looking forward to releasing an updated version of Ephesians in January. In the works are Nehemiah, Romans, and New Testament and Old Testament Surveys.

Follow and subscribe to get early access to new books and articles at TonyPortell.com.

Helping Others Heal

If you are facing challenges in your mental and spiritual journey, contact us at HelpingOthersHeal.org and we can connect you with a Mental Health Coach or Licensed Therapist.

ABOUT THE AUTHOR
Tony Portell

It is my honor and privilege serve as the Lead Pastor of Vineyard Life Church (VLC) in Indianapolis, which my wife Lori and I established in 2006. VLC has campuses in both Indianapolis and Plainfield.

I hold a Master's degree in counseling and biblical studies. Besides my pastoral duties, I serve as a Chaplain for the Indianapolis Fire Department and a member of the State of Indiana's Mental Health Crisis Response Team. I also support churches and pastors throughout Indiana as an Area Leader for Vineyard Churches.

My book, No Longer Stuck, is an Amazon bestseller, and my latest book, Battle from Above, Paul's Letter to the Ephesians, is a #1 New Release on Amazon.

Contact information

Tony Portell

612 N. High School Rd.

Indianapolis, IN 46214

(317) 222-5510 | office

www.TonyPortell.com

BOOKS BY TONY PORTELL

A FINAL FAVOR...

Our goal is to help as many people as possible discover the life transforming message of God's Word. You can help by leaving a review on Amazon for any of Tony's books. The more positive reviews, the more Amazon promotes his books. You can search for Tony's books on Amazon and then scroll down and see where to leave a review.

www.ingramcontent.com/pod-product-compliance
Lightning Source LLC
Chambersburg PA
CBHW060512230426
43665CB00013B/1492